Contents

Acknowledgments

$\mathcal{I}$ need to take a little space to say thanks for those who helped me on this journey. I've already cited my wife, Julie, and brother, Bill, who waded through it with support and encouragement.

Special thanks to:

KWMU radio in St. Louis for its support

Ralph Keune of Epic Video in St. Louis for transferring some ancient videotape into usable freeze frames used in this publication. What's lacking in quality is not his fault. Time's a thief in more ways than one.

My thanks to local newscaster John Auble for refreshing my memory on the Paula Sims incidents, and to former colleagues Betsey Bruce, Dennis Riggs, Donn Johnson, and Paul Schankman for responding to my calls for help.

Preface

*I*t was almost fifty years ago that I began a career in journalism, a career that has taken me from the country clubs in New Jersey to the Cold War in Europe, to the Civil Rights struggle in this country, to the domestic political wars, to Bonn, to London, to Baltimore, and, finally, to St. Louis. Individual assignments have taken me to much of this country and abroad to Central America and Africa. I have rubbed elbows with the famous, the infamous, and many who were anonymous until I became a conduit for their celebrated fifteen minutes. I remember most of them while fully understanding that few likely have any recollection of me. Yet, as I have reached a point in my life when looking back is more pleasurable than looking forward, flash frames of my experiences pop in and out.

After starting in radio, then spending the next forty years or so in television, the water under those particular bridges has now pooled for me in the world of public radio.

These days, I am associated with the local National Public Radio station, KWMU. In NPR, I have found a world that I had not experienced since those youthfully idealistic days.

NPR and KWMU are one of the few bastions of journalistic honesty in the country today. They are populated by dedicated professionals who bring balance, credibility, and substance to journalism. It is done with a commitment of long standing and because reporters and interviewers are given a luxury not provided in commercial broadcasting. That luxury is time. They are given time to prepare material and given airtime to present it. The result is detailed reportage, which goes a long way toward the lofty objectives of giving the listeners the information needed to make intelligent decisions about their lives, their community, and their nation.

I have often said that I have never listened to NPR and my station, KWMU, when I did not learn something. I'm only sorry it took me so many years to learn that.

What is a flash frame? It is a single, isolated frame of film that appears for a millisecond between two unrelated scenes. Some memories are like flash frames. They come and go at unexpected times. I'm not working from notes; just the flash frames of whatever recall ability is left, and Google. Any omissions or embellishments are simply the result of faulty recollections. You have my word that nothing is being overtly overblown or underplayed for effect. What follows are the flash frames as I see them today, in most cases, many years later.

My broadcasting career began in reverse, essentially as a foreign radio correspondent at a young age, then on to a career in television news. I am not nationally known or recognized. It's more like Roger Miller's *Kansas City Star*—a medium fish in a small pond. I'm a local news guy. But I have bounced around since television news came of age. Some of the bounces have been high and satisfying. Others have been lower to the ground. I have done quality work, and I have done crap. Such is the lot of those in my trade.

I write this with no presumption that anyone outside of my immediate circle gives a hoot about my experiences. However, I have come to realize that these experiences have been wide-ranging and, in many cases, interesting and even important. Granted, many have been more interesting than important, more humorous than enlightening, but some have been on the fringes of history.

It is in this spirit that I write of my journey. It is not about me. It is about where I have been and what I have seen. The hope is it will give you a better understanding of what life is like for thousands of the people who bring you your news every day, a better appreciation of some unconnected yet fascinating historical events, and, I hope, a laugh or two. Please join me on this collection of recollections. Feel free to jump on or off the ride at any time.

Flash Frames

Frankfurt

*F*or those of you old enough to remember Ted Baxter from the old *Mary Tyler Moore* show, you may recall that he was fond of telling anyone who would listen that, "It all began in a 5,000 watt radio station in Fresno." He said it as if it were the most important thing someone had to know about him, as if it explained everything.

In that spirit, let me begin by saying it all began in a dingy office in Orange, New Jersey. It was home to *Suburban Life Magazine*, a small monthly that specialized in engagement announcements and wedding pictures of the well-to-do, with an over abundance of information about unimportant meetings and obscure organizations. College was no match for the chance to join a journalistic enterprise and take on the heady title of "Managing Editor." It was a title that seemed to fit the only employee. "Owner and Publisher" was awarded by default to the occupant of the only other desk in the office. He was an elderly gentleman who awarded me the title because he needed someone to help sweep the floor, cut and paste, cover an occasional "story," and help out on the monthly trek to Baltimore where the magazine was put to bed and printed. His wife handled advertising, but she worked from home.

The nine months spent there may have established a record for anyone specializing in writing captions for wedding photos, or misspelling names of garden club members. Nonetheless, it was a beginning. One could only go up from there.

In this case, "up" was away. Far away to Germany.

Far away came on the last day of the spring of 1960, the day after Floyd Patterson knocked out Ingemar Johansson in the fifth round of their title fight to regain the world championship. It was the day I left for Germany for what I hoped would be a job as a civilian newsman for the American Forces Network (AFN). The network broadcast over 150,000 clear channel watts to some half a million GIs and their families in Europe. With that kind of unobstructed firepower the signal went a lot farther than the western part of Europe. It bounced around the ionosphere like a ping pong ball in a windstorm ultimately reaching audiences as far away as the Philippines.

1960! It was a hell of a year to begin a career in journalism. Ahead was the Kennedy election, the Bay of Pigs, the Berlin Wall, the Cuban Missile Crisis, Vietnam, the Kennedy–King–Kennedy assassinations, the civil rights struggle, and seismic shifts in American social and political attitudes. Not only did I not know any of this was coming. I didn't have a job.

With an old Volkswagen sold and a modest wardrobe stuffed into an old suitcase, I left for Frankfurt on the chance that I could fill an opening in the AFN news department. It was somewhat more calculated and less spontaneous than it might appear. My brother was a news editor with AFN, and I had been interviewed by the station's program director in New York some weeks earlier. No job was promised. Nonetheless, the twenty-one year old who was too naive to be practical and too young to be smart, headed across the ocean when big brother announced a writer's job was opening. And it was. Unfortunately, by the time this would-be newsman arrived, it had been filled, leaving me with no job, no prospects of employment of any sort, and, sadly, very limited financial resources.

There was enough money for hanging around for a couple of months. Ah, but youth looks no farther than that. I stayed, taken in by a compassionate brother, Bill, and his even more compassionate wife, Ingrid. Monte Wooley was the "Man Who Came to Dinner" in the movies. He came to dinner and stayed six months. I halved that with Bill and Ingrid, though to them it undoubtedly felt like six years, which was how long I was to stay in Germany.

The waiting game was actually advantageous. It gave me a chance to learn one of the basics about the job I was hoping for. It was radio after all. It might be a big help to learn how to read a news story in front of a microphone. Practicing on a tape recorder between visits to the local beer gardens, I began to get the hang of how to read out loud. Practicing on a typewriter (you do remember typewriters don't you?) I learned the basics of how to write a radio news story. While I was certainly not very good at it, I was at least comfortable enough to think I might do all right in a promised audition. There was still the real possibility that there would be no job opening, but I held on to the fragile hope that an opening—if one occurred—would happen before I ran out of my paltry savings and before my patient relatives lost their patience.

I hung around with the guys in a "guys only" news department. As a group they probably averaged close to thirty in age. They seemed worldly, mature, together, and tolerant of the intrusion of youth. In my mind, they were the 1960 equivalent of "Murrow's Boys." I saw them as dashing civilian journalists living and working a glamorous overseas life, serving a noble purpose by delivering news and information to a sizable American audience as well as to those Germans who cared to eavesdrop.

Germans did listen. Many learned or perfected their English by listening to AFN, which they affectionately (I think it was affection) called the *Affensender,* or "monkey radio station."

The station was located in a castle in the Frankfurt suburb of Hoechst. The building was right out of medieval central casting complete with turrets, a (dry) moat, and ivy meandering across the façade of ancient stone. Adding to the local color and chronological contrast was its location next to a twentieth-century complex, the giant I.G. Farben chemical factory. Farben was an important company in postwar Germany just as it had been thirty-five years earlier when it produced the Zyklon B gas used in Hitler's concentration camp gas chambers. Plumes of smoke from unknown particulates drifted into the European sky from Farben's smokestacks often leaving a greasy residue in the neighborhood. That was, of course, before anyone really worried about such phenomena as air pollution.

The castle was populated by the civilians who constituted the bulk of the news operation, and by military officers and enlisted men who ran and maintained the radio station. There were several Army and Air Force personnel who were the on-air talent at AFN. Programming was pretty much as it was stateside but it was more of a composite of the stations back home. There was a lot of music, but AFN also carried much of the transcribed programming that was popular in the United States: *Arthur Godfrey and Friends, Don McNeill's Breakfast Club,* and other programs that were popular in

Von Bruning Castle, Hoechst, Germany, AFN Frankfurt Headquarters

the states in those years. Occasional live sports events were beamed in from such familiar places as Crosley Field, Fenway, and Wrigley. Transcribed drama was another staple. A little bit of everything to bring "a bit of home" to the hundreds of thousands of Americans stationed in Europe and therefore within earshot.

For the most part, the enlisted men were draftees who were more than happy to be assigned to a radio station rather than a tank along the border with the communist East. The AFNers could come and go pretty much as they liked as long as they met programming demands, which were demands in name only. There was an accommodating number of taverns, *Gasthäuser*, in the little town of Hoechst and they were well supported by the troops. By all standards, AFN was considered good duty.

There was a great deal of camaraderie among the enlisted men

and the civilians. Most civilians had long since done their obligatory two years in the service. They worked side by side as equals
with a lot of animation and teasing, though the civilians all had
Government Service (GS) ranks that made them equivalent to officers. An entry-level civilian news writer, for example, was a GS-8,
the equivalent of a second lieutenant, and the station's program
director was a GS-14, the equivalent of a colonel. I remember one
prank-prone civilian taking a call from an Army announcer and be-
rating him for not sounding like he was standing at attention on the
other end of the line. This particularly gullible GI took him seriously
and swore that he was in fact standing at attention.

The newsroom was small, loud, and smoky. Everyone smoked,
which may be why no one complained about the hyperactive smokestacks next door. Three to five writers flanked an editor at a horse-
shoe-shaped desk and ground out copy for the hourly five-minute
newscasts as well as for the fifteen-minute and half-hour versions
aired at strategic times of day. The constant chatter of noisy AP and
UPI wire machines matched nicely with the staccato of the typewriters and gave the room a rhythm that proved more than attractive
to a young man wanting to be a newsman. Periodically, a German
national employee tore copy from the wires, brought it to an editor
who evaluated it and, if it met his approval, assigned it to a newswriter who put it into broadcast form. To say the team "churned"
out copy would be an overstatement. There was plenty of time for
cigarettes, jokes, coffee, and general grab-ass.

Humor was an important ingredient in the newsroom. The walls
were covered with old wire copy of unusual stories, the more risqué
the better. There were photos too. Some were carried by the UPI
photo wire, some had been cut from newspapers, and all were af-
fixed with irreverent captions. On the back of the newsroom door
was a chart that would never be permitted in a newsroom today.
It was not quite a joke. Someone, somewhere along the line, had
decided it would be instructive for newsmen to be able to put the
value of American life in perspective. The chart featured a long list
of various nations with the United States at (where else?) the top.
The chart specified that one American was worth two Britons, three
Frenchmen, four Germans, and down the list until the value ranking placed one American as equal to five thousand Pakistanis, ten

thousand Indonesians, and so on. The idea was that the death of ten thousand Indonesians in a typhoon carried as much news weight as the death of a single American. Political correctness was a long way off. But in all honesty, the "journalistic equation," as outrageous as it was, found general acceptance by many journalists in those days. Many might concede that this formula remains in effect, *sotto voce* of course, in many newsrooms today.

Absent from the news department itself were the civilian correspondents stationed in bureaus across Europe. Reporting from their bureaus in Berlin, Bonn, Munich, Paris, later London, and other smaller but key European cities, the correspondents contributed news reports and information to the newsroom throughout the day and broadcast news of their beat each night on a fifteen-minute program called *Report from Europe*. Correspondents were the marquee players in the news department. The writers were the grunts. And if they were "Murrow's Boys" in my mind, the correspondents were "Murrow's Men."

By the way, the Soviets listened to AFN too. In later years, as the Cold War intensified, it was not unusual for "Murrow's Boys" to

1770 Sketch of Hoechst Castle, Johann Wofgang von Goethe

hear edited versions of themselves coming back at them late at night over Radio Moscow. The Russians taped AFN, judiciously edited material that could be altered to their advantage, and broadcast it themselves when the edited version did them the most good. It was a pretty good propaganda stunt.

When a radio newswriter job finally opened, I was ready. More importantly, I was *there*. That was a huge advantage. No one to hire from the states. No one to transport. No matter that this guy standing in the door was soaking wet behind the ears. He was there and there now. So I was offered the opportunity to audition. That meant being given a full day's worth of wire copy, culling from it the most important/interesting stories, putting them into newscast format, then reading it in a recorded audition. The news director, who conducted both the written and reading audition, was no stranger to me. I had hung around for three months. I was, therefore, less intimidated than I might have been otherwise. He was a highly respected newsman from Des Moines, Iowa. As fate would have it the reading audition included a story about his home town. He hadn't selected it, I had. I read it as "Da Moinz." I knew better, but in trying to articulate precisely, I overdid it. I almost read the dots in the "i"s out loud. It gave him a good laugh, but I got the job anyway. They must have been more desperate than I knew. I was put on the payroll as a GS-8, at $5,600 a year, and moved into the Bachelor Officer's Quarters (BOQ). I spent the better part of the next year and a half working the overnight shift grinding out news of the world and feeling like Scotty Reston.

So it really all started in a 150,000-watt radio station in Frankfurt!

Sinatra–Martin

*W*e used to hear stories about new factory workers who were sent out by old timers to find and bring back "an assembly line." It was part of the rites of passage. The old timers got a good laugh, then everyone would wait for the next rookie. It's like that sometimes in newsrooms. Guess who was the rookie? Instead of an assembly line, this rookie was dispatched to find and interview Frank Sinatra and Dean Martin.

It was August 1961, and the rookie had been on the news desk writing copy and reading newscasts for ten months. It was a difficult time in Europe. On August 13, the East Germans, with the blessing of the Soviet Union, began constructing a wall and barbed-wire barrier around the Western sectors, effectively separating the Soviet sector from those of Britain, France, and the United States. The Soviets were obviously interested in isolating West Berlin, which was located about 120 miles inside the Soviet Zone and which Russian Premier Nikita Khrushchev described as "a thorn in my side." Berlin was a source of constant friction between the Western allies and the Soviets, and Moscow was continually looking for ways to assert its authority over the former German capital. If the relationship among the four powers was unstable before construction of the wall, it reached flash point on August 13. Berlin was thought by many to be the spark that could ignite a third world war.

Enter Sinatra and Martin.

Dean Martin's son was a serviceman stationed in Germany. Martin and his good pal Sinatra had been visiting England, and while there they decided to visit Dean's son in Germany. However, Martin did not know exactly where the young man was stationed. All he had to go on was the younger Martin's Army Post Office (APO) address. Martin, or his representatives, contacted AFN for assistance in locating the singer's son. In fact, that was accomplished, and there was a reunion. But a deal had been struck. Someone at AFN had gotten Martin to agree to do an interview after the reunion before he and Sinatra returned to the states.

Now, anyone who has ever read anything about Sinatra and Martin might remember that they were not overly press-friendly. Sinatra had had many celebrated run-ins with reporters. He, and to a lesser degree Martin, were often targets of tabloids. They found it difficult to move about in public without a hoard of reporters, photographers, or both, in their way. They rarely gave interviews. If the Berlin Wall was formidable, the barrier that these two entertainers built between themselves and the media was no less so. And, like the wall in Berlin, there was occasional bloodshed at the barrier that Sinatra and Martin had erected to keep the press at bay. This was especially true with Sinatra who had, on more than one occasion, taken swings at reporters.

All this, of course, was known to the folks in the AFN Special Events Department, which produced all the feature material broadcast by AFN. Despite the promise of an interview in return for AFN's help in finding Martin's son, the Special Events folks knew better. It wouldn't happen. But just in case, send someone—anyone—to try.

Hello.

Frank Sinatra was huge in 1961. Dean Martin somewhat less so. His return to better days were ahead when television made him at least as big a star as he had been with Jerry Lewis. But Sinatra was at the top of his game. *Some Came Running, Never So Few, From Here to Eternity,* and *Pal Joey* were just some of the more recent contributions to the Sinatra legend. And, as always, the music. So, here comes the rookie assigned to find two movie and singing stars and do his first-ever recorded interview. No intimidation factor here. But the first problem was to find them. The only information we had was that they were at the Frankfurt/Main Airport. That's a little like saying there's the haystack, go find the needle.

We had no clue where they were. We had neither their airline nor their departure time. Nothing. All we did have was the fact that they were returning to the states that afternoon. Amid the bustle of tourist, business, diplomatic, and military people rushing to make flights, or rushing to find taxis, was the sporadic guttural of a language that was still new to me. It came from all around: passengers, pilots, public address speakers. It took some time to check departing flight schedules for afternoon departures. This reporter carried no pen and no notebook, just a Nagra reel-to-reel tape recorder valued at about $2,000. Yes, the government even provided rookies with the finest equipment tax dollars could buy. Nagras were so good, they were often used to record sound in movies. I was so new to this part of the radio news business I wasn't even sure how to turn it on. So, all I had to do was find Frank Sinatra and Dean Martin in a large, crowded airport, figure out how my equipment worked, then interview two of the biggest names in show business. Nothing to it. All in a day's work.

I found a TWA flight that looked promising and headed for the gate, protecting my Nagra like Emmitt Smith going over the middle. Perspiring and nervous, I managed to find the gate while trying to figure out whether I was more hopeful I would, or would not, find my prey. Except, I'm sure I was not thinking of them as my prey—more likely the other way around. I guess I expected to find them sitting at the gate waiting for the flight to be called just like the rest of us mere mortals. Of course, they were not. Stars would be given star treatment. I asked some airline people if they knew where the two men were. Shrugs all around until someone in a uniform and a friendly smile said, "They're probably in the VIP lounge."

"Where's that?"

A long finger pointed at a door. I went to it, turned the knob, and walked through, fully anticipating it would lead me anywhere but directly into a lounge where film stars were cooling their heels. It led me to a small room with a sofa and an easy chair, occupied by two men I had only seen before on television or in the movies. A third man in uniform, possibly a flight officer, stood off to the side. He looked at me, put down a drink, and almost knocked me down as he scurried from the room, leaving me alone with THEM!

Sinatra looked like he had just popped off the cover of an album. The usual hat with the wide hatband—paisley, I think. It was pushed back on his head. The knot of his tie, which was as wide as his neck was pulled down from an open collar. He sat hunched forward, a drink cupped in both hands. He looked at me as if I had stepped in manure. He did not seem surprised, just disgusted. I think I remember him turning his head from side to side as if he were thinking, oh no, not this again.

Martin looked relaxed seated in the easy chair, legs crossed. He was impeccable in a gray suit. His expression was not unlike it might have been in a scene where Jerry Lewis was trying to explain the theory of relativity. He had not picked up the odor of manure yet. That would come.

I stammered and mumbled. I was nonplussed. I hadn't expected to have just walked through a door to find the two of them sitting there. But there we were. Just the three of us. I tried to make an apology for barging in. I'm guessing it sounded like I was speaking Zulu. Returning to English, I identified myself, my organization, and my mission. I reminded Dino that we had helped him find his son and that it was time now to pay the piper. I'm sure whatever I said it was poorly done, but, before I knew it, he was taking a deep breath and saying, "Okay."

As I have indicated, the Nagra is a fine, top-quality, professional apparatus; however, the microphone cord on this one was little more than eighteen inches long. This meant I had to get on my knees next to Martin so that I could turn on the recorder (a simple twist of a conspicuous knob as it turned out) and hold the microphone close enough to pick up his voice. Get the picture? Nervous kid, first broadcast interview ever, on his knees, sweating, probably flushed to a degree that could have brought in a landing plane, next to Dean Martin with Frank Sinatra just a few feet away. With a click, the Nagra was on. The interview began.

(Allow me to point out that up to this point in the narrative, I have referred to the two celebrities as "Frank Sinatra and Dean Martin." That's because I was then, and have forever remained, a Sinatra fan. When it comes to the two of them, Sinatra was number one, Martin number two. However, I was there to interview Martin. This led to an unfortunate lapse in judgment which I attribute to nerves and a certain lack of sophistication in such matters. Did I mention that I was nervous?)

"Hello, this is Don Marsh at Frankfurt Airport speaking with Frank Sinatra and Dean Martin." I can still hear the shimmering tone in my voice.

"Not me, buddy." It sounded, at first, like a line from *From Here to Eternity*. It was not. It was instead, Old Blue Eyes letting me know that he was not going to be a part of my script.

"Ah, please Frank. It's for the troops."

"Nope." He turned his back to me.

"Hey kid, we run away from this stuff in the states. Where did you say you were from?" It was Martin. He had finally caught a whiff of the manure.

"AFN," I responded. Our eyes locked. There may have been tears in mine. His were as unflinching as two bullet holes in the snow.

"I have a few questions," I said. There was no response.

I started again. "This is Don Marsh at Frankfurt Airport with my guest Dean Martin." So far, so good. I had not been challenged. "Dean, what brings you to Germany?" I hate to admit it, but that was the question.

"I'm on vacation," he said. Silence for a moment.

"You were visiting your son?"

"Yes."

Now, keep in mind, the communist empire and free world were standing toe to toe about 250 miles to the northeast. A wall was going up, dividing a city that might have been the flash point for war. Troops were on alert. The world was watching. If the balloon went up, his son would be in the middle of it.

"Dean, as a father and as an American, how do you feel about what's going on in Germany right now?" Finally, a real question. But, apparently, it wasn't good enough.

"Rough man, it's rough. Are we through now?"

I think I mumbled something like, "I guess so." He might have mentioned something, but he was very clearly showing me the door with his eyes. I quite willingly complied with his unspoken instruction and could not get out of there soon enough. Fortunately, I didn't have ten feet of microphone cord to wrap up. I shot a glance at my man Frank. His back was still to me. Skinny prick!

I was bitterly disappointed, but as I drove back to the station I began to feel a little better about my failings as a newsman-interviewer. I rationalized that the mission might not have been accomplished as I wished or intended, but I had gotten through to the two and had even talked to them, however briefly or badly. I had accomplished what my buddies from Special Events had not even attempted. In a relatively short time, I had managed to pull myself from the depth of a stomach-twisting depression to the point where I was feeling quite proud of myself. Go figure.

When I got back I announced that I had gotten the interview. Jaws dropped and eyes widened. The expressions betrayed the skepticism. Someone reached for the Nagra. I explained very briefly what had happened as the tape was rewound. It didn't take long.

The knob was turned to "play" and in a moment, I heard my voice. Except, it wasn't my voice at all. It was a distorted version of it. The tape was running slightly faster than the intended speed making us all sound as if we were swallowing helium. Glances were exchanged as we listened to the few seconds that constituted the entire interview. My heart was in my loafers as a bad situation slumped beyond the previous low. What had happened to that earlier pride?

"I think we should run it," said one of the guys. "Quality stinks, but what jerks."

"We can't run it," said another. "The quality is too bad. Folks should hear what these guys are really like, but we just look stupid if we put this on the air." More glances all around as all in the room agreed. It would not air. I don't remember if I was relieved or not. Sinatra and Martin were not at their best, but neither was the interviewer. Aside from being unable to handle that difficult situation well, the rookie had not turned on the Nagra properly. It was set between the two possible speeds causing a recording too fast for one setting and too slow for the other. Stupid machine! The result was distortion. Fact is, had the interview gone on for any length, it would never have aired except perhaps as a blooper intended to make Frank Sinatra and Dean Martin sound like Munchkins.

The incident was unfortunate for me professionally. Not just for the moment. This was a long-term problem. I was actually quite shaken by the reception the two had given me. In fact, it would take a couple of years, yes years, before I was ever comfortable interviewing celebrities, particularly in the entertainment field. I was always concerned that I would be rebuffed, insulted, or otherwise humiliated in the face of such celebrity. Ultimately, I worked through it, largely because so many of them were genuinely nice people. Since that August day more than forty-five years ago, I have interviewed hundreds.

In the mid-1970s, I even walked away from David Soul and Paul Michael Glaser. Who? They were just beginning their run as *Starsky and Hutch*. It was just before season one. They weren't even stars yet. The interview was part of an ABC promotion for their new program in advance of the coming season. Stars typically did not like the format, which meant spending a long day being interviewed separately by dozens of reporters from all over the country. It most certainly had to be tiring and boring, answering the same questions over an eight-to-ten-hour period. But the whole idea was to give them, their programs, and their network maximum exposure, which in turn would enable them to live the life celebrated people live. In other words, it's akin to overhead, an investment of their time; it's the cost of doing business, a business that would enable them to live in luxury for the rest of time—or until the program was canceled.

I started the interview with these two with a basic question of some sort. Not only did they not look at me. They did not respond at all. They just continued talking to each other as if they were alone in a bar. The bartender would have gotten more attention than I. I tried again. Again, they ignored me. It pissed me off.

"Do you mind if I get in on this fellows?" I asked. Again I was ignored. So, I unclipped the microphone stood up and walked away.

An ABC publicist saw my premature departure from the interview set and rushed over to find out what was wrong. She asked, and I told her about their antics. "St. Louis is an important market for us," she said. "Please go back and do the interview."

"No way," I said. "If they ask, tell them I'll come back when they're stars. If they ever become stars."

Of course they did, and I spent the next twenty-five years in St. Louis as a local news guy.

Quick Cuts

I've found that the stars who have been around a while are unfailingly receptive to the interview. Why not? It's their bread and butter. I do remember an interview with pianist Van Cliburn after he had won yet another international competition. It was about two years after the Frankfurt Airport experience.

He was the Jesse Owens of the 1950s when he won the International Tchaikovsky Piano Competition in the Soviet Union in 1958. He was not supposed to win. It was an enormous triumph. As *Wikipedia* puts it, "It was supposed to go to someone to demonstrate Soviet cultural superiority and to expand on the recent Soviet success in space." He was so good that judges asked for, and received, permission from Nikita Khrushchev himself to give Cliburn the first prize. Our interview (with Cliburn, not Khrushchev) covered all the necessary bases. When I asked him if he ever just sat down at the piano and "played a little jazz or something for his personal amusement," the interview went south. Had I asked him if he liked to fondle little children, the response might have been the same. He lifted his nose, placed the tip of a long piano player's finger on the top of the microphone, stood up, and walked away, the fingertip trailing behind. I assumed the answer was "no." There was that Sinatra-Martin chill again. What made it worse was the fact that I had to hustle to another part of the hotel to do an interview with actress Angie Dickinson.

She was at the top of her game in the 1960s. Her acting ability didn't have anyone calling on her to play Joan of Arc or Lady Macbeth, but Hollywood publicists had managed to get her legs insured for a million dollars. We would learn years later that a relationship with John Kennedy was in full bloom at about this time.

I guess I was a little nervous when I got to her. She was even more gorgeous in person than she was on the screen and must have sensed my nervousness. She greeted me with a perfect smile and put her hand out to take mine. She said something about looking forward to our interview, put her arm around me, and suggested we go to a corner of the room where it was less noisy. Although I don't remember exactly what was said, that's what we did. Who could remember the words of a babe like that draping her arm around you? I was in love.

Another setback occurred about this same time. Again, I was on my knees, which brought back memories of the Sinatra-Martin chill. Andres Segovia, the Spanish classical guitarist, was at the top of his career when we crossed paths. The interview was uncomfortable for me, and presumably for him. In another scene reminiscent of the Dean Martin fiasco, Segovia sat in an easy chair while I knelt before him on the floor, extending my microphone cord to its full three-foot length. I had learned at the Frankfurt Airport that short microphone cords are a no-no, but apparently I still had not caught on to taking a seat next to the person being interviewed. What I knew (know) about the classical guitar can be put between two frets. I asked what I assumed were the typical, uninformed interviewer's stock and trade. He did not turn me away, so either my questions were acceptable or his English was not as good as it seemed. I asked him to tell me when he began playing the guitar. His answer: "In my mother's womb." My rejoinder was probably more disrespectful, and less funny than I intended, but I said, "Good thing you didn't play the piano." He didn't laugh. I guess he didn't have a sense of humor.

Don Marsh interviewing pianist Van Cliburn

Tommy Cash

A number of the GIs assigned to AFN had been broadcast professionals before they were drafted or enlisted in the service. They brought a high level of professionalism to the network, giving it a good sound. Some were career soldiers who had perfected their talents at various AFN stations around the world. Some of the draftees went on to garner some celebrity after their AFN–Germany days.

Tommy Cash was a small guy with a big brother: Johnny Cash. Tommy was another of the Army announcers at AFN Frankfurt. His hair was dark, his teeth straight, and his Arkansas twang unmistakable. He was personable and popular. He had dabbled in show business before entering the Army. Although "The Man in Black" was his brother, Tommy didn't make much of it and neither did anyone else. He could have. Johnny Cash had become a force to reckon with in the entertainment world in the late 1950s. The luster on his star never diminished for almost fifty years. Tommy played a role in that.

But our worlds collided, literally. Our paths didn't cross often, though we both worked in the castle. We were on opposite ends of the clock. When I was sleeping, he was working and vice versa. Our stars intersected one night, however, when we played out a scene reminiscent of John Wayne and Victor McGlaglan in *The Quiet Man*.

Tommy and I were separate visitors to a local club popular with young GIs and known to be frequented by ladies of limited virtue. This was not a traditional Oom-pah tavern. Beer didn't come in liter steins, but rather in little green bottles with high price tags. The ladies who delivered them weren't dressed in colorful, traditional frocks, but rather in tight dresses with low necklines. And if you spent any time there, it was expected that you would spring for a drink for one or more of them. In return, you got some conversation and whatever else you could bargain for. They were known as "B Girls" then, and I suppose they still are.

The exact circumstances are a little fuzzy, but somehow Tommy and I wound up buying drinks for the same young lady. A tribute, no doubt, to her salesmanship and decolletage. Somehow, we got into an argument over who had "rights" to this particular *fräulein*. One word led to another and the next thing either of us knew we had rolled up our sleeves and taken our discussion outside where we started throwing punches. I don't think any of them landed. We groped and wrestled and went to the ground a couple of times, working our way up and down the street. We did not rumble over hill and dale like the combative movie Irishmen. Instead, we wound up fifty yards from the club out of breath, disheveled, and remarkably unhurt. No doubt we considered ourselves lovers rather than warriors. In reality, we were neither. Both of us likely realized that it would only be a matter of time before MPs showed up, so we went our separate ways. The dispute was unresolved, unsettled, and clearly unimportant. I guess we both knew that the young lady who had inspired us to street warfare had, by now, sidled up to someone else.

When Cash finally returned home, he apparently found a successful life. He was, as I recall, his brother's manager for a while. Ultimately, he went on to a celebrated singing career of his own. Although Tommy never achieved the level of success of his brother, he had some recording hits and is still performing. I often wonder if he remembers our rumble. It may have given him the confidence he needed to succeed.

Arnold Zenker

Remember Arnold Zenker? He was a draftee who did a mid-day record show at AFN–Frankfurt. That was long before he garnered some national notoriety in 1967 when he substituted for Walter Cronkite on the CBS Evening News. Cronkite had honored an AFTRA (American Federation of Television and Radio Artists) picket line during a national strike. Zenker, a member of the CBS legal staff, was recruited to fill in for Cronkite because of his AFN on-air broadcast experience. Zenker appeared as a serious, buttoned-down presenter of the news. His glasses gave him a Robert Q. Lewis look. He got some nice reviews during the thirteen-day strike. Our paths crossed again a few years later when he did a morning talk show on WJZ–TV in Baltimore.

Gary Collins

Gary Collins was another disk jockey at AFN. He was determined and destined to be a star. Perhaps not of the first tier, but I'll bet you've seen him on TV. Collins was not considered a man of any special talent at that time although he was affable and articulate. He was tall, lean, blonde, toothy, and handsome, and his colleagues will confirm that he was well aware of these attributes. He wanted to be an actor. I remember his wandering the halls of the castle singing the score of *Oklahoma* when he was selected to play Curly in a military club production of the Rogers and Hammerstein hit. Let's just say that "Surrey With the Fringe on Top" does not necessarily play well in a military barracks setting. His fellow GIs got him to sharply reduce these hallway concerts.

Collins was married and lived off post with his wife who was a teacher in the military school system. It was her income that allowed them the luxury of a civilian apartment. Collins divorced her shortly before he was discharged. He took his release from the military overseas so he might pursue a career as an actor in some of the spaghetti westerns and other productions being produced in Europe. No one gave him much of a chance. Show business is a long shot.

I was working the overnight shift shortly after Collins' separation from the Army when he dropped by to ask if he could share my tiny BOQ apartment. It consisted of a bedroom and a small sitting room with nothing larger than a couch. He needed a place to sleep while I worked, leaving the place to me during the daytime. The inconvenience factor seemed low, and he promised it would last only until he left for Italy a week or two later "to make a movie." I was among those who figured it was just more Gary Collins BS, but I reluctantly agreed to let him use my place. "Use it" he did. He kept a parade of beautiful women moving in and out with such frequency that I sometimes thought I was on a Givenchy runway.

Typically, I would come home around nine in the morning, tired after the overnight grind. I'd let myself in and find a necktie on the door knob to the bedroom. My bedroom! And my necktie! It was the universal "do not disturb" sign that few young men could not read. I would try to be conspicuous and stomp around, cough loudly, take a noisy place on "his" couch, turn on the radio, and wait. Eventually, a stunning blonde, brunette, or redhead would emerge, smile, and leave without saying much, or anything. Gary would appear a little later, scratch himself, yawn loudly, mumble something that I rarely understood, and then leave, giving me an opportunity to straighten up the disheveled bed and go to sleep around the wet spots.

He would return a few hours later and take a noisy shower. Of course it woke me up. This went on for ten days or so until I told him I'd had enough and that he should be on his way. He was pretty good about it and was on the move fairly quickly. He told me he was off to Italy to try out for a part in *Cleopatra*. I learned years later that he did, in fact, get a small part, but I've never been able to spot him. Of course, it's a hard movie to watch more than once, and he more than likely found his mark in the middle of a legion of Roman soldiers.

The next I heard of him—I never heard *from* him again—he had gotten a bit part in *The Longest Day*. When I saw the movie, I found him on screen for about a minute drinking coffee and listening to Rod Steiger muse about the impending invasion. Collins had no lines. He must have nodded effectively, because he went on to co-star with Dale Robertson in a TV series called *Wells Fargo* and eventually wound up with a short-lived series of his own. I've forgotten its name.

He ultimately went on to become the television host of the Miss America Pageant in Atlantic City succeeding Bert Parks. He did that for nine years while guesting on a number of television series. He had an important role in *Roots*. He also had his own interview show for a time and won a daytime Emmy for that. Although he never achieved superstar status, he was quite successful and is still active. You can even find a Gary Collins star on the Hollywood Walk of Fame, but his biggest walk of fame as far as I was concerned was when he left my place, enabling me to get some sleep. And sleep I did, while Gary Collins went on to become a star.

Munich

*I*n the early 1960s, much of the Bavarian city of Munich appeared as it had hundreds of years earlier. Postwar construction was putting a more modern frame on the picture, but the Old World charm was everywhere. The Alps loomed to the south like a shadow on the horizon, and it was somehow comforting to know they were there. It was a landscape one never tired of.

Known as the "City with a Heart," Munich's history was showing a pulse during the days of the Roman Empire and early Benedictine monks. It survived colossal fires and medieval warring. The old downtown is dominated by the *Frauenkirche*, a twin-towered Gothic cathedral that has stood watch over the city-center for eight hundred years. It has been drawing tourists, artists, and worshippers in the predominantly Catholic region ever since.

The people of Munich are among the most friendly in Germany. In fact, they are quite different from all Germans, with the possible exception of the Berliners, who, collectively, have their own distinct, engaging personality as well as their own language. Bavarians are outgoing and wear their emotions on their sleeves as distinctly as they adorn the outside walls of their homes with colorful, pastoral murals. The hospitable nature of Bavarians may have been the result of almost (but not quite) mandatory employer-sanctioned beer breaks traditionally taken at mid-morning. They would typically wash down a snack they'd brought from home, usually a sandwich of some sort. (Interestingly, although everyone ate them, the Germans had no single word for sandwich at the time. Since my Munich days, the word *sandwich* has become a part of the language, although there is something of a compromise agreement on which article to use. Some call it *das sandwich*, while for others it's *der sandwich*. If you were in a restaurant and wanted, let's say, an

American-style ham sandwich, you'd have to say, "I would like ham put between two slices of bread put together." in German, it's *ein belegtes Brot mit Schinken zusammengeklappt*. (Why use one word when six will do?)

The region was prosperous and, to a young reporter, seemed to have survived the stains of recent history by sheer force of beauty and personality. Munich had nurtured the Nazi Party, hosted the abortive Hitler putsch, and was just twenty-five miles from the Landsberg prison where Hitler wrote *Mein Kampf*. Another chapter was written in the history books in 1938 when British Prime Minister Neville Chamberlain, meeting with Hitler in Munich, agreed to the Nazi leader's demands for the annexation of Sudetenland in Czechoslovakia in order to assure what Chamberlain would later hail (and still later regret) as "peace for our time." This acquiescence led directly to the Nazi takeover of all of Czechoslovakia. His famous speech came five years after a concentration camp at Dachau—a Munich suburb—was built.

My approach to Munich was not as a historian seeking ties to the past, but rather as a young man interested in participating in the vibrant present. The city offered so much. The wide boulevards bustled with activity, much of it produced by a large student population at the city's university. The historic panorama provided a beautiful set; handsome young men and pretty girls were omnipresent scenery.

My role as Munich correspondent responsible primarily for coverage of Eastern Europe was to gather information and analysis from researchers at the Munich-based American radio station Radio Free Europe (RFE). My reports were broadcast nightly on the AFN network program *Report from Europe*. In addition, I did a daily newscast for the local military audience, which consisted of military and community news. I also produced and hosted a weekly fifteen-minute feature program called *Assignment Bavaria,* which contained material of interest to the military audience. Years later, I learned that the young German engineer for that program was arrested, tried, and imprisoned as an East German spy. I never got a whiff of that during my eighteen months or so in Munich. I had no idea, making him a better-than-average spy, or me a less-than-average reporter.

Eventually, a new program was added to the network called *Weekend World*, which originated in Frankfurt. Its format was not unlike NBC's old *Monitor* program, which was a radio staple for many years. Our version aired for three hours on Saturday and Sunday afternoons and offered a variety of material from hard news and weather to entertainment segments and other human interest pieces. This program had an enormous appetite. It would gobble up almost everything that correspondents and in-house contributors were able to produce. It was extremely well done with a talented host who could have been valuable to any network back home. I spent much of my time during the week doing interviews and features for the two longer-form programs.

But my main focus was keeping on top of what was going on in Eastern Europe. I did so by gathering material from RFE which in those days was headquartered in Munich. RFE's mission was to broadcast to target nations behind the Iron Curtain— Czechoslovakia, Bulgaria, Hungary, Poland, Romania—broadcasting the West's version of world events to counter the slanted versions they were getting from their own government-controlled media.

The information from the West came from traditional wire services. However, a great deal of information came into the RFE offices from the East. The overwhelming majority of employees at RFE had been born and lived in the targeted nations, refugees who had fled to the West. They monitored the media in their former nations so completely that they were essentially reconstructing them on paper in Munich. Newspapers, magazines, and radio were scanned for political, economic, and other news. Every event, whether it was a political change in a remote town or the building of a new factory someplace equally obscure, would be monitored, tracked, and filed. Analysts "watched" the rise and fall of political personalities and monitored the political and social trends in their former countries. This enabled them to accurately identify future political leaders or dissidents. What may have seemed like innocuous information to the uninitiated proved highly valuable intelligence in the hands of analysts. The Central Intelligence Agency gathers much of its information the same way. RFE was officially divorced from the American intelligence community, though it certainly was a rich source of material for it.

Each day I picked up hundreds of pages of material assembled by the RFE news department. It was called the "Daily Budget."

Information therein was shared among the five Eastern European "desks." The material was also used by the news department either as background or, when warranted, as news and transmitted to the five targeted nations. I could not myself travel as a correspondent to Eastern European nations, so the RFE budget was a rich and single source of information for my nightly segments in *Report from Europe*.

Life was good, relatively easy, and at this stage, very much a learning situation for a young man in his early twenties. Although I was spoon-fed the Eastern European material, there was a challenge in going through it, evaluating it, and trying to understand so I could help others understand some of the things going on in the closed society in the East.

It was at RFE that I met Ingrid Gallmeister.

Steve McQueen and Ingrid

*I*ngrid was with RFE's Special Events Department, which put together feature material to be broadcast eastward. Her job was both administrative and secretarial with no on-air responsibilities.

She was German, very intelligent, spoke several languages, and admitted that her parents had been Nazis. Few Germans ever admitted any connection, no matter how obscure, to the Nazi Party. In fact, in almost seven years in Germany, she was the only person who ever admitted to me that she had a direct Nazi connection. And I met only two others in that time who admitted fighting against the Allies in World War II. One was a bartender who would have put on the uniform again at a moment's notice. The other was my brother's father-in-law who was conscripted in 1939 and fought in Russia and Italy.

Back to Ingrid. She was the exception to conventional wisdom that the Nazi Party produced nothing of beauty. Ingrid was a stunningly beautiful twenty-five year old who was the prototypical German with long blonde hair and blue eyes. She was a 10. Tall and athletic, with a body that would fuel any man's fantasy and any woman's envy, there was a movie-star quality to her look. If you remember the actress Susan Anton (about whom we'll hear more later), you will have an idea of the look. Yet, women seemed to enjoy her company, perhaps because she seemed oblivious to her attributes and therefore less threatening.

She did not dress to be overtly provocative, but that's what it was. She wore the typical costume of the young, modern Bavarian woman: usually ski pants and sweaters which accentuated her assets. There seemed to be no pretense. Her natural, spontaneous manner was engaging. Some interpreted her outgoing style as flirtatious and encouraging. Coupled with a hearty laugh and winning smile, it tended to lure platoons of male admirers until they realized her manner was more naturally friendly than flirtatious, or fell off the bus in confusion. She was one of those women who, most men will recognize, are approachable but unreachable. Ultimately, admirers came to realize in frustration that they had little chance with Ingrid—perhaps if they were a prince, or as it turned out, a movie star.

Of course I was infatuated with her, even if I took my place at the rear of a line of hopefuls. I used to see her every day during at least one of my two daily trips to RFE to pick up the budget. In fact, I made it a point to see her. We flirted, chatted easily, and became friends just as easily.

My hope for a more intimate relationship was fueled by her fascination with my job and her eagerness to visit our studios and watch a broadcast. Her ambition was to do work on the air as a feature reporter. There was little opportunity for that at Radio Free Europe. Her language proficiency was in German, English, and French. RFE broadcast only in the languages of its East European target nations. Nor was there any chance of broadcasting for AFN, which she knew. Her hope was to broadcast for German radio.

I eagerly accommodated her wish to visit during our broadcasts and spend time observing the other things we did, such as editing audio, recording material, and writing newscasts. She indicated she was impressed, but she was infatuated with radio, not me, and her visits only reinforced her ambition. Ingrid's time at AFN also ultimately defined the lines of our relationship, which was evolving, sadly, into nothing more than a solidly platonic friendship. We'd have an occasional beer, and I began to get the picture she drew of a tragic love. Seems she had had a torrid relationship with an American race car driver who was killed driving on some European track. Ironically, his name was Lucky. I kid you not.

In any case, she was not quite over that. As well as we got along, and in spite of the fact we enjoyed our times together, it was clear that, as she saw it, her next non-platonic relationship was on a distant emotional horizon well beyond me, and, as I would realize soon enough, well over my head. For the moment, she was in love with radio and seemed obsessed with finding a way to make it a career.

In order to put the rest of this story together I must digress.

A major motion picture was about to be shot in Munich. It was to star several actors who were at various stages of their careers when the shooting began, including Steve McQueen, James Garner, Charles Bronson, James Coburn, and Richard Attenborough (now Sir Richard Attenborough), just to name the main players. *The*

Great Escape was released in mid-1963 to great reviews and is considered by some to be a classic. None of this was foreseen by any of us who frequented the set. For me, during the several weeks of shooting, it was an opportunity to regularly fill my feature bag with material for *Weekend World* or that insipid weekly *Assignment Bavaria* radio program. I made the movie a regular assignment. I found it heady stuff.

It was filmed at a studio in Geiselgasteig just south of Munich. The entire property was a set or a potential set. A small replica of the Brandenburg Gate greeted the visitor just inside the main gate. In 1961, Billy Wilder was making the film *One, Two, Three* in Berlin. He was nearing completion when construction of the Berlin Wall began. Wilder still had several critical scenes to shoot involving the Brandenburg Gate, which is one of the great landmarks of the city and which was located on the line separating the eastern from the Western sectors of Berlin. Since he no longer had access to the gate and the angles he needed for his scenes, Wilder built a smaller replica of it at the Geiselgasteig studios and finished his filming there.

Just one of the tricks Hollywood was and is capable of. *The Great Escape* is a World War II German prison camp drama. The set included a partial reproduction of a wartime prisoner of war camp, including a row of prisoner barracks. More accurately put, they were façades of barracks built to face in various directions.

The Brandenburg Gate

The layout appeared odd to the visitor until it was explained that they were constructed to accommodate the day's shifting light. This would enable them to shoot all day in front of one façade or another, keeping shadows and lighting relatively constant. Because much of the movie involved exterior shooting, this made for a more efficient shooting schedule. I visited the set frequently and got to know the principal players fairly well. Nothing social, but they knew me and were apparently comfortable with my hanging around. I was certainly comfortable basking in their glow, and I was productive with the microphone interviewing stars, directors, producers, and all sorts of behind-the-scenes people. Frankly, it was exciting being in this Hollywood atmosphere and among the celebrities. We were all on a first name basis. All this just two years after Frank and Dean.

It was in the middle of all of this when Ingrid stopped me at RFE. She wanted a favor. Seems she had a chance for a radio job and wanted to do an audition. She asked if she could accompany me the next time I visited *The Great Escape* set so she could do some interviews and make them part of an audition package. That certainly was no problem for me, and I was happy to help. She also wanted to use my equipment, my precious Nagra, to do her recording. That was also no problem. I gave her more instruction in its use than had been given me before the Sinatra–Martin "interviews," and she caught on quickly. It was probably a few days before we actually went to the set. On the way out she told me how excited she was about the job prospect and about the good fortune of having a big-time movie being shot in the area. An audition tape is always enhanced if you have people on it who are well known. It punches up the reporter's credibility and makes it more likely that the person reviewing the tape will actually listen to it. There were plenty of well-knowns at Geiselgasteig, so her prospects were bright.

On arrival, she went right to work ingratiating herself with the publicity people and those she interviewed or wanted to interview. I don't remember exactly whom she interviewed initially, but I do recall that she had set her sights on Steve McQueen. He was involved in a scene and unavailable on our arrival. However, he ultimately agreed to an interview. He was known to have an eye for the ladies, and I suspect that when he saw who wanted to do the interview it didn't take too much persuasion. Ingrid and I had been sharing the Nagra, and she was excited about the promised interview, so she took the tape recorder and was off.

I occupied myself watching them set up to film a tunnel scene as I waited for her. I had some time before I had to get back for that daily newscast and the rest of the routine. But ten minutes stretched into twenty. Half an hour became an hour. All of a sudden time was beginning to be a problem. I found one of the women handling publicity and asked if she knew where Ingrid and McQueen were. She did not. I wandered around to some of the areas where interviews were often conducted. Nothing! Time had picked up speed, and I was almost at a point of no return. I needed to get back. I needed my Nagra. And, because she had traveled with me, I needed Ingrid, though at that point I would have gladly settled for two out of three.

Someone finally got the idea that they might have gone to McQueen's private dressing room. These sanctuaries, which were actually more like small suites, were off-limits to all but the most chosen on this, and I assume, most movie sets. I had never been to any of the private areas, but soon I was on my way with a publicist and a security guard.

We knocked when we got to his door. I'm sure I was checking my watch every few seconds by then. No answer. More knocking. More silence from within. The publicist and the security guard moved away and conferred. It was clearly a very serious conversation. I was not a part of it nor could I understand anything that was being said. They wore worried expressions, as did I. At one point in the proceedings I remember making it clear that a very valuable piece of recording equipment was involved in our little quest and that I had no intention of leaving without it.

Finally, a decision was made to enter the room. The security guard produced a key and knocked loudly on the door once more. He was nervous and the publicity lady was apoplectic, probably thinking that she was watching her professional life flash before her eyes. After the last echo of the last knuckle-rapping faded away, the lock clicked with the turn of the guard's key. The door swung open. The woman and the security man stepped inside. I stood at the door.

From where I stood I could see that the room was empty. I could also see the Nagra on a small table in the middle of the room. I was transfixed watching the two reels turn. One was empty. The other was producing a thakata-thakata sound as a tail of tape slapped against the plastic wheel that was supposed to guide the tape through the recording mechanism. I stepped into the room, shut off the machine, and slung it over my shoulder. Because the room was empty, my two companions seems a little more relaxed. They were edging toward the door as I was, anxious to put their intrusion behind them.

I thanked them as I made my way toward the exit and my car. I had no idea where Ingrid was, although I had a pretty good notion.

I had her tape and out of curiosity listened to her interview later that day. It's hard to describe my feeling hearing her voice coming from the speaker. Oddly enough, it made me feel lonely somehow. It was like hearing the voice of someone you long for who is far away and cursing the distance between you. Or perhaps it was more like hearing the voice of someone close who had died. Conflicting emotions that were hard to define washed over me. I was sad and angry. I was bitter and even a little envious that she had pulled it off and handled herself as one might expect Ingrid to. She was, as usual, flirtatious, in a subtle and engaging way. I recognized the technique quite well although the interview itself was unremarkable. Unremarkable until the end.

That's when McQueen propositioned her. It came out quite naturally, as I recall, as if it were part of the interview. It ended with her quick acceptance. So quick in fact, she forgot to turn off the Nagra.

Years later, I watched the famous Steve McQueen movie, *The Thomas Crown Affair,* in which McQueen co-starred with Faye Dunaway. There is an extraordinarily sensual, suggestive, and provocative scene in which McQueen and Dunaway's steamy game of chess is a metaphor for raw passion. Dialogue was extraneous as the music of Michel LeGrand enhanced the sexual tension, elevating it from warm to torrid. I always considered it one of the most sensually provocative scenes ever filmed. The sensuality was established with the eyes and sexually charged gestures. When I first saw that film I sensed that it must have been similar to Ingrid's interview with McQueen.

My next meeting with Ingrid was a frosty one. I had not heard from her for several days after the trip to the movie set. I called, but there was no answer. I looked for her at RFE during my daily trips there, but she never seemed to be around. Her colleagues made what I thought were obvious excuses: "She's in a meeting," "she's sick today," or "she's on an errand." I guess my feelings were hurt that she was avoiding me.

She called about a week later and sheepishly asked if she could have the tape. She didn't ask if I had listened, and I don't believe she cared one way or the other. She explained that some German radio executives were interested in hearing her interview with the movie star and wondered if she could have the tape. Ingrid was Ingrid. She seduced me just as effectively as McQueen had seduced her, and the next thing I knew I was in my car heading for RFE with the tape. When I got there, there was nothing more than a "thank you." No mention of the tryst, no mention of the visit to the studio at all. In fact, she left the office with me just standing there within seconds of receiving the tape. I can only guess she was taking it to an editing suite to expunge the incriminating sequence.

Shortly after that, Ingrid left Radio Free Europe. I learned years later the terminating officer cited her for frequent absenteeism and tardiness and that it was a tearful departure. I also learned she invited him over for drinks hours after he fired her in an apparent attempt to get her job back. He refused.

At the time, I was uncertain whether she had joined German radio or what had happened. Our relationship had tailed off since the visit to *The Great Escape* set. I made a few fruitless calls to her apartment. She, of course, had no particular reason to contact me. Former co-workers at RFE were vague as to her whereabouts. I was getting the message. My own work and the passage of time put more and more distance between thoughts about Ingrid Gallmeister and the routine of my life.

She was about the farthest thing from my mind when I saw her next. I had been on assignment in Berchtesgaden in Southern Bavaria, a town close to Hitler's infamous Eagle's Nest retreat. My assignment included an interview with General Maxwell Taylor, President Kennedy's top military guy. I was sick as a dog when we sat down together. I almost fainted during the interview and couldn't have been happier when it was over. I knew something was wrong and that I needed medical attention. Seems I had come down with pneumonia during the trip although I didn't know it. Nonetheless, I drove back to Munich later in the day, feeling lousier with every mile. I tried to sweat it out in my tiny BOQ, but ultimately I had to call for help and was taken to the hospital by ambulance.

A day or two into the stay, I had a visitor. Ingrid! It had been a couple of months since I had seen or heard from her. She had apparently called my office where she learned of my illness and somehow made her way out for the visit. The hospital was a good twenty miles from downtown Munich. She had no car. I don't remember how she got there, but the means may, as it turns out, be significant.

I was happy to see her. We made small talk. No mention of the Geiselgasteig incident. She was doing some freelance public relations work, she told me, and the radio job was still pending. I guess we must have chatted for half an hour when she made a very unusual request, prompting my equally unusual response. She asked if—since I was laid up in the hospital—she might use my car for a couple of days. She wanted to visit a friend in nearby Austria. Remarkably, I agreed, even though letting a German national use an auto bearing a military license plate, was absolutely verboten. Since I worked for the military as a civilian, my car carried the distinctive maroon license plate of U.S. forces.

It was absolutely the wrong thing for me to do, but I did it. I told her she could take it for a couple of days. I was expecting to be in the hospital for another three or four days anyway. Shortly after I agreed, she left in my car. It was only after she was long gone that I began to worry about what I had done. If she were stopped at the border or had an accident, I would be in a lot of trouble and would probably have my registration and military driver's license pulled. It could even be worse than that. And had I known then what I would later learn, I would have been frantic.

However, she was back in time to drive me home from the hospital. There had been no incident. I asked cautiously if there had been any problem crossing the border. Her German papers would not have matched the registration. She just smiled in response. No doubt the same kind of smile she would have offered a smitten border guard. That's the way she was. A wink and a nod and a brilliant smile could take this young lady a long, long way, borders or no borders. Then, she was out of my life again. The next time I saw her would be the last.

Oh well, I still had *The Great Escape*. The occupation of Geiselgasteig by the stars, the sets, the publicity people, and all the trappings of movie making was about to end as producers sought to wrap it up before fall. But one of those stars and I found ourselves caught up in a drama of our own that was, and was not, of our own making.

Jim Garner
and the Munich Riots

*T*he student district in Munich is a wonderful area. In those days, as it is now, it was alive and vibrant with the palpable energy of youth. The university stretches in part along one of the grand boulevards of the city: Leopoldstrasse. It is a broad thoroughfare crowded with vehicular traffic and a steady parade of pedestrians who populate the street at all hours of the day and night. Sidewalk cafes stretched like open arms waiting to embrace, and, when the weather permitted, the embrace was mutual, as students filled the entire area. Young lovers held hands and swooned at tiny tables. Students drank beer or wine nearby stretching their intellectual muscles with arguments about anything worth, or not worth, arguing about. Others drank coffee and read papers or studied. A walk down the street was a dream come true for a linguist. Dozens of languages were in play at all times, and an assortment of tongues from all corners of the world could be heard from one table after another. One attraction of the cafes was that a patron could tarry at a table for hours over a single cup of coffee without fear of eviction, which played very well among the traditionally impoverished students

Such was life on Leopoldstrasse day and night during the nice weather of spring, summer, and fall. It was student turf, but older residents ventured into the hospitable environment as the sun went down for the same reasons as the students. Coexistence was typically peaceful. There was plenty of room. And if it was crowded, strangers would share tables.

But as can happen, a small incident on a summer evening served to intrude on the normal tranquility. A student with a guitar found a place on a busy sidewalk and established squatter's rights. He cradled the instrument in his arms and began to play and sing. It was all very pleasant and very innocent until some passersby found it inconvenient to walk around the musician. Some took exception to the music itself. It led to an exchange of words, which, in turn, led to a further exchange that quickly got ugly.

People nearby and passersby began to take sides, and the exchanges became more heated and vociferous. This, in turn, drew the attention of others who had earlier been oblivious to any exchanges, and before long they were drawn in. Soon the verbal jousting became more physical. Pushing and shoving led to some punches. In some cases, blood was drawn. It became raucous enough that police were soon on the scene trying to break up the crowd. That only exacerbated the situation and more people were drawn to the area, some as onlookers, others as participants. Within a very short time the crowd numbered in the hundreds.

The few officers present found it increasingly difficult to establish control. They called for reinforcements, which only resulted in protests from jeering students. Within less than an hour after the original incident, two dozen police were using batons to prod people out of the area. Students found the tactic unacceptable and voiced their displeasure in an ever-increasing crescendo. Other students who had not even been in the area earlier were drawn to it by the noise and word of mouth. Police suddenly found themselves surrounded by thousands of angry, shouting students who would not comply with orders to disperse. Few things make police officers more angry. They called for more reinforcements. Before long, dozens of officers arrived. The appearance was menacing as they arrived on a phalanx of horses deployed across the entire breadth of the boulevard.

Students watched the officers position their steeds flank to flank a block away, then slowly make their way down the boulevard toward the young people. The line of horses and their riders stretched from one side of Leopoldstrasse to the other, so close together that there wasn't enough space for a small man to walk between the horses. The strategy was clear. The mob was being approached by the four-legged police line and was forced to retreat as far as the riders chose.

But the students resisted and refused to move. Then it really got ugly. Horsemen walked into the unyielding crowd. The big animals shouldered young people aside and stepped on and, in some cases, kicked them. The horsemen maintained their line and swung rubber truncheons striking their targets in the heads, shoulders, and upper torsos. Many of the students fled bleeding and screaming as the mounted patrol forged onward. It was a mismatch. Students had the numbers but the police had the muscle. The officers on foot who'd arrived earlier made their way into the crowd to support their colleagues on horseback. They were no less enthusiastic in their handling of the students and arrested many after beating them.

Students quickly lost their taste for the beatings and had an equal distaste for arrest. They sought out the escape valve, the side streets, literally avenues of escape from the horses. They left behind bits of clothing, eyeglasses, and books. Also left behind were small pools of blood and blood spatters in those parts of the street where contact had been most intense. It had all started with an impolite verbal exchange and escalated quickly into out-and-out street warfare.

The next night, the guitar player was out again, this time with an audience. Thousands of students swarmed into the area before the sun went down. When it did, the horsemen were back, two lines this time and the battle was joined before the street was dark. Rocks and other missiles were brought into the fray this time, and blood was drawn among the policemen on horseback. It took several hours to clear the streets. If the first night had been a rout, this was closer to a draw, but the students still got the worst of it.

The next night was even worse as two lines of police on horseback converged on the students from opposite ends of Leopoldstrasse. On this night, ambulances were behind them at both ends to tend to the inevitable wounded on both sides. There were also dozens of officers on foot who came into the combat from side streets, cutting off previous escape routes. The anger spawned on previous nights had turned to furor, and they turned their clubs on the students with the strength borne of that anger.

By now, it was a national story making headlines all over the country. And as such incidents tend to do, the predictability of the event was drawing a crowd of its own. People were drawn to the violence as onlookers, which presented dangers of a different sort. In the minds of the police, being near the conflict was being a part of it.

The police presence left few places of refuge. Anyone on Leopoldstrasse, or near to it, risked a confrontation with an officer who was on horseback or on foot. Many reporters, myself included, felt the sting of those rubber clubs while trying to get out of the way. Many other innocent onlookers found themselves in the middle of the melee as the students, pursued by the horsemen, spilled into side streets, where they were intercepted by policemen who had been posted there to plug the escape routes. By the third night, the officers were clearly more interested in doing physical damage to the students than they were in merely clearing the streets. It was a very unflattering episode for Munich policemen.

The street action was getting a lot of attention from Innsbruck to Berlin. And even at Geiselgasteig. James Garner came to town to catch the show. He unexpectedly found himself a player in the drama. And because of it, so did I.

As a reporter, I covered the student-police clashes every night. I was there with my trusty tape recorder gathering sound and interviews for my daily newscast and for *Report from Europe*. It was rare that the Munich correspondent had breaking news for that broadcast.

It was on the third or fourth night of the clashes, a Friday night, that I ran into Jim Garner in the crowd that typically gathered on the periphery of the Leopoldstrasse confrontation. Sightseers usually retreated to safety on the side streets that funneled into the main boulevard once the troubles started. But dozens of police gathered on many of those side streets awaiting the call to enter the fray. It was a tense time for the officers as they anticipated the clash. I think it is fair to say, based on my observation and recollection, that far too many of them were impatient to join the free-swinging melee. Because it was a Friday night most people in the area were anticipating the largest demonstration likely to lead to the most violent confrontation.

When I bumped into Garner, he was furious. He recognized me from my many hours on the movie set where I had frequently interviewed him. He was surrounded by Germans who had obviously recognized him and was accompanied by at least two stunning young women. Garner was complaining to the few onlookers that police had confronted him as he parked his car on one of the less busy side streets. He was unaware that I was recording him at first. When he realized I was recording, he turned his attention to me and told his story.

He told me that several officers had approached him. Garner thought they recognized him, or were attracted by his car, a late-model Jaguar. Rather than approach him as a celebrity, he said they spoke to him harshly and seemed to be on the verge of getting physically abusive. They demanded his passport. It was in his wallet and when he withdrew it from his jacket, one of the officers grabbed it. Not only did the policeman take the passport, Garner told me, he emptied the wallet of some eight hundred dollars in cash.

Garner said he protested, but the officers would not listen. Instead, they told him they were keeping his passport and that if he wanted it he would have to go to police headquarters "later" to retrieve it and to face "possible charges." Apparently, that led to a shouting match. Garner demanded identification from the officers as well as the return of his passport and cash. The officers refused and ultimately left, returning to the fun.

The actor was livid. He had no personal identification, no money, and no idea what possible charges might be filed against him. He had, he said, done nothing more than get out of his car with his friends, then comply with the police request for his passport.

Jim Garner had worked up a full head of steam during his conversation with me. He became angrier as he spoke. He said that when he had been making a film in Japan (*Sayonara*, I believe), Tokyo was experiencing ongoing student protest demonstrations. These too had received international coverage primarily because the police were particularly harsh in dealing with the demonstrators.

Garner told me that as badly as the Japanese students had been treated by police, it was nothing compared to what was going on in Munich. The police were out of control in this city, he said, and much more brutal than their Japanese counterparts. Then, he added, "What I'm seeing here reminds me of what it must have been like under the Nazis in the thirties." To me, that was a pretty good sound bite, and I knew just what to do with it.

The following day, Saturday, offered the perfect vehicle for the story. AFN's *Weekend World* ran for three hours during the afternoon. Its voracious appetite enabled longer-form reportage. The ongoing Munich "riots," as they were now being called, was big news in Germany, and the Garner interview was perfect for the format.

I spent much of the night putting together a piece and fed it to the network headquarters in Frankfurt to be broadcast Saturday afternoon. Once on the air, it set into motion a series of events that almost cost me my job and almost had Jim Garner thrown out of Germany. Inasmuch as *The Great Escape* had not yet finished its Germany shooting, with several scenes remaining to be filmed, the incident almost undercut the production of a major Hollywood film.

The German government took serious exception to Garner's characterization of the Munich police as Nazis or Nazi-like. German sensitivity to the Nazi era was acute, and this reminder was more than unwelcome. An apology was demanded. German public opinion was squarely behind the government, and not only because of Garner's comments.

Garner was a Korean War veteran. While filming *The Great Escape*, as I recall, he had been made an honorary member of the famous 24th Infantry Division that was then headquartered in Augsburg, Germany. It was a famous military unit and was stationed in the German Federal Republic as a visible and tangible counterpoint to any post–Berlin Wall Soviet military intentions in Western Europe. Many Germans apparently thought Garner's comments on the streets of Munich sullied the revered division because of his honorary association with it. It also proved an embarrassment for commanders of the division. But it was what Germans considered the actor's insulting reference to their country's Nazi past, linked to the troubled present, that government officials and citizens alike found most irritating and unacceptable.

An apology was demanded, but Garner was defiant despite threats to kick him out of the country. He stood by his remarks. There was a lot at stake for him, not the least of which was the completion of his movie. Garner was apparently as stubborn as he was proud. For several days he stood by his refusal to apologize for what he believed was an accurate observation. I have no idea what sort of pressures he was subjected to, but he ultimately did issue an apology, which sufficed to put the issue to rest.

I was caught in the undertow for having reported the comments in the first place. I was advised that it could lead to my being asked to leave Germany as well. I was never asked to make any kind of apology; however, I was led to believe that somehow my fate was linked to Garner's response. It may or may not have been, but the bottom line was that he got to finish his picture and I got to stay.

Betrayal

$\mathcal{A}$nd then, Ingrid Gallmeister was back in my life. The riots ended when students decided that the show was not for them. *The Great Escape* tent had folded. Routine had returned to my life, only to be disrupted by yet another call from Ingrid. It was the last I ever received from her.

She called me at the office. Her voice was uncharacteristically nervous. She explained that she had a problem and asked if I could meet her. Her choice of a meeting place was also unusual. It was not at one of Munich's innumerable sidewalk cafes, which was a typical meeting place for us (back in the days when we'd meet at all). She chose a busy department store. I didn't think too much of it at the time, although later I theorized she favored being in the midst of a crowd.

It was not the same Ingrid. She was clearly nervous and somehow looked less glamorous than usual. It was a tentative Ingrid who showed none of her customary confidence. She was slightly unkempt. The long, blonde hair needed to be brushed. She wore no makeup. Her clothes just weren't right. It was as if she had been taken apart and put back together just slightly differently. She was biting her lips and paying close attention to the shoppers when I found her. When I arrived, her appearance changed. It was less a look of relief than of impatience.

She put a hand on my arm and directed me to a less busy aisle. "I need to borrow some money," she said. It was not a request and not a demand but was closer to the latter than the former. It was quintessential Ingrid, a woman not used to having requests denied. There was nothing coy in her attitude, just impatience. I suppose she knew there was less likelihood that there would be a denial from me than most. Knowing that probably made her even less patient. I asked what she needed the money for. More lip-biting. She said something about her mother being sick and Ingrid's need to travel to her hometown of Mönchengladbach near the Dutch border.

I was the customary putty in her hands. I never carry much cash, but I had a one hundred mark note in my wallet. That was about twenty-five dollars in those days. I told her that that was all I had on me. She snapped it as I pulled it from my wallet. "I'll pay you when I get back," she said, and quickly melted into the crowd, where, within seconds, she was lost among the ambling shoppers. That was that. It all happened in less than a minute. No small talk. No goodbyes. No thank you. No mention of when she would be back. In fact, she would not be back. I never saw her again after the following day, when her picture was on the front page of the nation's leading tabloid. It told an incredible tale.

A certain amount of background is necessary here. These were the days of Charles de Gaulle's France. The French president's ongoing crisis concerned Algeria and its drive for independence. For almost a decade, Algeria had been engaged in a violent, anti-colonialist campaign against France. Paris considered Algeria French territory and was unyielding in its efforts to hang on to what it considered its North African real estate. What began as an Algerian terrorist operation against French settlers in Algeria and the French Army there evolved into a full-scale war that deeply divided France, and in many ways still does. Even de Gaulle, who came to power with the promise of maintaining Algeria as part of the French family, eventually came to understand that France could not hold on to its colonial property. He swung toward independence. The political opposition swung back with a mailed fist.

Right wing generals who opposed independence for Algeria quickly came to despise the former war hero and colleague. They established a violent network to work actively against him. Many of those generals and other dissident officers were responsible for unspeakable reprisals and torture against Algerian patriots. They formed what was called the Secret Army Organization, or OAS, which sought to overthrow de Gaulle and worked actively in opposition to agreements that ultimately granted Algeria independence.

One of the leading officers in this cause was Colonel Antoine Argoud. At one time he was a ranking officer on the general staff in Algeria and was close to those opposed to de Gaulle's new policies. Initially, he was secretly involved in various efforts to derail independence. When his sympathies became less secret, Argoud was recalled to France and put under surveillance. He secretly returned to Algiers and was eventually exiled from France after an abortive effort with fellow plotters to thwart de Gaulle's plans to cut Algeria loose. Argoud remained active in the cause and from outside of France helped set up a committee of national resistance. He was a thorn in the French president's side and went into hiding. Unbeknownst to any but those closest to him, his base of operations was in Munich.

In the winter of 1963, Argoud returned to Paris. However, it was in the back of a small van. He had been kidnapped from a hotel in Munich and spirited across the French border. The van, on information provided by an anonymous tipster, was located just a few blocks from the police headquarters in Paris. As promised by the informant, the "most wanted man" in France was found inside the van. Argoud was bound and gagged and immediately placed under arrest.

The German newspaper I was reading a few days later was recounting this story. It showed a picture of Argoud and the van in which he was found. There was also a picture of a woman believed to have worked for Argoud in Munich who was said to have participated in a plot to return him to France. I could not believe my eyes. It was Ingrid Gallmeister. There was no mistaking her. The quality of the picture was poor, either a mug shot or a driver's license photo, but there it was over her name.

The story was based mostly on interviews, conjecture, and speculation. However, there was no doubt in my mind that it was true. Given her fluency in both German and French, she had apparently gone to work for Colonel Argoud and his resistance movement in Munich. She had taken one of two sides. If she had betrayed Argoud, that would have put enraged loyalists on her scent. If she were working for government agents, her role might well have proved awkward for them, something they would prefer to live without. Either option guaranteed that she would have dangerous enemies. The people supporting de Gaulle played at least as tough as those who opposed him. Developing scenarios in which either side would find it expeditious to eliminate Ingrid for her role in the abduction was not difficult. She was either a traitor to a cause, or a potential embarrassment.

Whatever her motive was, the limited available information showed that Ingrid and a male friend had abducted Argoud in Munich and drove him to Paris. There seems to be little dispute about that. Some early news reports said he was brought to France by French secret policemen. So perhaps she was on the government payroll. We will never know for certain because Ingrid Gallmeister was never heard from again. The newspaper story said simply that she was missing.

The crowd she may have betrayed included any number of cut-throats and killers. The rebel military had killed and tortured and maimed opponents in Algeria. Their heroes were people who led them, and Colonel Antoine Argoud was one of those leaders. It is not too much of a stretch to imagine they caught up with Ingrid and meted out the ultimate punishment for her "treason." Argoud's supporters would not likely have been lenient, or to have fallen for that wink and a smile. On the other hand, operatives on the other side might have had their own reasons for eliminating their linkage.

The whole story brought me back to those few days when she was cruising in my borrowed car. Had she used it for a dry run of some sort to see how she could handle border operations? Had she gone to Austria in my car, or had she made a dry run to France? And what if it had been my car used in the abduction rather than a small van? Where might that have led? There were more questions than answers, but that is as close as I ever hope to get to foreign intrigue at that level.

Poor Ingrid. I am convinced she is dead and has been since shortly after I lent her the one hundred marks. The incident certainly explains her appearance and nervousness the last day I saw her. Beauty does not hold up under fear. I still have a clear image of her in that final minute we were together. She was obviously nervous and worried. Knowing that ruthless thugs would be looking for her would do that and more. It also could explain why she wanted a meeting in a crowded place. She may well have feared her own abduction. That might have been the last day of her life. On the other hand, that one hundred marks might have gotten her out of Munich in time. I doubt it, but I would like to think so.

Argoud, by the way, was sentenced to life in prison later in 1963. However, he was pardoned by de Gaulle five years later as the French president faced students in another summer crisis. There were fears that some army officers still smarting from France's loss of Algeria might join the students making an already very bad situation a lot worse. Colonel Argoud was pardoned as a gesture to keep the military in line. Argoud died at the age of eighty-nine in 2004. Ingrid Gallmeister could have been no more than twenty-five or so. That's how well I knew her. I never even knew her age.

The Great Escape
Actors Emote

*A*number of flash frames come to mind when I think back on the Munich period. I was doing a lot more feature reporting than covering hard news. It was not unusual that I, as a correspondent responsible for covering Eastern Europe, had no access to Eastern Europe. Thanks to the scholars and journalists at Radio Free Europe I was able to stay abreast of developments throughout the area, and I managed to become quite proficient in both pronouncing and spelling the names of leaders pulling the strings behind the Iron Curtain. Names like Enver Hoxa, János Kádár, Georgie Georgiu Dej, Władysław Gomułka, and Nicolae Ceauescu were prominently featured every night. Quite an alphabet soup! However, since I was totally detached and separated from my "beat," I focused on those things that were more accessible. Usually, that involved interviewing celebrities who came to town.

The mother lode was to be found on the set of *The Great Escape*.

At one point, I was asked to approach the stars—Steve McQueen, James Garner, Charles Bronson, and James Coburn—and ask them to record some public service messages for Labor Day. Basically, I requested that they do thirty-second spots encouraging GIs and their families to drive safely over the holiday. It was felt that this would be especially meaningful coming from McQueen who had something of a reputation as a speed merchant on four wheels or two.

The actors readily agreed so I wrote several spots for them to read. It was no big deal and was designed to involve a minimum of time for all involved. It didn't quite work out that way for unexpected reasons.

We got together outdoors on the prison camp set. I doled out the scripts and started recording. One by one they read them. And one by one, I was forced to ask them for additional takes. They were awful readers! They sounded unnatural and as if they were reading the scripts. That's a no-no. It's supposed to sound like the reader is just talking to the audience, not reading. There was no natural rhythm. Their words were halting and uneven. In fact, each of them sounded a lot like children learning to read by picking out words one at a time. Additionally, the timing was way off. They were either well short or well over the required thirty seconds. I was startled by the amateurish performance by these established stars, and I knew I could not put the material on the air as they read it. It was that bad. It was also embarrassing for me to ask them time and again to repeat the readings. Who was I?

They took me, and themselves, off the hook. They listened to the playback, and I'm sure they were hearing what I was hearing. They did not attain their star status through poor performances. One of them, I think McQueen, said something about the way it sounded. They all agreed that it did not sound as they would like.

I don't remember the exact words, but as the others nodded in agreement, McQueen explained that as actors they were not used to reading scripts aloud. What they did was memorize scripts, then emote . . . or "act" them. He asked if I minded if they just looked the scripts over then put the message in their own words. Was I going to disagree? No way.

They each did so and within a matter of a few minutes I had all the scripts on tape. They had "said" the message perfectly and within the time frame that was necessary. The transformation from the original readings was extraordinary. Bottom line was they could have let the original readings go and not worry about it. But they did worry. They were too professional to allow an admittedly inferior performance to hit the airwaves. So they figured out a way to make it work.

"She's going to be a star!"

*A*t the time *The Great Escape* was made, co-star Richard Attenborough was not well known in the United States in spite of an illustrious two-decade film career in his native Britain. His career has been remarkable as an actor and Academy Award–winning director (for *Gandhi*). His credits fill pages. He was knighted by Queen Elizabeth in 1976. However, he was all but unknown to me in the early 1960s.

During one of my visits to the set of *The Great Escape*, Attenborough approached me and asked if I would be interested in interviewing a friend of his who was visiting the set. He pointed to a young woman on the other side of the room. She was petite and attractive though somewhat short of leading lady looks. Attenborough allowed as how she was a huge singing star in Britain and that it was only a matter of time before she was big in the United States. She had a peculiar name. I had never heard of her. I was busy. I turned down his offer. I think he was more surprised than hurt by my rejection.

It was only a matter of months before I was hearing that unusual name singing one of the biggest hits of the 1960s just about every time I turned on the radio. The name was Petula Clark. The song was *Downtown*. She was good enough to earn a Grammy, but not good enough for my pitiful Bavarian feature program.

Other Celebrities

*I*f nothing else, I was consistent. During those days in Munich I felt as if I were actually being stalked by another recording artist. I started getting phone calls at the office and even at home from a young singer who was on the military club circuit and looking for publicity. He wanted to be on my humble *Assignment Bavaria* program. It was not quite the right format for entertainment, so I turned him down. He was persistent. On one occasion, he even managed to reach me at a party at a friend's house. The phone rang. It was for me. It was Roy Orbison. Again, he wanted to be on the program. Again, I turned him down as I did every time until he stopped calling giving him the time to advance from star to superstar status.

I was much more receptive to established stars. It was my pleasure to spend a day with Duke Ellington in Munich. I went to the airport to interview him upon arrival in town for a concert. I was surprised when he came into the terminal alone. He looked somewhat lonely and confused as I approached him. He readily agreed to the interview, which we did at the airport. Then he asked if I would give him a lift to his hotel. I did, and en route I offered to show him around. He seemed grateful for that, and we spent the better part of the day hitting many of Munich's points of interest. For a few years thereafter, I received Christmas cards from him signed with the signature phrase "I love you madly."

Louis Armstrong was equally gracious. I intercepted him in front of his hotel on the morning of a big performance. He had just arrived from Paris by train and looked exhausted. The rest of his musicians were flying in later. Nonetheless, he agreed to an interview "for the boys." I thought he might fall asleep during our talk, yet that night he was refreshed and at the top of his game on stage. The Germans loved him, as they did all the Americans who performed for them with great regularity.

There were many performers of diverse reputations and accomplishments who came to Munich to entertain both Germans and Americans. People like Rita Moreno, Martha Graham, Carlos Montoya, Tony Curtis, Erroll Garner, Count Basie, Chubby Checker, virtually every country star alive at the time, and many, many more. Unlike Messers Sinatra and Martin, they were all always happy to spend a few minutes at the microphone to say hello to the troops.

Dachau

*T*he tiny village of Dachau was just a few miles from my apartment in Munich. It was a typical charming Bavarian market village with the obligatory onion-shaped church steeples and colorful farm scene murals on the sides of buildings. The cobbled streets were narrow and lined with shops, making it easy for the women to walk from their homes to the butcher or baker. The men wore leather shorts and green hats with feathers in them; the women favored their colorful dresses, Dirndls. The children had rosy cheeks and played games in the streets as parents worked or shopped nearby. It hadn't changed much over generations. The postcard charm belied its sinister history as home to the infamous Dachau Concentration Camp.

The camp site is a short distance from the picturesque village, which made it convenient for those village residents who were involved in the camp's activities and operation. The camp was built in 1933 on the site of a former munitions factory, but it was under constant expansion during its first decade. Certainly, villagers were employed there during the various expansion projects, performing labor not suited for either the prisoners or the troops who manned or administered the camp.

Yet, when the camp was liberated, villagers denied any knowledge of Dachau's past or purpose. They wanted the world to believe they never questioned the foul and greasy smoke that poured from its smokestacks, nor did they ever question the steady stream of prisoners behind the barbed wire. In the early days, executions were carried out by shooting prisoners in the back of the head as they knelt beside what was called the "blood trench." Villagers never questioned what was going on. Many said they never heard the gunshots. Their denials so infuriated the American officers who liberated the camp that the villagers were made to clean it up.

Dachau was Hitler's first concentration camp on German soil. It received its first prisoners in 1933 and continued to do so until the last days of World War II. In its dozen years of operation, some 200,000 prisoners from thirty countries were housed there. About

Dachau, Germany, 1962

10 percent of them were executed. While a large number of Jews were imprisoned there over the years, the prison population comprised primarily of German dissidents, communists, homosexuals, gypsies, resistance fighters, clergymen, writers, intellectuals, some allied prisoners of war, and any others who offended the Reich.

Dachau was the prototype for other camps in Europe. It was at Dachau where the infamous gas chambers and crematoria, "showers" and "ovens," were developed for the most efficient death and disposal. These methods were put to use throughout Europe in the concentration camps that followed. The physical layout of the camp and its facilities proved so workable that they were replicated elsewhere. Auschwitz, for example, was a larger version of Dachau.

Ovens at Dachau Concentration Camp

In 1962, the camp was more or less intact and much as it was when liberated in 1945. Structures remained in various stages of disrepair. The setting was dismal. Plans to upgrade were something of a work in progress. It eventually became a memorial to the camp's victims. If such a place of historic misdeed can ever be called tastefully done, the Dachau of today would qualify as a totally respectful shrine to those who suffered so much or died there. It was nothing of the sort during the days when I would bring visiting friends to Dachau. Despite the condition of the camp, it was on the itinerary of many tourists who wanted to see a vestige of this particularly horrific part of history for themselves and to pay respect to the victims. Tourists plodded solemnly along the paths, stopped briefly at points of interest, then moved on, many with tears in their eyes. On each return I was astonished by three things in particular.

Located at the entrance to the camp was a *gasthaus*, the German version of a tavern or pub. Its name? Gasthaus am Krematorium! (Crematorium Tavern.) What a charming place to have a beer or two before visiting the ovens, the blood trench, or the infamous windowless, air-tight showers where prisoners were given bars of soap that were actually made of stone.

Barrack at Dachau, 1962, which were still occupied by former prisoners

Those shower rooms were themselves nothing short of aston-
ishing. Thousands were gassed and died in them then taken to the
ovens' fires. The visitor in the early 1960s could enter these very
same chambers and try to imagine the horror inflicted on those un-
fortunates who died in heaps, one upon the other, seconds after the
gas was released. But the walls were nothing less than a sacrilege.
They were covered from top to bottom with inscriptions; the names
of visitors and dates of their visits. Numerous inane and inappropri-
ate comments had been scrawled on the walls by visitors including,
of course, "Kilroy was here." The languages and alphabets showed
clearly that most nations of the world were represented. It seemed
the ultimate in disrespect, reminding some visitors of men's rooms in
the United States where tasteless inscriptions flank the urinals.

Perhaps even more startling were the barracks themselves. There
were some twenty of these buildings inside the camp. When Dachau
was liberated, 32,000 prisoners were housed in these buildings.
Each had been built to accommodate 250 prisoners. At war's end
each housed 1,600 souls. What was astounding to the visitor seventeen years after the camp had been liberated was the fact that dozens
of squatters were still living there. The population comprised home-

less Germans and former prisoners from Eastern Europe. Many had been unable or unwilling at the end of the war to return to their homelands, since communist governments had taken over or were about to. These people, whom the Nazis had considered undesirables, were fearful they would also be categorized as such by new regimes.

So they chose to remain as squatters at the liberated concentration camp, making it their new home, this time by choice. Some Germans who had lost their homes in the war moved into the camp and remained for years. Who could miss the irony of former captors and captives thrust together in a new twist of fate?

It was strange to see laundry hanging from lines stretched between the wooden buildings and children playing in the dirt streets. It looked like a fairly self-sufficient refugee camp, which, in fact, it was. These people ate, slept, and even went to their jobs from there, day after day, year after year, for seventeen years. The Germans hoped for an eventual better life in a country that was prospering for all but them. The former prisoners, apparently hoping for the day when they might return to where they had lived before being taken prisoner, remained until work on the victims' memorial forced them all to leave later that decade.

And as further evidence that time marches on, we must mention the golf course. Yes, golf course. The Americans built one at Dachau for use by military personnel. They played there at bargain rates. The course occupies an area of the former concentration camp that was once occupied by German officers and non-prisoner workers. The golf course has since changed hands and is now controlled by the Germans. The greens fees are no longer a bargain for the Americans.

Bonn

*I*f there were ever an important world capital that was geographically misplaced it would have to be Bonn. Known as the *Bundesdorf* (Federal Village), Bonn was selected as the postwar capital of the Federal Republic of Germany for two reasons: Berlin, the prewar capital, was located some 120 miles behind the Iron Curtain in the Soviet Zone of Germany, and because Germany's first chancellor, the man running the show, wanted it in Bonn. Although Berlin was administered by the four powers, the United States, Britain, France, and the Soviet Union, its location, and Moscow's ability to put the squeeze on access, made it an unacceptable location for the West German government.

Bonn, on the other hand, was favored primarily because it was the choice of *Der Alte* (The Old Man) Konrad Adenauer, the former mayor of Cologne. Cologne was located just a few miles from Bonn. Adenauer was in his sixties when he began his career as leader of the Federal Republic, an age when most men are retiring. He favored the tiny town on the banks of the Rhine River. Frankfurt, about one hundred miles to the southeast was considered a more logical choice. However, Adenauer prevailed.

What Bonn lacked in size, it made up for in village charm and history. It was the birthplace of Ludwig von Beethoven in 1770 and home to a fine university. Roman legions established a settlement there before the birth of Christ. And it is rich with important elements of Teutonic Mythology.

A small range of hills that some call mountains is just across the Rhine. They include the *Drachenfels* (Dragon's Rock). It was on the *Drachenfels* that Siegfried is said to have slain a fierce dragon and won invulnerability by bathing in the beast's blood. It was a mirror-myth to the Greek legend of Achilles and is just one example of many similarities between Teutonic and Greek mythology.

Bad Godesberg, an even smaller village just south of Bonn, became a district of the capital city in 1969. Its place in mythology is as secure as the Greeks' Mount Olympus. It was here that the gods of the Germanic and Norse mythological era dwelled. It should be noted that while the power of the legends is still strong, the *Godesberg* and *Drachenfels* are fairly unimpressive. They are rather unlike the craggy mountains bathed in lightning bolts that artists have depicted and that many associate with their storied past. Bad Godesberg was also home to the U.S. embassy, which contributed its own less colorful pages to the local history during difficult Cold War chapters. And one of the early Hitler–Chamberlain meetings took place in Bad Godesberg.

The muddy Rhine lazes by carrying barges heading to Cologne and on to the North Sea to the north and to Rhine wine country to the south, and eventually to Switzerland. The river flows south to north from the Alps and is flanked from Mainz to Koblenz by picturesque and storied castles as well as world-famous vineyards. Those heading south would pass the famous Lorelei, a rock formation at the narrowest portion of the river. It was here that legend insists many sailors were fatally enticed by the siren songs of local maidens who lured them to the rocky shoreline and a frothy demise. Again, there is a strong resemblance to the Greek myth of the Sirens, who were ultimately done in by Odysseus.

Modern travelers are lured by the more tangible famous local wines poured at every riverside village and town. Each of these places proudly presents local vintages consumed by locals and visitors alike in quantities up to and surpassing excess. One of the towns, Bingen, apparently outpaced its neighbors in this regard. Bingen gave us the word *binge,* which has been long associated with imbibing.

Bonn became one of the more important capitals in the world during the post–World War II era. It was from Bonn that the country's "economic miracle" was directed. Economic resurgence, four-power occupation, and geography gave West Germany a prominent seat at the table at which Western leaders formulated Cold War strategies.

The Germans sat at that table with several agendas. They were desperate for reunification with that portion of Germany to the east that had been sliced off for Soviet occupation. It was called the German Democratic Republic, or GDR. The West Germans were also, with good reason, paranoid about the potential for Soviet forces to send waves of tanks and troops from the east, across Germany, and on to the English Channel in an ultimate potentially nuclear confrontation with the West. In that regard, and as a member of NATO (North Atlantic Treaty Organization), West Germany hosted tens of thousands of American military personnel to counter the Soviet threat. It was widely understood that the Western forces would have little chance of doing much more than slow down any such sweep by the Red Army.

West Germany's inclusion in NATO led directly to the establishment of the Warsaw Pact, the communist bloc's military counterpart to the Western alliance. It comprised East European Soviet satellite nations, which more or less formalized the adversarial relationship. It put a line in the sand, a line that ran along the Federal Republic's border with the German Democratic Republic and the rest of Eastern Europe. The result was an even stronger bond between the United States and West Germany and fixed a potential flashpoint for an East-West conflict.

The Federal Republic had emerged Phoenix-like from the ashes of World War II to become a major player on the world stage. It all served to make the Soviet Union, which had suffered the loss of some 12 million people in the war, extremely nervous and bellicose. It wanted nothing more than to keep Germany divided. East and West stood toe to toe along the border of a divided Germany. The potential for war was a daily fact of life in postwar Western Europe.

The Bonn government was also a champion of European economic unity. As a cornerstone member of the Common Market (European Economic Community), it was intent on helping bring about the economic integration of Western Europe.

It was into this environment that I moved to the West German capital in the late spring of 1963. The staid and sleepy Bonn contrasted with Munich's energy just as a sleepwalker differs from a dancer. Munich's energy was in its youth and in the streets. The energy in Bonn came from old men sitting behind closed doors. It was political, defensive, and desperate.

Flash Frames

"Ich bin ein Berliner"

*T*he comings and goings of international political leaders and their functionaries was ongoing. The most famous, of course, was the visit to West Germany by President John Kennedy in June of 1963. The early part of his historic visit took him from Bonn to Berlin and the famous *"Ich bin ein Berliner"* speech delivered before tens of thousands in the Rudolph Wilde Platz before the Schoeneberg City Hall.

Prior to the trip to Berlin, Kennedy visited Bonn briefly. I was not part of the coverage during his short appearance downtown. I was the rookie and relegated to other chores outside the immediate area of presidential excitement. My task was to gather sidebar material from members of the American community living in the area. Easy duty, inasmuch as anyone who was anyone was somewhere near him, including the more seasoned AFN correspondents. In short, I was essentially assigned to cover those unable to be at the center of things. Even miles away, however, I could hear the cheering downtown. Nonetheless, I was really no closer to it then than I was as watching him on television later in Berlin. I was as moved as any by his stirring words, the crowd's reaction to those words, and to him.

What is true of this city is true of Germany—real, lasting peace in Europe can never be assured as long as one German out of four is denied the elementary right of free men, and that is to make a free choice. In 18 years of peace and good faith, this generation of Germans has earned the right to be free, including the right to unite their families and their nation in lasting peace, with good will to all people. You live in a defended island of freedom, but your life is part of the main. So let me ask you as I close, to lift your eyes beyond the dangers of today, to the hopes of tomorrow, beyond the freedom merely of this city of Berlin, or your country of Germany, to the advance of freedom everywhere, beyond the wall to the day of peace with justice, beyond yourselves and ourselves to all mankind.

Freedom is indivisible, and when one man is enslaved, all are

56

not free. When all are free, then we can look forward to that day when this city will be joined as one and this country and this great Continent of Europe in a peaceful and hopeful globe. When that day finally comes, as it will, the people of West Berlin can take sober satisfaction in the fact that they were in the front lines for almost two decades.

All free men, wherever they may live, are citizens of Berlin, and therefore, as a free man, I take pride in the words "Ich bin ein Berliner."[1]

The roar was deafening. With that simple German sentence, Kennedy had captured Germany as completely as any American general in World War II. It was an embrace that was to last the rest of his life, which, unknown to anyone, was only five more months.

A few in the crowd might have been chuckling amid the cheers. For one thing, the president's Boston-American accent gave his German pronunciation a distinctly non-Germanic twang. Also, he had been tossed a linguistic curve ball. A well-intended American correspondent had provided the president with the line that would deliver the speech's most memorable moment, *Ich bin ein Berliner.* The intention was for Kennedy to proclaim, "I am a Berliner." However, the American's German was incorrect. *Ich bin Berliner* translates correctly to *I am a Berliner.* Therefore, by adding the article *ein,* that famous closing line translated to something quite different than intended. A visitor to a bakery in Berlin ordering *ein Berliner,* will get a jelly doughnut. So, on that sunny June day in 1963, Kennedy actually pronounced to the world that *"I am a jelly doughnut."*

The Kennedy visit was part of a five-nation trip to promote Western solidarity. I was to become part of the coverage of the Italian leg of his journey where he would be meeting with officials of the latest of that nation's many postwar governments.

However, other events were capturing headlines in Italy during that time. The day that Kennedy was scheduled to arrive in Rome happened to coincide with the installation of Pope Paul VI. Cardinal Giovanni Montini had been elected Pontiff, succeeding Pope John XXIII who had died in early June. The new Pope was to be crowned on June 30, the day of President Kennedy's scheduled arrival. Kennedy, not wanting to deflect any of the attention from the planned outdoor ceremony in St. Peter's Square, decided to spend the day and overnight near Milan, then travel to Rome the following day to pick up his schedule of meetings and ceremony.

The change in schedule enabled me to cover the Papal ceremony. It was bonus coverage for me and for the AFN audience. My brother Bill and I were the correspondents assigned to Rome for the Kennedy visit. We traveled separately from the presidential party to be in place in Italy when the president arrived. Bill had been in Berlin for that presidential visit, giving him the opportunity to observe and report on two of the most emotional and significant events in recent European history.

The Papal coronation in St. Peter's Square rivaled the Berlin success in terms of scope and emotion. Hundreds of thousands squeezed into the square to applaud and pray for the new Pontiff. The cheering was no less enthusiastic for the Pontiff in Rome than it had been for Kennedy in Berlin. The meaning to those in attendance in Rome was no less palpable.

It is fair to assume that no one in the crowd, and certainly not the two AFN correspondents, had any inkling of the presidential backstory to be played out to the north. For this, we have to rely on Seymour Hersh, one of the premier investigative reporters of this generation. The president's detour to Milan was an improvisation, necessitated by events at the Vatican. According to Hersh, the president had also planned a stop in the Milan area on the way home.

By way of background, I must explain that earlier in the year, Britain had been rocked by the John Profumo scandal. The British defense minister had been associated with two prostitutes, at least one of whom was also linked to a Soviet official. Had Profumo leaked important secrets during his assignations? It was a tremendous scandal, made more so by news reports that "a high ranking U.S. official" was also linked to one of the prostitutes involved. Gossip and speculation bounced back and forth across the Atlantic as if on a bungee cord. News reports, most notably in *The New York Journal American* danced around the speculation saying Bobby Kennedy was trying to find out if "a man who holds a very high elective office in the Kennedy administration" and linked to a prostitute in the John Profumo scandal in Britain was the president.

Hersh says the investigative reporters who wrote the story told Bobby Kennedy it was, in fact, the president. According to Hersh, Kennedy had had liaisons with one Suzy Chang, a hooker well traveled in upscale circles, as well as with Maria Novotny, another prostitute involved in the Profumo scandal. Novotny said years later that she and Chang had serviced Kennedy before and after the 1960 election.

Hersh wrote in his book *The Dark Side of Camelot*:

"Jack Kennedy carried on as usual while his brother struggled to keep the lid on at home. The last stop (of Kennedy's historic European visit where he made his famous Ich bin ein Beliner speech) was Italy, where the president was to meet with government leaders and the newly elected Pope, Paul VI.

The president had worked hard to arrange a long-planned dalliance at Lake Como with Marella Agnelli, the wife of Gianni Agnelli, a prominent Italian businessman. He had been forced to ask (Secretary of State) Dean Rusk, not one of his usual go-betweens, to arrange the perfect hideaway.

Years later, Rusk described the painful incident to Pat Hold a senior staff member of the Senate Foreign Relations Committee. While planning the trip, Hold told me (Hersh) in a 1994 interview for this book, "Jack said to Rusk, 'Mr. Secretary'—he never called him anything else—'can you find a place that's sort of quiet and restful where we could stop on the way home?'"

Rusk was conflicted about recommending a villa at Lake Como that was owned by the Rockefeller Foundation. As a former president of the foundation, Rusk knew that there were long-standing rules against the use of its facilities by public figures. 'Nonetheless,' Hold recounted, "they made it available, and Rusk was looking forward to it. He hadn't been in office very long and he hoped to spend a day or two with the president, letting his hair down.

The plane stopped in Milan and Rusk is thinking they're going to Lake Como. Instead, the president says, 'Thank you, Mr. Secretary for arranging this. I'll see you back in Washington and he goes off."[2]

But I digress. Very vivid in my recollection of Kennedy's brief time in the Italian capital was his appearance at the Victor

Emmanuel monument in Rome. It is a tribute to united Italy's first president, and it also houses the tomb of Italy's unknown soldier. It is a massive white marble structure. Though impressive, architectural critics scoff at the block-long monument. Nonetheless, it is *de rigueur* for visiting dignitaries to pay their respects.

The president did so, placing a large bouquet of flowers at the site. Unbeknownst to anyone there, times would be changing within a few months on matters of presidential security. As a reporter, I stood within thirty feet of the president as he placed the bouquet and then stood at attention before the monument. He was tall and tan and strikingly handsome. It was hard to think of him as a man with widely reported back problems. There was no hint of it as he stood ramrod straight. He moved easily and gracefully, more so than many of the journalists who stood on the periphery.

My position at the monument was selected independently. There was no press cordon, behind which members of the fourth estate were required to congregate. Other reporters also had freedom of movement and were scattered nearby. Some were closer to him than I, others farther away.

Eventually, the president moved away to his waiting open-topped limo. The president got in with a wave and the vehicle slowly moved away from the site. Secret service agents trotted alongside the car, which was moving so slowly that they could have probably walked and kept pace. The crowd, which was sizable, began to press in toward the car. There was no apparent alarm on the part of the accompanying agents. However, they were using their elbows with some force to keep the closest onlookers from moving beyond their loose line. The elbows were less instruments of force than a means of control to discourage the pressing crowd from coming in too close. The tactic worked with no apparent anger or ill will on either side, and within moments, the president was out of sight.

In later years I could not help but think back on the innocence of those moments. In November of that year, President Kennedy was shot down in his own country, and presidential security would never be the same. It will never return to where it was that June in Rome.

I would also think of it later when I recalled the many visits of French President Charles de Gaulle to Bonn. De Gaulle was not the most popular politician in Europe in those days of discontent over

Algeria or his independent position on European economic unity. It is safe to say that he was a high profile target for any number of adversaries, and he was, in fact, an assassination target that year, 1963, in a plot concocted by military officers opposed to the independence of Algeria. A few years later, a fictional assassination plot against de Gaulle was dramatically portrayed in the novel and film *Day of the Jackal*. Nonetheless, when he came to Bonn, he typically landed at the tiny airport outside the German capital. It was accessible to anyone—any potential "jackal"—who might choose to wander toward the runways.

While I suspect de Gaulle was traveling with a hefty contingent of security people, they were not obvious. Nor did they discourage reporters and well wishers, or for that matter anyone who might have been a potential assassin, from pressing toward the imposing, uniformed figure of the French president. I myself moved on occasion to within three or four feet of him as he moved from his plane to the waiting limousine. He even stopped to answer reporters' questions as they pressed round him en route. It was all very informal. On one such visit, an incredulous Associated Press reporter, familiar with the depth of animosity some held toward de Gaulle, remarked to me, "This is incredible. He is like a cigarette in a pack. Someone could slip a knife between his ribs and he wouldn't even fall."

Ted Kennedy

Comings and goings in and out of Bonn by political and diplomatic celebrities as well as by the more conventional kind during this period was commonplace. Leaders of Common Market and
NATO nations were often in the capital. Some, like de Gaulle, Queen
Elizabeth, Averell Harriman, Henry Cabot Lodge, any number of
Kennedys, including Robert and Rose, stand out in my memory,
and the youngest of the Kennedy boys, Senator Edward Kennedy, is
particularly prominent.

As of this writing, Ted Kennedy is the second-longest serving
member of the U.S. Senate. His start in politics was carefully choreographed by his famous father, Joe, who wanted his youngest son
to take the senate seat his brother John vacated when he was elected
president in 1960. However, the younger Kennedy was not eligible
until he reached the age of thirty. That would not be until February
of 1962. A carefully selected caretaker was appointed to keep the
seat warm until Teddy could legally step in. He won a special election in 1962, then ran for and won the full term in 1964.

It was in 1963 that the young Senator arrived in Bonn on the
kind of visit that is most often described as a fact-finding mission.
He arrived at the same tiny airport used by other dignitaries such as
de Gaulle. Again, I had no problem walking from the tiny terminal
directly to the small plane carrying the senator. He stepped from
the plane and walked directly to where I stood waiting. I was, to
my surprise, the only reporter there. An embassy photographer was
also present. I'm not sure why Kennedy's arrival did not draw a bigger crowd of journalists or dignitaries, American or German. His
brother, after all, was president. I recall no other opportunities for
reporters to have access to him during his brief stay in Bonn.

My assignment was to record a generic arrival statement to be
broadcast to our American audience, and I was expected to be able
to ask him a few questions. We never got to the questions because
the traditional "it's nice to be here" statement proved fairly difficult.
I asked him something easy like the purpose of the visit. He began

Edward Kennedy interviewed by Don Marsh and an Embassy engineer in Bonn

to say something simple about looking forward to having a dialogue on Germany's role in Europe and NATO. He stumbled and mumbled a few words. Then he stopped, waved his hand as if trying to erase them, while announcing that he would start over. He did, and the same thing happened. There were three or four false starts before he stopped altogether. He then pulled out an envelope or piece of paper from his pocket and began writing something down. After a few minutes, he read his arrival statement from that paper. I don't remember what he said, other than it was very routine about "being happy to have the opportunity, etc." It was nothing memorable, nor was it expected to be, which may explain the lack of reporters. I do remember that the statement was well under thirty seconds long. It may have been the only time that a Kennedy was at a loss for words, especially this one. It's interesting to contrast Kennedy and *The Great Escape* actors. They tore up their scripts. He wrote one.

It would have been a stretch at that time to foresee the development of Senator Kennedy's oratorical skills. As he and I crossed paths over the years, and as I have observed him during almost half a century in the public eye, I often think back on that awkward first meeting. Some years later, I mentioned it to him. He had no recollection of it. Of course, he evolved, becoming a magnificent orator, perhaps one of the best of the late twentieth century. Unfortunately, he came of age under tragic circumstances, the deaths of his two brothers. He was a stoic but more or less mute presence at events surrounding the president's death in November 1963. His comments at brother Bobby's funeral five years later moved a nation to even more tears as he struggled to control his own. Some scholars place his eulogy at St. Patrick's Cathedral in New York on June 8, 1968, as one of the country's one hundred greatest speeches. Who can forget the chokingly emotional conclusion:

My brother need not be idealized, or enlarged in death beyond what he was in life; to be remembered simply as a good and decent man, who saw wrong and tried to right it, saw suffering and tried to heal it, saw war and tried to stop it.

Those of us who loved him and who take him to his rest today, pray that what he was to us and what he wished for others will some day come to pass for all the world.

As he said many times, in many parts of this nation, to those he touched and who sought to touch him:

"Some men see things as they are and say why. I dream things that never were and say why not."[3]

However, he was a relative newcomer to the stage when he came to Bonn. He clearly lacked the self-assurance that was to come. I also think back to his arrival in Bonn in a small plane, probably having flown in from Frankfurt or some other European city. Some months after his trip to Bonn, while campaigning for the full senate term, Kennedy was almost killed in the crash of a small plane. The pilot and an aide were killed. He suffered a broken back and other serious injuries, some of which plagued him for the rest of his life.

Mourning JFK

$\mathcal{T}$he bullet that killed John F. Kennedy wounded much of the world. Nowhere, including the United States, could the wound have been more deeply felt than in the Federal Republic of Germany. The November 22, 1963, murder in Dallas came almost five months to the day after Kennedy's visit to Germany and the historic Berlin speech. I have no doubt that his popularity in West Germany following that visit was higher than it was in the United States. Germans claimed him as their own. If the shock waves of assassination caused an emotional earthquake in the United States, it was a tsunami in Germany.

The American president was much on the minds of Germany that fateful November day. Chancellor Ludwig Erhard was returning from an official visit to France. He was to touch down briefly then fly on to Washington to meet with Kennedy. Given the political climate in Europe, such visits were always deemed important and watched closely. This planned meeting was no exception.

My principal role as Bonn correspondent for AFN was to gather information for daily newscasts, but also for the nightly program *Report from Europe*. Fellow correspondents from Paris, London, Berlin, Bonn, and other locations contributed nightly to the fifteen-minute report. It was one of the broadcast jewels in the news department crown and was an important source of information for our predominantly military audience.

My office near the parliament building in Bonn was some twenty minutes from the U.S. embassy, whose broadcast facilities were made available to AFN for the nightly program. About an hour or so before my broadcast, because I was in transit, or preoccupied with last-minute details of my report, I was in something of a communications limbo. When I arrived at the embassy, I was stunned and inclined toward disbelief when the marine guard informed me that the president had been shot. He was unaware of the seriousness of the president's wound or wounds. At that time, a few minutes before 8 p.m. Central European Time, the status of the president was unclear to anyone but those attending Kennedy at Parkland Memorial Hospital. I rushed to the studio hoping I could learn more from colleagues at AFN Headquarters in Frankfurt. Our Frankfurt studio was the point of origin for our Europe-wide broadcasts.

It put our broadcast plans into some disarray as material gathered for the report had to be discarded as we correspondents reacted from our respective capitals. It was reaction based on the shooting, not on the president's death, which was not confirmed until a few minutes after the broadcast. We had no reaction to the event, but we reacted ourselves, putting the shooting into some perspective relative to where we were and how the news was being received. I had a somewhat easier perspective because my story was to have been the imminent Erhard visit to Washington and the economic, diplomatic, military issues that were to have been the basis of the discussion between the two nations. News of the shooting raised some questions as to how U.S.–German relations would be affected by the assassination.

The next few days were a nightmare, not only because of the rapidly developing events in and around Dallas and Washington, D.C. There was considerable uncertainty. Even after the capture of Lee Harvey Oswald, nothing was known of the motive for the assassination or who bore responsibility. Because of Oswald's time in the Soviet Union, it was not much of a stretch to speculate that the Russians might have been involved. And even if they had not been, wasn't it conceivable that they might attempt to take advantage of confusion within America's executive, legislative, diplomatic, and military establishments?

Full-scale military alerts were immediate. The Soviets had multiple tank and infantry divisions within easy reach of the West German border. Was the killing a precursor to war and a Soviet sweep across Western Europe? War game scenarios anticipated that in the event of conflict, divisions of Soviet tanks would attempt a dash to the English Channel to extend the Iron Curtain across the entire European continent. None of those scenarios held much hope that NATO forces could do much more than temporarily slow such a red wave. A Soviet attempt to capitalize on events was not considered such an outrageous possibility given the tense state of East-West relations. These were issues that could not be answered immediately but which had to be considered.

As the world waited for clarification, the issue became increasingly unsettling as one shock followed the other in Dallas. Oswald was shot and killed. What did this mean? Who was his murderer, Jack Ruby? Was it all part of an incredible international plot?

Those of us covering events in Bonn had plenty to report in the way of reaction to all of these events. The government prepared to send its chancellor and president to the funeral. The American community in Bonn/Bad Godesberg, which was sizeable, was reacting in very much the same manner as Americans at home. There was shock and dismay accompanied by the uncertainty and fear that we all could be in harm's way if the Soviets did have plans to take advantage of the situation and expand their position in Western Europe.

Within forty-eight hours of the shooting in Dallas, it became relatively clear that no Soviet aggression was likely. The Russians were as startled by the assassination as the rest of the world. The fact that they were not prepared for a military sweep westward lent credence to their informal insistence that they were in no way involved in the death of the U.S. president. As this became more apparent, Americans and Germans alike turned their full attention to the United States and the assassination aftermath.

A two-week period of mourning was established for Americans in Europe. The American embassy in Bonn was the largest diplomatic mission in the Federal Republic and one of the two largest in the world. There were hundreds of employees. Their job descriptions covered the many facets of the 1960s diplomacy game, while a sizeable intelligence apparatus operated in the shadows.

With few exceptions, the employees were housed in a complex especially constructed for embassy personnel. Located on the banks of the Rhine with a wonderful view of the Drachenfels, Plittersdorf was a veritable little America with all the comforts of a suburban American neighborhood. This contributed to a certain degree of isolation from the Germans, whose homes, businesses, and entertainment venues surrounded this U.S. enclave. If they so chose, Americans who lived there need never have ventured out of the complex and interact with the Germans residing all around them. Unfortunately, a large number of Plittersdorf residents never left the community at all unless there was a critical need to do so. They made do with a recreation center, movie theater, restaurant, supermarket, and other amenities all built to American scale and standards.

This little patch of America was self-contained and included living accommodations suitable for all ranks—except for the ambassador, of course. He lived in a mansion directly on the Rhine River between the community and the embassy.

Much of the activity came to a standstill during the two-week mourning period. Entertainment facilities were shut down to wait out the two weeks. Once the state funeral for President Kennedy was over, there was some grousing about that, primarily from parents with kids who complained about having nothing to do.

I, like many of my American journalist colleagues, lived in this community under special arrangements made with the State Department. I didn't think much of it at the time because I was technically a government employee, and most of my journalist colleagues, those associated with Western broadcast networks, newspapers, and other publications, also didn't give it much thought. But it has since struck me as exceedingly odd that so many journalists allowed themselves a landlord about whom they were reporting on a daily basis. I recall no discussion about it. Perhaps it was no issue at the time. It certainly would be today.

During this immediate funeral-mourning period, a remarkable thing was happening on a relatively frequent basis in my own household. Although I lived in the American community, my telephone service was provided by the local German phone company, and my name and number were in the regional telephone book.

In the immediate assassination aftermath I began receiving telephone calls from strangers: Germans. There were many such calls, and in every instance they were from Germans who had taken the trouble to look in the telephone book for "American-looking" names. They called those they found with the specific intention of expressing condolences over the death of the president. It had to take some time and effort to accomplish this. It also took some courage, for all who called spoke in English with varying degrees of fluency. It's not something I believe many Americans would attempt in a foreign nation. It was very moving, and I believe it spoke to the entire nation's admiration and respect for the murdered president. When he said he was a Berliner, "jelly doughnut" or not, Germans took him to heart and kept him there. Many of my acquaintances said they had received similar calls and were similarly moved.

After two weeks, the official mourning period ended and the Americans once again had access to the conveniences of the community. Many had waited impatiently for the movie theater to reopen. It was a principal source of entertainment and was always well attended. Entertainment starved and largely unwilling to go to a

German theater, men, women, and children flocked to the American movie theater for the reopening.

The first film selected to end the official mourning period for the assassinated president was a remake of *State Fair,* that old 1945 Dick Haymes and Jeanne Crane musical, which was itself a remake of a 1933 non-musical version starring Will Rogers. This third incarnation was another musical starring Pat Boone and Anne Margaret. It was not a memorable film, but at this particular time and place, and under the circumstances, it became notable because of its opening sequence, which included an aerial shot of an American city most Americans were trying to forget: Dallas.

When patrons digested what they were seeing, an audible gasp emptied the theater of its air. Incredible! Those who had gone to the movies innocently trying in some degree to put events of the past two weeks behind them were assaulted with yet another reminder of what they had just been through. Critics called this version of the film "forgettable." Not to this crowd.

Almost twenty years later, when I was in Dallas covering the Republican National Convention, I visited Dealey Plaza. I was developing a pre-convention story about the Republican Party bringing the faithful to a city which Democrats seemed to claim as sacred turf. The Republican ticket was assured. There were certain to be many references to Kennedy and many reporters looking for stories outside the predictable convention. It struck me as odd that the GOP would select a city that would be forever linked to the assassinated president no matter what the Republicans did. (What they did was renominate Ronald Reagan and George Bush. Texan Bush's role on the ticket may have had some sway on the Dallas choice. It was the only time any party ever held its national presidential nominating convention in that city. Eight years later, the GOP convened in Houston. Perhaps not coincidentally, George Herbert Walker Bush was then a sitting president awaiting renomination.)

I was struck by the size of the area in which one of the most significant events of modern history had occurred. The event was huge, but the stage was not. Because the event had loomed so large in the minds of so many, I had in my mind magnified everything to match. It did not magnify. Dealey Plaza was what it was, just another street corner in another town, but like another formerly anonymous place, this was home to a date and event also destined to live in infamy.

Flash Frames

The Queen Is Coming

*W*hat better place to meet a queen than on the banks of a river with a mythic past whose hillside banks are infested with castles that have survived the centuries. So it was to be in the Rhine Valley when I met a queen: *the Queen,* Elizabeth II. It was at a gathering hosted by the British ambassador to the Federal Republic on the occasion of the first visit to Germany by a reigning British monarch in more than a half-century, since before the dark days immediately prior to World War I.

Her visit was scheduled to symbolize the restoration of relations between two nations that had fought two bloody and comparatively recent wars. The cost in terms of blood, treasure, and trust had been enormous on both sides. The wounds of the most recent war had hardly healed, which brought some criticism of the queen at home. Nonetheless, the geopolitical realities of the time (and perhaps the House of Windsor's own Germanic bloodline) brought the monarch to the decision that it was time to try and heal those wounds and reestablish the frayed trust. The result was a well-publicized and symbolic eleven-day official visit in May of 1965.

I was both surprised and delighted to receive the invitation to attend a press reception for *"Her Highness and Prince Phillip at The Petersburg Residence at four-fifteen p.m. on the 18-th of May,"* the day of her arrival in Germany. The invitation stipulated that the reception would last precisely one hour, that men should wear dark suits, and that anyone arriving without the actual invitation would be sent packing.

The reception was clearly designed to give journalists who would be covering her visit the opportunity to see the queen up close and personal. It might also serve to curry some favor among those who would be detailing her every move for readers and listeners around the world and, perhaps more importantly, in her own country. Ironically, the reception was to take place about a mile from the Hotel Dreesen, the Bad Godesberg hotel on the west bank of the Rhine where Hitler and Neville Chamberlain had met in 1938, paving the way for their

E II R

On the occasion of the State Visit of
Her Majesty Queen Elizabeth II
and His Royal Highness, The Prince Philip, Duke of Edinburgh
The British Ambassador
is commanded by Her Majesty to invite

Mr. Don W. Marsh

to a Reception at The Petersberg Residence,
on Tuesday, the 18th of May, 1965, from 1615 to 1715 hours.

A reply is requested to:—
The Press Attaché
British Embassy,
Bonn.

Dark Suit
Presentation of this invitation
and enclosed name card at the
entrance is obligatory.

infamous "peace in our time" negotiations in Munich.

There was no shortage of journalists in attendance, all murmuring in anticipation as they waited in a large hall. The Bonn foreign press corps was sizeable. Then there was the contingent traveling with the queen. My impression was that these world-traveled fourth-estaters, typically cynical, worldly, acerbic, self-important, and often slightly arrogant, who had covered cold and hot wars and all manner of East-West confrontations, were abuzz over this imminent event, about which most would probably write little. But few had ever met the Queen of England. Restraint was palpable, betrayed only by nervously polite chatter conducted at the lower end of the audio spectrum.

Before Her Majesty entered the hall, all of us in attendance were given instructions as to how the event would unfold. Clearly, this was to be a highly controlled happening. The instructions were specific and included some choreography. Those assembled were placed in groups of four. The groups were to remain in place engaging in quiet conversation. When the queen arrived at the hall, she could be expected to move from group to group making every effort to visit with each one as time allowed. It was made quite clear that no one was to address the queen unless she initiated the conversation. She would be addressed as Ma'am. No questions of journalistic substance, please! No photographs! She would likely offer her hand, as would Prince Phillip. But the royal hand would only be shaken if offered by one or both. A concise "how do you do?" would suffice unless further comment were encouraged by the royal couple. Bending slightly from the waist was not discouraged. After chatting for a moment or two, the queen and prince would move on to the next group, whereupon the quartet just visited would remain intact and in place for the remainder of the reception. They were left to watch Her Majesty and Phillip glide from group to group until the royal entourage left the hall.

I have no recollection of specifically what was said during the few seconds the royal pair joined our group. I suspect it elicited no comment beyond the state of the weather and the anticipated wonderfulness of the next eleven days.

What I recall more completely is my impression of England's first couple. She seemed smaller than I anticipated, almost petite, although her height is listed officially at five feet four. I was surprised to learn too that Phillip was less than the somewhat imposing figure I had expected, although he is listed at six foot two. He appeared to me to be closer to my height of six feet or less. There is something about people, and places too for that matter, who seem larger than life as they appear on the world stage in photos or video. Put in a real-world perspective, or on more or less equal footing, they often scale down considerably. Then again I remember being listed in the program on my high school football team as being a little bigger and heavier than was really the case (at least it was the case then). That was a tactic teams used to try and intimidate opponents. Could it be the keeper of royal vital statistics was attempting to make Britannia's first couple, already larger than life on the world stage, larger than life?

My other impression was how attractive she was. This queen was never regarded as a beauty, nor would I describe her as such. However, I was surprised at how attractive and animated she was in person. Her eyes were the deepest blue and appeared even more so in contrast to her creamy, almost translucent, skin. I have heard all my life about "a peaches and cream complexion." I never quite knew what that meant until I met her.

Any woman of my acquaintance could and would remember exactly what she was wearing on a significant occasion, even after forty years. While "frumpy" is an adjective frequently applied to the queen, suffice it to say she was dressed in something appropriate for late afternoon in the mild weather of mid-May. The dress was of a lighter fabric and something close to beige. Those who might have expected a dramatic touch, like a tiara, would have been disappointed. Instead, she wore a small hat tilted at a rather jaunty angle, while the prince wore a simple conservative dark suit. I associate no color with his attire.

Her smile was warm, welcoming, and disarming. So different from what we had all come to see as the typical unsmiling, almost stern, personality which stared back at the world from countless magazine covers and newspapers. My conclusion was a simple one: the queen of England just does not take a good picture. In fact, she takes such a bad picture that, whenever I tell people how pleasantly attractive and unlike her photographs she is, the usual response is that I am crazy, blind, or that I never met her.

On the Other Side of the Wall

Robert Frost had it wrong. What might have worked in New England was a calamity in Germany. Good fences might make good neighbors in Vermont.

Walls dividing neighbors, relatives, lovers, and friends make for tragic division, desperation, and diplomatic intransigence in the middle of Europe.

Before the queen's visit, I had occasion to travel to Berlin with my brother. In 1965, this remarkable city was a magnificent study in contrasts. By day, the energy and personality of Berlin's Western sectors could rival any major city in the world. There were still signs of its destruction in World War II, but what one observed in the mid-1960s was not what had been, but what was, and what would be. The Western sectors were thriving despite the wall. A city had risen from the rubble created by Allied bombers more than twenty years earlier. Skyscrapers, shops, restaurants, and pedestrian and automobile traffic gave the city a heartbeat.

Berlin is located more than one hundred miles inside what was then the Soviet Zone of East Germany. Following the war, the country had been divided by the four powers into four zones, each administered by one of the four victorious powers: the British, French, Americans, and Soviets. Berlin, having been the former capital, likewise was under four- power control. It was divided into sectors controlled by each of the four powers. The wall was built to separate the Soviet sector and zone from the three Western sectors. The city, therefore, was a four-power island in a figurative Red Sea surrounded by territory under the control of the Soviet Union.

Prior to construction of the wall, traffic between East and West Berlin was relatively unimpeded. East Berliners entered the Western sectors to work, to visit relatives, and to shop. Over the years, however, East Berliners, and Germans from other parts of the Soviet Zone, as well as non-Germans from other parts of Soviet-controlled Eastern Europe, had access to West Berlin. Increasingly, many who ventured into the Western sectors did not return. East Berlin and

The Berlin Wall

East Germany, and to a lesser extent Eastern European countries, were losing population. And it was an important demographic. Younger residents of the Soviet East, laborers and intellectuals alike, were opting for a new life in the West, incrementally depleting an important human resource in the Soviet-controlled world. The wall was built to stem this flow of strong backs and brain power. And it succeeded, except for those scores who attempted to flee by challenging the wall. They did so by going over it or under it.

From the very moment it became clear that the barrier was going up, the diplomatic temperature went up. Volatility was high. Allied and Soviet troops took threatening positions. The Allies protested. The United States extended overseas tours for military personnel. Thousands of soldiers, draftees and volunteers of all ranks, had nothing to say about it as additional months of service were tacked on to their tours. It was as close as the world had come to another conflagration since the Chinese entered the Korean War. It was a very dangerous time.

The wall and barbed wire barrier followed the borders of the three Western sectors for almost one hundred miles, effectively isolating West Berlin from the rest of Germany. The barrier carefully followed the sector boundaries to keep it from encroaching on Allied territory, where it almost certainly would have been torn down. With Germanic precision, the line took it along the sector borders, just inside Soviet territory, rendering useless the Allied protests. Buildings that straddled the border were sometimes literally cut in half or, more often, torn down. On a map, the barrier took the shape of a hangman's noose. It was, as one of our presidents said, a wall not designed to keep people out, but to keep people in. A carefully pruned strip on the communist side of the barrier gave guards a clear field of fire at those attempting to flee. More than a thousand would-be refugees died trying to escape to the West.

There was limited and carefully controlled two-way traffic through crossing points into each of the three Western sectors. That traffic was limited to what was perceived as a necessity by the authorities in East Germany, who ultimately approved a complicated permit system for relatives on both sides of the wall, but only in instances of family emergencies or, later, over certain holidays. Traffic was held to an absolute minimum, allowing hundreds to cross east to west and back, whereas tens of thousands had done so before the wall. The communists had put the cork back in the bottle.

For Allied personnel and for non-Germans who had reason to travel into the Soviet sector, passage was basically restricted to one

Checkpoint Charlie in Berlin

checkpoint—Checkpoint Charlie at Friedrichstraße. Checkpoint Charlie was made famous for what it was, and by any number of books and movies that portrayed it with dramatic effect in Cold War spy dramas. Use of this route was subject to four-power agreements stipulating that American military and government personnel could pass through on official business, or even on sightseeing trips, without the need to show passports, as would be required at a normal state frontier. Military identification sufficed for passage to the east. This was an issue of enormous importance and delicacy to the Western Allies and West Germans, since showing passports would give East Germany the de facto status of a legitimate state, thereby undermining the Western contention that East Germany's existence was a temporary phenomenon under temporary occupation by the Soviet Union. Recognition as a sovereign state was something the Soviet-backed regime coveted, but this was regularly and zealously rejected by the United States, Britain, and France. Government employees were told in no uncertain terms that showing passports crossing in either direction was verboten!

Visiting East Berlin as a tourist was not uncommon among American government employees during visits to the divided city. There was a strong curiosity among many to observe the sharp contrast between the two parts of Berlin. That contrast was most pronounced at night. While lights blazed and nightlife thrived in West

Berlin, the darkness to the east was dramatic. Seen from the west it was as if a curtain had been drawn. From above, it looked like a half moon on a dark night; one half bright and vibrant, the other invisible in the shadow. The reality was that the energy-poor Soviet sector did not have the juice to power the neighborhoods. Few ventured out at night anyway. East Berlin, joyless and drab by day, put on its darkest coat by night. When the sun shone during the day, it could not punch its way through a dreary, colorless landscape. It lost its luster where it fell, whether it be on a sullen citizenry or the uninspired government-issue architecture.

Nonetheless, for many Americans, it was something of an adventure to travel to East Berlin. It gave them a chance to transit Checkpoint Charlie and visit the bleak landscape that stood in such marked contrast to the Berlin they were temporarily leaving. It was a chance to have a beer in a vacant beer garden and gather material for a cocktail party's conversation. It was to live an illusion of danger in the comfort of relative safety. It was a chance to play John le Carre's Alex Leamas or another fictional character stepping through a dark looking glass, confident in the knowledge that they could return the same way they had entered, perhaps bringing back a good story from "the other side."

I was just such a tourist traveling with my brother and our wives. It was an excursion, a brief sightseeing trip made for all the aforementioned reasons, plus some limited insight into the territory we were called upon to write about or reference in our professional lives. We did what visitors do, marveled at the lack of imagination in the Soviet-inspired architecture that dominated the area. Even in the middle of the day, the drab neighborhood apartment and office buildings looked as if they were standing in the shadows. There was little in the way of foot or vehicular traffic. What little there was added nothing to the ambiance.

The people exhibited non-committal "jailhouse stares" devoid of any curiosity about the strangers among them. Such curiosity had long since been stifled in favor of avoiding risk and suspicion. It was this fear that caused them to pass by quickly to avoid any contact. Delay came only from the limited vehicular traffic that might cause them to stop and wait before crossing the wide boulevards. Most of the automobiles were small and had strange names. Like everything else in the Soviet sector, the automobiles were colorless, reminding a visitor of Henry Ford's assertion that early American car buyers "could have any color Ford they wanted, as long as it was black."

An hour or two of drinking in the local color, or lack of it, and after a beer that seemed watered down compared to the more robust brew on the other side of the wall, we decided we'd had enough. We concluded that East Berlin was just as it appeared in the newsreels and was described by those colleagues or friends who had been there before.

The return to West Berlin required retracing our steps, since Checkpoint Charlie was the only way back. As we approached the wall, we were aware that civilian traffic was far lighter than in the neighborhood we had just left, and that the closer we got to the wall, the few people we did see were likely to be in uniform. These were the infamous *Volkspolizei* (People's Police). They were called VoPo's and were the thugs who policed East Germany. In the eyes of the free world they had become the villainous face of East Germany because of their brutality along the wall. It was they who "protected" the integrity of the wall by stopping those who would attempt to breach it. They were just as capable of gunning down a teenager attempting to scale the wall as they were of casually scanning activity at Checkpoint Charlie behind large binoculars. GI's made fun of them, but they were no laughing matter. They may have been called policemen, but in reality, they were both the criminals and the jailers.

Traveling back to West Berlin involved passing through a checkpoint on the East Berlin side. It was here that we, as civilian employees of a four-power government, were to show our government identification cards to the East German officers manning the post. The officer who stood between us and the walkway to West Berlin asked for our passports. Passports? The rules were clear: no passports! We knew the rules and had no intention of becoming the source of East German propaganda. We were certain that showing our passports would be photographed and that we would be cited in the East German press as Westerners who had accepted East Germany's contention that it was a legitimate state.

This was not a minor issue in the ongoing bickering between East and West. If East Germany could assert and establish nationhood, it could then move to absorb all of Berlin located within its "national" borders. The ramifications of such a claim would be enormous and bring a new dimension to the tension between Washington, Paris, London, and Moscow.

This is not to suggest that we four would have triggered such a confrontation, but we did think that showing passports, acceding to the VoPo demand, and violating a State Department directive was something we could not and should not do. So, we refused, explaining the official position.

In turn, we were told we could not cross the border without doing so. The officer was armed with a nasty looking weapon that I would identify as a machine pistol or grease gun. It was an automatic weapon that looked to have considerable short range firepower. He held it menacingly. We demanded to see a Russian officer to set the record straight and insist on our right to travel unimpeded on the basis of existing four-power agreements.

"There are no Russians here," he said. I'm sure our thoughts ran along the line of "there are no coals in Newcastle" either. We suggested that he or one of his colleagues go and find a Soviet officer and bring him to us so we could clear things up because we had no intention of producing passports. He walked a few paces away and started a conversation with one of his colleagues. We had hopes he was sending that other officer to find us a living, breathing Russian.

Fifteen minutes later, he was still chatting with his comrade, and we were still standing at the entrance to the crossing point. Finally, one of us told the VoPo officer that we were not showing passports and were going to cross.

The conversation between the two uniformed men ended abruptly. They turned toward us and moved slowly our way. While doing so, they each racked a round into the chamber of their respective machine pistols. They shifted them to the "ready" position, which means they were more or less pointed at the four of us. The officer we had been negotiating with moved one step closer to us than the other. "You can stay here for as long as you like," he said. Then he added, "But if you take one stop in that direction," he said pointing to the west, "I will shoot you while you are still in East German territory." His hard eyes met ours, one by one. Was he bluffing? Would he shoot us if we moved to the west? These are questions we were asking ourselves.

None of us thought he was bluffing. He was convincing enough that we stayed right where we were, and for the next thirty minutes or so we talked about it, hoping something would happen to change the status quo. It didn't. We had two choices: stay in place until the Cold War was over or violate the State Department order. Funny how logic can be influenced by the business end of a loaded automatic weapon pointed at you.

Moments later, after showing our passports and watching as they were duly stamped by our smiling VoPo captor, we crossed through to the small shack that housed the Americans manning Checkpoint Charlie. Our rationale was that we had shown our passports under duress. It was, we thought, our obligation to report "the incident." We were throwing ourselves on the mercy of the court. A young lieutenant was in charge of the checkpoint detail. He listened politely, though he seemed slightly preoccupied with some paperwork he was shuffling. We explained the conditions under which we had produced our passports and failed our country.

The verdict was immediate. After listening to details of our ordeal, he said, "Don't worry about it. Everybody does it. No big deal." Eyes were downward, papers were adjusted, a not so subtle sign for us to scram. Which we did.

So, there you have it. We were not the object of an international incident. I have no idea whether pictures were taken as we acknowledged "East German sovereignty" at Checkpoint Charlie, but we all came away from the incident with the clear impression that there is as wide a divide between the people in Washington making the rules and those on the front line who have to live with them.

My recollections of the incident, and of many experiences in Germany, were rekindled almost thirty years later when I covered the appearance of former Soviet President Mikhail Gorbachev at Westminster College in Fulton, Missouri.

It was at Westminster that Winston Churchill delivered his famous "Iron Curtain" speech in 1946, declaring on that day that "from Stettin in the Baltic to Trieste in the Adriatic an iron curtain has descended across the Continent." A reminder of that Iron Curtain is also present in Fulton, where huge chunks of the wall have been assembled by Churchill's granddaughter, Edwina Sandys, in a massive and impressive sculpture. Titled *Breakthrough,* the sculpture consists of silhouettes of a man and women carved into a graffiti-strewn wall. The college has been the sculpture's permanent home since the Gorbachev visit. His trip to Westminster was a book-end of sorts, symbolically proclaiming an end to the Cold War at the very spot where it had first been declared.

Twenty thousand people clogged the campus to see and hear Gorbachev on that day in May of 1992. Few if any of the students in attendance had even been born when the Berlin Wall went up in 1961. His remarks were broadcast live to 132 countries. I was there to anchor our live television coverage. The sculpture was a more-than-appropriate backdrop for Gorbachev, who had been the subject of Ronald Reagan's historic entreaty, "Mr. Gorbachev, tear down this wall." Gorbachev did, and the world breathed a little easier. As Gorbachev put it in Fulton:

The goal today has not changed: peace and progress for all. But now we have the capacity to approach it without paying the heavy price we have been paying these past fifty years or so, without having to resort to means which put the very goal itself in doubt, which even constitute a threat to civilization. And while continuing to recognize the outstanding role of the United States of America, and today of other rich and highly developed countries, we must not limit our appeal to the elect, but call upon the whole world community.[4]

In 1989 while working for a St. Louis television station, a young news producer who was responsible for putting together a newscast seen by a quarter million people every night, watched video of the Berlin Wall coming down. He said to me, "I don't get it. What's the big deal?"

Auf Wiedersehen

*T*he decision to leave Germany after six years and return to U.S. soil was neither easy nor based on any single circumstance. The story remained an exciting though somewhat predictable one. Although there were certain blips in the relationship between East and West— the charged atmosphere that followed the Bay of Pigs, the Cuban Missile Crisis, the Kennedy assassination—Nikita Khrushchev's departure led to a period of relative calm. Khrushchev's successor, Leonid Brezhnev had decidedly Stalinist tendencies, but his attention was primarily on domestic politics and solidifying his position internally. His first serious foreign adventure came in 1968 when he moved troops into Czechoslovakia to abolish Alexander Dubcek's liberal regime in Prague.

I was also doing some "stringing" work for Westinghouse Broadcasting during those years in Bonn. It involved providing radio reports for the small Westinghouse radio network. I approached Westinghouse about employment back home, and it was received positively.

This job inquiry came at a time when there were some disturbing shifts in the way the American Forces Network operation was being structured. During my six years with the network, the news department was essentially a civilian operation and relatively autonomous. The overall network operation was run by the military, but there was little interference in the journalism we civilians were producing. However, it became increasingly apparent that greater Pentagon involvement was on the way. I suppose, in retrospect, it was because of our growing entanglement in Vietnam. No doubt the generals were concerned about what American troops in Europe were being told about Vietnam. Some of the troops then in Europe might one day find themselves in the jungle. There were undoubtedly also concerns about how our adventures in Southeast Asia were perceived by our allies in Europe. News to both the Americans and Europeans on the military's own radio station could be managed.

Rumors persisted that the Pentagon was going to take control of news output in Europe. There was a very clear impression that AFN Europe's news content would be controlled by the Pentagon and that civilian autonomy at the network's newsroom in Frankfurt would be severely eroded. It seemed clear to me that this was not a time to be associated with an organization that was more likely to be producing propaganda than valid news.

Then there was a specific offer from the Westinghouse folks and an opportunity to look to a career in management with that respected broadcasting company. And the direction they wanted to send me was toward television. In the mid-1960s, what red-blooded American boy could turn down a chance at TV?

So it was this confluence of circumstances, plus a real feeling that I had been away from home too long, that influenced my decision to say "*auf wiedersehen*" to Germany and "hello Baltimore."

Baltimore

*I*t would not have been my first choice. Westinghouse Broadcasting had prestigious operations in New York City, Chicago, Pittsburgh, and Washington, D.C. Problem is, the choice was not mine except to accept or reject. It was Hobson's choice: I could have any city I wanted—as long as it was Baltimore.

I had begun my journalistic career in 1959 in my home town in New Jersey working for a monthly magazine that was actually printed in Baltimore. Once a month, the publisher, his wife, and I drove to Baltimore to oversee the magazine's production. At that time, I thought Baltimore was uninviting, a welcome milestone to be bypassed for those traveling from New York or Philadelphia to Washington, D.C.

Baltimore wore a blue collar and had its sleeves rolled up. It was rusty and needed a coat of paint. Downtown was old, deteriorating, and dingy. The waterfront's most distinguishing feature was neglect. The Inner Harbor was framed by dark wooden warehouses and other buildings in need of repair.

The city's history was important, impressive, and interesting, but Baltimore seemed content to hang onto the past rather than to forge ahead to the future. Hidden behind some of the downtown blight and beyond the periphery were Johns Hopkins, some wonderful restaurants, and relatively attractive suburbs. But they were invisible to this monthly visitor. Upon learning in Germany that I would be assigned to the Baltimore television station, WJZ, I was sorely disappointed.

My arrival in Baltimore did nothing to stoke my enthusiasm. The town had not improved much in the seven years since I had been active there. There were some signs that the city might be waking from its slumber, but only the most optimistic boosters might have foreseen what the city was to become. Within a few years, the development of the Inner Harbor turned out to be the kiss that turned the frog into a prince. It led to a surge in downtown development which ultimately transformed Baltimore into a very attractive place to live, work, and visit.

Getting a start in television news was heady stuff. It was a different experience from radio, but one for which radio can be a good teacher. I was put into the reporter-producer ranks immediately and was soon immersed in a story that grew for the rest of the decade and into the next, and that eventually changed U.S. political history.

Spiro "Ted" Agnew

*I*n the summer of 1966, prior to my arrival in late September, Baltimore was one of the major fronts in the civil rights struggle. The focus was on fair and open housing, and it set the stage for the political season to follow. At stake was the governor's mansion. The state's top job was held by Millard Tawes. He was serving his second and last term as governor. His departure would create a vacuum the Democrats expected to fill. The party traditionally held a firm hold on the state's political apparatus, and the Republicans saw his departure as an opportunity, if the right candidate could be found, to alter this tradition. Some might have regarded the Republicans' aspirations as ridiculous, or, given the Democrats' strength, as a mission of political suicide.

But the GOP found their man in Spiro Agnew, a relatively unknown politician statewide, even though he had been elected as Baltimore county executive in 1962. He did so following a bitter dispute with local Republican Party leaders. Running as a Republican outsider and outcast, he was nonetheless elected in the strongly Democratic county, the first Republican elected to the county executive's post in the twentieth century. He was considered moderate-to-liberal, and one of the hallmarks of his administration was the passage of an anti-discrimination ordinance, one of the first of its kind in the United States.

"Ted" Agnew was clearly ambitious, but he brought something to the table. He was swarthy in a way that reflected his Mediterranean heritage. His graying hair was combed straight back, reflecting the style of an earlier era. He was a natty dresser and carried himself well, exuding an unmistakable presence and sense of mission, not to mention confidence. He chose his words carefully, though he sometimes gave people the impression that he selected a word first, then built a sentence around it. Nonetheless, he was articulate and stylish, qualities that in later years would please headline writers, and his tone was measured and controlled.

His energy, style, confidence, and availability appealed to

Republican strategists. He was a full package. He didn't have much of a political history, but he had limited baggage. His record as a Republican renegade could encourage some liberal votes. And if he lost, damage to the party would be short-term, if at all. Republicans were not expected to win in Maryland. No one was expecting an "accident of history."

History, however, was lining up against the Democrats as candidate after candidate entered the primary until no fewer than eight were seated at the primary table. While the lineup ranged from poor to adequate as potential nominees, two were considered exceptional. One, Tom Finan, was the sitting attorney general. The other, Carlton Sickles, was a sitting U.S. congressman.

An all too familiar name, George P. Mahoney was on the very fringe of this Democratic stable of candidates. Mahoney was a successful real estate developer with a lucrative contracting business. He was active in party activities and was a fixture at Democratic National Conventions of the era. And he was also what could kindly be called a perennial candidate. He had run no fewer than five times for the senate and four times for governor with nothing to show for it—nothing, that is, but fairly widespread name recognition. In 1966, he was outspokenly opposed to integrated housing, and he got a lot of attention from conservative Marylanders. In the primary campaign, his slogan was "Your Home Is Your Castle, Protect It." He became known as "George-P-Your-Home-Is-Your-Castle-Protect-It-Mahoney."

With the large number of candidates vying for Democratic primary votes, it was inevitable that a certain degree of bitterness and downright animosity would be generated during the campaign, creating a dynamic that salivating Republicans encouraged, and which would ultimately make George Mahoney an otherwise unlikely beneficiary.

If ever an election could prove that anything can happen when multiple candidates of divergent levels of competence are involved, this was it. Voters were casting ballots like farmers feeding the chickens. They were all over the place. Finan and Sickles were clearly the most qualified candidates, and they split the votes cast for them fairly evenly. But well after midnight, when all the votes had been counted, George-P-Your-Home-Is-Your-Castle-Protect-It-Mahoney had the most. He was the Democratic candidate.

The electoral exercise became academic. No self-respecting Democrat, whether voter or office holder, could abide by the openly racist campaign of their candidate. The campaign worked to Agnew's advantage, making him more attractive than he otherwise might have been. He was portrayed as a reform-minded, outcast Republican who tilted left of center. He looked like a flaming liberal in comparison with Mahoney. The situation could not have played out better for Maryland Republicans. Democrats who could not abide the segregationist instincts and Mahoney rhetoric were reminded by candidate Agnew that he had been raised a Democrat. Democrats flocked to the Republican candidate. It was a slam dunk: an election victory in excess of 82,000 votes. The fact that a huge number of them were cast by blacks would ultimately become significant. He was their man, but his political and philosophical stripes were about to change.

He was inaugurated in January 1967. He worked reasonably well with the Democratic legislature, particularly on racially sensitive issues. He signed an open housing law, which was the state's first, and even presided over repeal of laws prohibiting interracial marriage. Something of a populist, he was a conspicuous figure at Baltimore Colts football games during the glory years, and he was frequently seen waiting in line outside a popular Italian restaurant with dozens of others. Because he was willing to stand outside the restaurant with "the proletariat," Ted Agnew was seen as an egalitarian, and he occasionally continued the practice of standing in lines with the voting populace after he became vice president of the United States.

H. Rap Brown and Cambridge

Q can mark the beginning of change in Spiro Agnew from personal observation, and it didn't take long.

It manifested itself in Cambridge, a sleepy town on Maryland's Eastern Shore. Cambridge is separated from the rest of the state by the Chesapeake Bay, but in this case it's more than a geographical divide. Cambridge is nestled at the mouth of the Choptank River, which feeds the bay. Fishing and agriculture dominate the town's and the region's paltry economy. Cambridge fit in nicely with the way of life on the Eastern Shore. It is as different from the rest of Maryland as Mississippi is from Massachusetts.

When it came to racial attitudes, many, with more than a little justification, compared the area to the Deep South. Indeed, a century earlier, Maryland's Eastern Shore was populated by plantation owners and their slaves. No less a personage than Frederick Douglas wrote bitterly and graphically of slave life there. Given social attitudes of that day, it is not surprising that the Eastern Shore was sympathetic to the South during the Civil War, while the rest of Maryland, although a slave state, supported the Union. Attitudes fron 1867 were alive and well throughout this Maryland exclave in 1967, when blacks across the nation were becoming increasingly militant in their demands for equal rights. Descendents whose ties ran in a straight line to the previous century found this "uppity" attitude unacceptable, and they were poised to defend historic prejudices.

A town of about ten thousand, Cambridge was sleepy but not asleep during the mid-1960s at the height of the civil rights movement. There was a growing impatience with ineffective sit-ins. As blacks took a more militant approach in other parts of the country, Cambridge was being led away from earlier tactics. A young black Howard University graduate and Cambridge resident, Gloria Richardson, fanned the flames of protest, encouraging a more militant approach. Testimony to Richardson's powers of persuasion is not only what followed her activities in Cambridge, but also the fact that she ultimately was hired by the Madison Avenue advertising powerhouse, J. Walter Thompson.

Richardson's leadership was followed by a Cambridge crescendo. Demonstrations rattled the town in 1963 over the usual grievances, lack of jobs, as well as inequities in education and public accommodations. Martial law had been declared at that time. Attorney General Robert Kennedy, hoping to put out the fire quickly, got into the act in Cambridge. His intervention led to a shaky truce of sorts. The fuse that was to ignite the explosion four years later may well have been lit during this time.

Racial tension that had simmered in the town for a century was reaching a violent boiling point by 1967. First, there were sit-ins, marches, arrests, and rock-throwing confrontations that ultimately led to exchanges of gunfire between demonstrators and police. The population was about equally divided between black and white, but that was the only hint of equality. Just as the Eastern Shore was separated from the rest of the state by the bay, Cambridge's whites and blacks were divided by a single street. Its name, ironically, was Race Street. For decades, blacks had lived in frustration and poverty on one side. Only slightly more prosperous whites clung to their traditional prejudices on the other. The conjunction of Cambridge's 1967 social dynamics aligned to put this otherwise anonymous but troubled town squarely into national view.

Ironically, I had been assigned to do a special report for WJZ in May of 1967, four years after the earlier troubles. At that time, I reported that blacks and whites in Cambridge were more optimistic and that conditions for the black population had changed for the better though there was still plenty of room for improvement.

Frustration trumped optimism as Cambridge came into public view once again in June 1967, when new demonstrations were encouraged by black leaders to protest the pace of progress or lack of it. Escalation was rapid between police and young blacks. The clashes reached a peak in mid-June, when demonstrations and protests led to full-scale rioting and gunfire. National Guard troops were ordered in. Martial law was declared once again. It was a Band-Aid on an open wound and did little to sooth an increasingly hostile environment. Nonetheless, within a matter of weeks National Guard troops were withdrawn from Cambridge. With the troops gone, H. Rap Brown moved in.

Deep-rooted racial restiveness across the nation was carried on a wave of self-proclaimed black power, making an increas-

ingly nervous country even more so. Brown had just come into
his own as a national figure, having taken the reins of the radical Student Nonviolent Coordinating Committee (SNCC), from
Stokely Charmichael. Charmichael was a firebrand leader who had
become a national celebrity preaching "black power." SNCC tired
of Charmichael's increasing independence, which was coupled with
a frustrating inability to further the SNCC's agenda. In the midst
of this internal strife, the organization basically expelled him from
leadership. Brown was expected to be less fiery, but the tension of
the times would dictate otherwise. His own rhetoric espousing self-
reliance and self-defense was increasingly bellicose and inflamma-
tory. He was soon widely quoted proclaiming that "violence was as
American as cherry pie."

That was the gist of his message on the night of July 24, 1967.
Brown had traveled to Cambridge to attend a rally. The sultry evening
was perfect for a hot message and some unforgettable images. A crowd
had gathered at dusk outside the local SNCC offices in anticipation of
his arrival. He appeared suddenly and dramatically just after dark to
face a crowd of some 350 blacks milling about in the street.

Like a cat, Brown leaped easily onto the hood of a car and began what might best be described less as a street sermon than as a
call to action. All black faces were turned toward him and attention
was rapt. Brown was tall and skinny with enough voice to reach the
edges of the crowd. He used his hands like a conductor, with each
long, thin finger a separate baton punctuating his every sentence. If
he had achieved his position with SNCC on the expectation or hope
that he would be less fiery than his predecessor, neither would survive this night of July 24, 1967. It was a call to arms.

"*Don't be trying to love that honky to death. Shoot him to death. Shoot him to death, brother, because that's what he is out to do to you. Do to him like he would do to you, but do it to him first. If this town don't come around, this town should be burned down.*

Ain't no need in the world for me to come to Cambridge and I see all them stores sitting up there and all them honkies owns them. You got to own some of them stores. I don't care if you have to burn him down and run him out. You'd better take over them stores. The streets are yours. Take 'em. They gave you the streets a long time ago, before they gave you houses. They gave you the streets. So we own the streets. Take 'em. . . ."[5]

I was grateful during these moments that my cameraman, who had moved away from me to get his shots of the event, had not brought the some two hundred pounds of equipment that would have been necessary to record Brown's remarks. These were the days before videotape and the eventual miniaturization of television photographic equipment. Our equipment was conspicuous, heavy, cumbersome to maneuver, and time-consuming to set up. The sixteen millimeter sound cameras required two cases to transport lights, batteries, and tripods. Not knowing exactly how events were going to unfold, he shot with a camera the size of a toaster that was incapable of recording sound. I took notes.

It was a nervous and frightening time for a white reporter standing in the middle of a black crowd, that, if not already hostile, likely soon would be. Brown's rhetoric about "honkies" was receiving his desired response. I was just a few feet from him, fearing at some point he would point at me as an example of the enemy that had to

be "taken." As if that concern wasn't enough, I was fully conscious of the presence of a man standing alongside me. He wore a look of admiration for Brown on his face and carried a ball-peen hammer in his hand. I fully expected it could be used on me as the "street sermon" continued.

The possibility of trying to distance myself from Brown and his disciples did not exist. As he spoke, the crowd pressed in toward the speaker, creating a gridlock for those of us closest to Brown. The only way to move would be if the crowd moved. Then, I would have to move with it, not against it.

With those long fingers pointing alternately at the crowd, the sky, and himself, Brown called upon his audience to take to the torch. He told his listeners that the town had turned its back on them, that it was time to turn their backs on the town, and burn it down. He pointed to a damaged school nearby. It had been victimized by arsonists earlier in the summer. He called upon his audience to finish the job. Members of the audience were apparently receptive to the mission. Before the night was over, they did, and then some.

He spoke for some forty minutes. Then, as quickly as Brown had appeared, he was gone. The crowd was left only with his words. It broke up slowly. People hung around in small groups and talked about what they had just seen and heard. There was a perceptible feeling of excitement but no apparent rush or even inclination to follow his call to action. To call it a party atmosphere would be misrepresenting the mood of the crowd. To call it a mob that appeared intent on serious mischief would be even more so. It actually struck me as more like congregants leaving the church discussing the preacher's sermon. It took several minutes before the streets were

empty, allowing me and my cameraman to move out of the area. I was relieved not to have the business end of that ball-peen hammer imbedded in my ear.

There was no way of knowing what might happen next. Brown's words were not ambiguous. It remained to be seen whether his challenge to the crowd to "take back the streets and the stores" and to "finish the job" were received as marching orders.

The first flames appeared an hour later. A flicker on the horizon at first, but within a few minutes it was clearly a major blaze. The fire started on the corner we had vacated only a short time earlier. It was also the site of an African American Elks Lodge that had been damaged earlier in yet another fire of suspicious origin. The Cambridge Fire Department, a volunteer unit, assembled several blocks from the fire. We were hearing reports of looting and gunshots. One police officer was wounded by gunfire during the first moments. Fearful of snipers, the firefighters refused to enter the fire zone.

The Maryland attorney general, Francis Burch, the first ranking state official on the scene, played an important role. He met with local officials and pleaded with firefighters to take on the flames. Most refused. Burch bravely donned fire gear and led some of the volunteer firefighters to the blaze, which by this time was roaring down Pine Street. It was two hours after the first flames had been spotted, and it was too late. The fire was too big. Burch and the firefighters retreated.

As they returned to a more secure area, reinforcements were on the way to Cambridge to reestablish order. Local police were arriving, soon to be joined by one hundred heavily armed state police officers. The first of nearly seven hundred National Guard troops

ordered to Cambridge began arriving. Governor Agnew, who had been vacationing in the resort town of Ocean City, arrived around dawn. Dressed more formally than the situation might require—a suit and tie—he seemed somewhat incongruous amid the smoke and grit and grime. He met with local officials, then with us in the media.

He was clearly angry, but controlled. His words were chosen carefully during the impromptu remarks, which he delivered in a measured monotone, apparently attempting to encourage restraint. His verbatim remarks follow:

"Unfortunately, the Negro citizens of this town have been victimized by a few rabble-rousers who caused a great deal of trouble. The property damage is considerable, including the Pine Street School, some residences, and a couple of stores.

We have to act quickly to protect our citizens, particularly the Negro citizens who sustained all this damage, victimized by this man Brown who came in from out of town intent on sowing trouble. We have a transcript of what he said, and I have directed the attorney general to take whatever steps are necessary to bring him to account for his irresponsible actions.

I think the time has come when we must cease to forgive and condone this sort of conduct. The people who suffer are those who can afford to suffer least. They are lives these people say they are trying to protect, but they're the ones hurting most. I visited the area not long ago, about an hour ago, and I see them standing on the street and they seem to be dazed and not understanding what has happened to them because of these people who come in and have sown discontentment in this state and all over the country.

If we, the public officials and the responsible Negroes and the people of the state don't take action against them, then we're headed for trouble.

Reporter Marsh: What plans do you have for the National Guard, governor?

I think the guard will be maintained here, probably not in great force, until we're certain the area has been restored to a peaceful situation.

Reporter: Can you explain the delay in sending in the fire department?

The firemen were, frankly, gun shy. They've read about firemen being shot at and sniped at . . . fired on and bricked and assaulted in other cities. This is a volunteer fire department and they just didn't want to go in there. I have to say I understand that.

Reporter: Could you not have sent the Guard in before the firemen?

The guard and the state police are not able to protect against sniping from buildings and the streets.

Let me say this, I think the Negroes of Cambridge are going to take action to see that they are not victimized by this kind of action again. And I have every hope that the responsible citizens of both races of this town will band together to stop these things from happening. The wave of this kind of outbreaks here and all over the country are just too much for the general public to endure. The general public is just interested in protection of their property and person and are not rioting for the sake of rioting, looting for the sake of looting, and killing for the sake of killing.

Reporter Marsh: Do you think you were remiss for not arresting Brown during his speech?

No, I do not. I don't think in a volatile situation like that is when arrests should be made. A lot of misunderstanding when that happens and a scuffle could just lead to misinterpretation of what's going on."[6]

There was no misinterpretation of what had happened overnight. Eighteen buildings had been burned to the ground. The damage stretched for two hundred yards on each side of Pine Street.

All of the damaged property belonged to the black residents of Cambridge. There were numerous injuries, none fatal. Rap Brown, like a misguided military officer of the era in Vietnam, had essentially told his audience that local blacks needed to burn down their town to save it. If that is not what he meant, that's what happened.

Brown himself was reportedly wounded slightly by a shotgun pellet. He was treated by a local doctor and left town that night during the fires. Warrants were issued for his arrest on arson and other charges linked to the riots. His fiery rhetoric, once unleashed, could not be stopped as he traveled the country. He was soon being quoted widely:

> *"America is on the eve of a black revolution."*
> *"Black masses are fighting the enemy tit for tat."*
> *"Neither imprisonment nor threats of death would deter me."*

And of President Lyndon Johnson:

> *"He nothing but a white honky cracker, an outlaw from Texas."*

Events that night in Cambridge helped change the tone and tenor of the civil rights movement. It unleashed a new pride in black America and incited a new, more militant approach. It also generated a backlash that would characterize relations between white and black America for years to come. Following Rap Brown's July speech, official white America had no patience for radical blacks. FBI Chief J. Edgar Hoover included Martin Luther King, Jr., among them and created what he called the "Rabble Rouser Index." It was a *Who's Who* of black militancy and included many who continued to preach non-violence. Congressional hearings into Cambridge riots and other violent demonstrations were becoming commonplace with Congress passing anti-riot legislation designed to stymie the militants. Politicians fed off of the unrest, setting the stage for the political balance to tilt right. And Spiro Agnew was tilting as much as any of them. Cambridge is cited by many as a major tipping point in the civil rights struggle as it set the stage for what lay ahead.[7]

Martin Luther King's Assassination

A critically important date in the political life of Spiro Agnew is April 4, 1968, the day Martin Luther King, Jr., was assassinated. It changed everything! Even though a less moderate, more conservative Agnew had emerged from Cambridge, the governor had been raising eyebrows that week during an ongoing conflict with black students at the University of Maryland campus in Princess Anne. The historically black school was located on the Eastern Shore of Maryland. That long-simmering part of the state had long since evidenced a less than hospitable response to people of color. The mutuality of the feeling was obvious nine months earlier, when Rap Brown had encouraged people in Cambridge to burn down the town. Agnew was likely still smarting from that.

The students had a long list of grievances alleging inferior facilities and accommodations at their state university campus. Their complaints matched those of blacks all over the country. It was an extension of earlier racial tension on "The Shore," providing further evidence of an ever-growing determination by blacks to demonstrate their displeasure. It was spring, they were angry and restive, and it was a time of heightened awareness and passion on campuses and in cities across the country. Many went to Maryland's capital, Annapolis, to give emphasis to their complaints and to demonstrate. They marched, carried placards, and sang. Agnew had had his fill of black intransigence. He would have none of that in the state capital and ordered mass student arrests.

Reporters from Baltimore were on the story—and a good story it was, especially for television. It had TV's most essential ingredient: dramatic video. Film was shot by the mile showing students being rounded up and arrested. In some cases they were taken into custody less than gently. I watched in some disbelief as they were hauled to a National Guard parking lot and placed behind imposing chain-link fences topped with barbed wire. It conjured up images that came from Germany a generation earlier. Good pictures for television. Bad pictures for state leaders.

It was during the coverage of this episode that word came that Dr. King had been assassinated. Reporters were notified in the field over two-way radios and told to turn their attention to Governor Agnew. He was sought out for a statement. He appeared as stunned and perplexed as any in his audience. As he was trying to put his finger in the dike between black anger and the white backlash in Annapolis, Memphis—and very quickly the rest of the country—was being overrun with emotion from all sides. In retrospect, it's possible that Agnew was beginning to realize that the King assassination was going to put him and the country on a history-altering course. Agnew obliged the journalists with the obligatory condolences. He had little to say about the roundup of students, an incident in which Dr. King most certainly would have applauded the students and decried Agnew's reaction to them.

But King's voice was stilled, and with it went considerable influence for his tactic of non-violence and civil disobedience.

The rage of an emerging generation of impatient and militant blacks filled the void. Blacks had decided that if life on an equal footing in America would not be granted voluntarily, they would force the issue on the streets. Baltimore's streets were an early battleground, joining Washington, D.C., New York City, Chicago, and more than one hundred others.

The Baltimore riots began on the evening of Saturday, April 6, two days after the King assassination. Baltimore had its own history of racial unrest and turmoil. King's murder, the usual grievances of the black community, coupled with festering discontent with the war in Vietnam, exploded as young blacks took to the streets just after the sun went down. But it was not dark on the edges of downtown and in the black neighborhoods. They were illuminated by flames. Fires created a surreal, artificial dusk. Silhouettes ran in and out of the shadows finding new targets for the torches and Molotov cocktails.

Early targets were the tiny shops and corner grocery stores where blacks had always claimed prices were high and the bread stale. Blacks believed shop owners exploited and cheated them. Some did. Many did not. All were early victims. It made no difference to the demonstrators and looters who made no distinction between shops where they had been cheated and those where credit had been extended to get customers through tough times. The commodity now was revenge, vengeance for generations of real and perceived economic outrages perpetrated against them.

Firefighters could not keep up with the number of torched buildings under attack north of downtown by separate bands of young arsonists. Camera crews were being assembled and sent into the turmoil with and without reporters by the local television stations. It was into the deepest part of the black community that I was dispatched early in the evening, fortunate to be accompanied by Wiley Daniels, the only black reporter on our staff. Our assignment was to get information to put with pictures later. However, the violence was so widespread that it was frequently necessary for reporters to cover the story without an accompanying cameraman. There was plenty to find. Eventually, reporters and photographers would be assigned and deployed as teams.

I'm not quite sure why Wiley and I were put together, but I was grateful we were. Wiley was my senior by about ten years. He was a celebrity in the black community because of his high visibility on television. To his credit, he was one of the few black reporters I have known who did not use the salary television afforded him to move out of the ghetto. Wiley stayed. Wiley could usually be found on his stoop at the end of a workday surrounded by neighborhood kids. He was revered and was a wonderful role model.

It was with no small touch of irony that one of my first jobs at WJZ was to work with Wiley on production and reporting techniques. I didn't know it at the time, but I was actually training him for an anchor job that otherwise would probably have been mine. When that eventually did occur, we both understood what had happened and why. While he was a lot happier than I was, it was never a source of friction between us.

I was especially grateful for our relationship that night of April 6. We walked through the neighborhoods facing acrid smoke, the sound of breaking glass, and the wail of sirens. There were occasional tense moments when we encountered small bands of young people. While Wiley was greeted as a friend, I was not, and more than once the unfriendly words directed at me were overtly hostile and threatening.

Wiley kept the lid on, making sure that the scofflaws and dissidents knew I was with him. "Cool it," he said over and over again, "He's with me brother, go on home. The police gonna lock you up." They didn't go home, but they didn't bother us beyond some pretty abusive language. They respected Wiley Daniels, and the respect they had for him was my security blanket. I shudder to think what my fate might have been had I been in those places alone or with a white cameraman. We had no black photographers on staff at that time.

Later that evening, when we paired up with separate cameramen, I had a chance to find out what it would be like to be cut off and alone. Wiley went one way, I went another. My new partner and I got to the scene of a firebombing before firemen arrived and while the arsonists were looting the store. When they realized that pictures were being taken of them—and by two white guys!—their attention turned to us. It was an extremely tense situation. They advanced on us, throwing rocks and bottles as we sought refuge behind our vehicle. Our only escape was to get into the car and take off before the attackers moved in. It was going to be close. The cameraman had trouble finding the car keys. We both thought we were finished just as a single fire engine rolled up to take on the fire this group had started.

The firefighters saw our predicament immediately. They pulled hose and got a full stream going quickly. That water was aimed at the would-be attackers, not the fire. They were long gone before the firefighters directed the water in a futile attempt to save a mom-and-pop grocery store that by then was fully enveloped in flames.

In the morning, the landscape had changed. Most of the fires were out, but smoke still rose in steamy plumes across black neighborhoods. Help for overtaxed police and other responders was beginning to arrive. Governor Agnew had called in the National Guard. Thousands of guardsmen were put in place throughout the day joining five hundred state police officers who had come in earlier. Agnew requested federal troops from President Johnson, and soon they began to arrive. They were all business, carrying bayonet-tipped rifles, chemical side-arms, and orders to restore the peace. In all, more than five thousand paratroopers from Fort Bragg, soldiers from Fort Benning specially trained in riot control, and even special sniper teams were put in place as other units arrived from other parts of the country. In all, some ten thousand guardsmen and Army troops were in town. Baltimore had become an armed camp.

There were rumors attributed to the FBI that H. Rap Brown had been in town the previous evening inciting young people to take the streets. It certainly fit both his strategy and tactics, but his presence was never proved. Over the next two days and nights, sporadic incidents of arson and gun violence were reported from various parts of the city. The heavy police and military presence was proving at least partially effective. However, the lid was not back on until Tuesday, after four days of violent confrontations and widespread incidents of arson.

The full extent of the story is in the numbers. Over the four days, six people had been killed in the violence. One thousand fires had been set taking out homes and businesses, almost all of which had been looted. The number of injured was placed at seven hundred. Federal troops and local police took nearly five thousand people into custody. The dollar amount in damage was placed at about $15 million, and this was when stamps sold for a nickel and gas was thirty cents a gallon. It's impossible to completely measure economic consequences. Many of the burned-out businesses never reopened. Many of the homes were never rebuilt or not rebuilt for many years. Baltimore had taken a prominent place on the national stage of civil unrest. To a large degree, the city had imploded. The governor, meantime, exploded.

One of the things I had noticed during my time on the streets over those four days was the number of black adults who were trying to rein in members of the mob. It was generational. The younger blacks were running wild. The mob's rage gave it a momentum that carried the fury for four days in spite of efforts to contain it within the black community. Older family members, church leaders, civic leaders, and business leaders were trying to stop it. There may have been some individual successes but it amounted to a finger in the dike effort. In spite of some almost heroic and dangerous individual efforts by these people, Governor Agnew was convinced black leaders had not done enough. He intended to take them to task for it. His own outrage may have clouded his thinking or he may have been given bad intelligence information. Or, as some have suggested, his next move may have been a carefully considered political calculation.

As it happened, I took the call to the news department from the governor's press aide as the rioting was winding down. He was announcing that Agnew had called a meeting of the top black civic, religious, and political leaders to discuss the previous days' mayhem and other civil rights issues. The press aide was a former broadcast newsman who had close ties with many of us covering Governor Agnew. Almost as an afterthought in our conversation he said to me, "It might be a good idea to bring two cameras to the event." When I asked why, he said, "It ought to be interesting to have one camera on the audience when the governor speaks. The reaction will be interesting."

Needless to say, my station complied as did the others, all of which had obviously been given the same invitation post script.

There were some seventy-five people in the audience. Most were recognizable to us reporters. There were politicians who were current or former office holders on the national, state, and local level. Many of those who ran social service agencies were present, as were many ministers of all manner of black churches from the most historic to tiny storefront places of worship. The average age of those in attendance was close to middle age. Most of those in the audience, perhaps all, had supported Spiro Agnew in his race for governor less than two years earlier.

Agnew started politely enough by thanking those in attendance for coming. It did not take him very long, however, to get to the point of the gathering. Agnew's outrage over events of the past days could not be contained and grew to crescendo proportions. He berated the audience, confusing those before him with the very rioters they had tried to contain. The implication was clear. They had been part of the problem rather than part of the solution.

Within a few minutes he was accusing those in the audience of not doing enough to stem the tide of violence. Although many of them had been on the street attempting to do just that throughout all of the rioting, he was tarring them with the same brush as the violent packs that had tried to burn down the town.

At one time he referred to his invited audience as "circuit riding, Hanoi visiting, caterwauling, riot inciting, burn America down type of leaders." His stinging, misplaced rhetoric at first stunned those who had honored his invitation in the expectation their efforts in the streets would be acknowledged or that they would be recruited to lead a community rebuilding process. However, as his words were absorbed and his meaning ever-clearer, they began to leave. First, one by one, then in small groups. Agnew had not yet finished speaking when the room was empty save for him, his aides, and a handful of reporters.

Spiro Agnew's transformation from liberal reformer and Republican outsider was forever set aside. His appeal to blacks and liberal Democrats was forever dashed on the rocks of ugly rhetoric. He had become the darling of the Republican right in just a few moments. Later Richard Nixon and his aides would admit that it was that speech that caught their attention. At that moment in time, Nixon was on the final lap to the Republican presidential nomination. He needed a running mate. He needed someone who would play in the South and someone to take the air out of third-party segregationist candidate George Wallace's high flying balloon.

Almost four months to the day later, I was anchoring our noon newscast at WJZ. The Republican Convention was in full swing in Miami. The big news for local stations in Baltimore so far had been that Spiro Agnew had placed Nixon's name in nomination at the convention. That in itself was quite a leap from his relative political obscurity of two years earlier. In the middle of the broadcast, the producer advised that we were going to cut away to a special report from Miami. I watched as Sam Donaldson in somewhat breathless fashion announced that Richard Nixon had selected Spiro Agnew as his running mate.

If the nation at large was stunned by the selection of "Spiro Who?" the surprise in the studio was at least as great. Perhaps more so, as most of us who knew him and his background and who had called him "Ted" just two years earlier, were left to consider what had happened and why.

Was Spiro Agnew a wily and shrewd politician who choreographed his way to the big table in politics? Or was he simply the beneficiary of difficult times, political naivety, and an honest transition of political philosophy? His ultimate disgrace following election as vice president and the revelations that he was taking money under the table may have blunted the debate. (There were also later disclosures that Richard Nixon had become disenchanted with

Agnew early in the first term. Nixon reportedly had concluded that Agnew was not intellectually or politically suited for the job and briefly considered dumping him from the ticket in 1972.) Agnew was, and was not, many things, but if nothing else, he was an accident of history. Had normal conditions prevailed in 1966, he would likely never have been elected governor. How might things have been different had he not been?

Ironically, a year or so later, I would find myself in a situation not unlike Spiro Agnew's, though on a much different level, when I was named news director at WJZ. It was a job for which I was neither suited nor qualified. I'll explain later.

Louie

*T*he contagion of national racial unrest continued to spread across the country. Maryland's Eastern Shore had been fertile ground for it for many years, even generations. Its largest city, Salisbury, was the next flashpoint, and it took only little more than a month after the King assassination for restive blacks there to take to the streets. A familiar pattern followed with National Guard troops sent in in the hope they would deal quickly with the trouble. If the rioters were learning from counterparts across the country, so were the responders. While Baltimore had registered high on the seismic scale of civil unrest, Salisbury was merely a disturbing blip.

We did not know that, of course, in Baltimore. So, I was part of a crew dispatched once again to an Eastern Shore community just a few miles down the road from Cambridge. It was more than one hundred miles from Baltimore, which was still reeling from events of a few weeks earlier.

We had no idea of how long we'd be in the Salisbury area, which presented me with something of a dilemma.

When news of the Salisbury rioting broke out, we were put on the road quickly, too quickly for me to make arrangements for my dog, Louie. Louie was a standard poodle and had been with me since my days in Germany. Don't jump to a conclusion that this was a custom-cut Foo-Foo with a rhinestone collar and painted nails. Louie was an outdoor dog, a throwback to the poodle hunters they were bred to be before people started sculpting their curly coats, opting for style over service. Louis was cut close so he could roam in the woods during our long walks without coming back carrying briars and brambles imbedded in a fancy coat. I mention this be-cause Louie looked rather nondescript to most and that turned out to be a good thing.

Because of the uncertainty of the Salisbury troubles and the un-expected nature of the assignment, I had to take Louie with me. I had no time to make other arrangements.

The trip to Salisbury was a couple of hours from Baltimore. We left in the early evening, when the first reports of street action were coming in. My cameraman and I talked about a reported incident that had taken place on the Eastern Shore a few days earlier. After all that had happened on that peninsula in recent months and years, many of the residents were more testy than ever, especially the older ones. A lot of the old farmers and fishermen wanted nothing to do with either the black troublemakers or the pesky journalists covering the trouble. Reporters were generally perceived as sympathetic to the "troublemakers." Locals thought news reports merely perpetuated the unrest.

The story we had all been hearing in Baltimore was either a frightening fact or a frightening myth. What we were hearing was that an out-of-town newspaper reporter had been gathering information for a story about attitudes and unrest on "The Shore." He stopped in a rural café and struck up a conversation with a bunch of good old boys. They turned surly and things quickly got ugly. The confrontation degenerated to frightening climax as the good old boys opted to end the conversation with a good old-fashioned lynching. The accounts were consistent on the point that the action seemed to have had something to do with the "nigger loving liberal press" and a certain tendency of "out-of-towners to stir shit." As the story went, he was on a table with a noose around his neck, when a state trooper coincidentally stopped in for a cup of coffee. He found himself facing an ugly scene as an equally ugly group of rednecks was about to kick the table from under a reporter with a noose around his neck. The trooper broke up the incident and escorted the trembling reporter from the scene. I was never able to corroborate the story and now believe it was very likely a contemporary urban legend borne of attitudes of the era.

That said, as a reporter heading for that dysfunctional part of the state yet again, it was a perfectly believable scenario. We had dealt with this attitude before on the Eastern Shore. It intruded on reporters' efforts to gather information. The animosity directed at us was undisguised but had not gone beyond the stare-down, epithet stage. Under the conditions of the spring and summer of 1968, the scenario was definitely not an unthinkable possibility in that area where lynching had been common only a few generations earlier and where attitudes had not changed much.

Was I certain that the alleged incident had occurred? Absolutely not. Did I believe it? Absolutely. And that is the way I was thinking as we once again drove eastward from Baltimore to cover yet another confrontation between blacks and whites. This trip was a little different. My dog Louie was part of the crew.

Louie weighed about eighty pounds. About seventy-five pounds of him was heart. He was loyal, obedient, and friendly. Louie was so people-friendly, in fact, that he had slept through an attempted break-in at my apartment. Had he wakened, he likely would have offered to show the robber around the place. Louie was quite content to sleep during the drive from Baltimore.

Somewhere between Cambridge and Salisbury, my cameraman and I stopped to pick up a couple of Cokes. We pulled up to a little place that was one of those all-purpose stores you find in rural areas. You could get breakfast there in the morning, gas and groceries all day, and longnecks all night. We had definitely arrived during the longneck phase. Five or six burley guys in bib overalls, flannel shirts, work boots, feed grain baseball caps, and surly expressions visible through two days growth, were sitting at a couple of tables in the middle of the room. When they saw us, their expressions told us in no uncertain terms that this was not happy hour.

Our well-identified news car was parked a few yards away from the pumps, but they had apparently seen it pull up and park past the front door. When we came into the place, the first words I recall were something to the effect of, "What the fuck do you guys want." One or two of them got up and stretched the way football players do before a game. This was a long time ago, and I must confess I do not remember exactly what these guys said to us. It may have had something to do with the fact that more than one was speaking at a time, and that our instincts told us to back up rather than follow plan A. The Cokes could wait. It was clear that we were unwelcome and that the language was not only unfriendly, it was also menacing. The media was unwelcome and was the "cause of all the trouble."

We backed out quickly, but these guys were with us as we maneuvered past the ancient gas pumps toward the car. They were in our faces with a rush of unintelligible verbiage. The message was still clear. They didn't like us. They didn't want us there. They didn't like what we did. They wanted to break at least a few bones, and getting about that business right then and there was okay with them. Our protests, if there were any, were probably unheard, and if they were, there were no available allies.

We had no place to go but toward the car. Not that it offered any real refuge. However, any object, however inanimate, was preferable to these guys especially if it could be put between us and them. I guess the commotion roused Louie, whose silhouette appeared in the back window and who delivered a challenging bark. No doubt he was protesting the interruption to his nap. If any one of these redneck jerks had realized that what was behind the glass was a French Poodle with a disposition rivaling Mother Theresa's, things might have turned out differently. However, Louie was a big dog, and he looked and sounded it in the car.

That was enough for the brew crew. One of them said, "Hey, they've got a dog . . . and it's a big one." We were close enough to the car by then that we could have loosed the monster inside with a flick of the handle. Thank God neither one of us did, otherwise Louie might have leaped out and started licking their curled fists.

Instead, one of the bozos said something like, "Whoa." That was all it took. It gave us the time to jump into the car and kick up a little gravel as tires dug into it and screeched back onto the roadway. We breathed a sigh of relief. Louie went back to sleep.

I have always thought that if the near-lynching of a reporter was in fact a true story, it happened where we had just escaped either a beating or worse. If not, it would have happened at a place just like it, involving people just like the ones we had encountered.

Salisbury

S alisbury was the minor leagues compared to what we had been through in Cambridge and Baltimore, and what much of the rest of the country had experienced, was going through, or was to face. We got there an hour after our close call in the middle of nowhere. It was just in time to get shot at. Local police were looking for someone who had done something that was bad. We found ourselves with them at one point as they were searching a lightly wooded area in a part of the city's outskirts. It was an area that was not well populated.

We, including our hero Louie, trod with them through the brush and trees when one of the cops said he'd heard something. He asked the cameraman if he could help with some light. He was as much of a rookie at this sort of thing as we were. The fairly powerful and intense power-pack light went on and did nothing more than bring two gunshots. Nothing like a bright light to offer a target. We heard the "pings" as the bullets struck within twenty feet or so.

How fast can you say, "lights out?" That's how fast ours was out.

The National Guard was into Salisbury quickly. Order was established in a very short period of time. That is not to say that grievances were satisfied. It was just another case of just another place in America where the pot simmered as it would, and in many places still does, some two generations later.

London

_W_ithin weeks after the Baltimore riots, and days after Salisbury, my situation changed dramatically. Because of my reporting background in Europe, I was selected to temporarily fill a vacancy in Westinghouse Broadcasting's London Bureau. It was a radio operation only. London was a full-fledged bureau in its own right, but it was also the conduit through which flowed material from correspondents and stringers in Europe and other parts of the world. News reports were filed to London from those outposts throughout the day. Then, at prescribed times of day, we would turn them around, "feeding" them to our station in New York. It, in turn, would provide the material to other Westinghouse stations, and those stations across the country, and oddly enough, Australia, that subscribed to a Westinghouse radio news service.

Although I had been hired initially by Westinghouse during meetings in London, I was a stranger to the city, and the city to me. As an English History major in college, the thought of (with apologies to Roger Miller) "Westminster Abbey, The Tower, Big Ben . . . not to mention the rosy red cheeks of the little children," London was an incredible opportunity to bring to life the many text books, history books, and novels I had read over the years. Why else would a young man seek out 221-B Baker Street within days of arriving?

The world of Shakespeare, Wren, the monarchies, the castles, the parks, the pubs, the wrong-way traffic was suddenly mine to absorb. Every cockney cabby sounded like a college professor to me. That would have made them all laugh. One could walk around the entire city, visit the nooks and crannies, figure out the "undergrounds," pop in to the museums, eat bad food and eat wonderful food. London is a cacophony of sound, color, and diversity with history and historic references shaking a visitor by the lapel at almost every turn.

An added bonus for this stranger was that 1968 was one of the warmest summers on record in England. Coming from Baltimore's heat and humidity to a heat wave peaking at 82–84 degrees did not seem like the hardship the locals were complaining about.

My assignment was for an undetermined period of time, likely to be several months. Pretty good temporary duty. I was in London about a month after the Baltimore rioting, where, with few exceptions, my role was more technical than reportorial. I received and recorded the material from our people in Europe and Asia, set it up for rapid (less expensive) transmission to the United States, then awaited the next round.

It was routine but interesting given the reported details on world events that passed through our recording equipment several times a day. There were daily reports on the ever-intensifying war in Vietnam. Students were restive in France as a young leftist Daniel Cohn-Bendit, known as "Danny the Red," was leading massive student demonstrations and convulsing the de Gaulle government. We watched the tension build in Czechoslovakia during "The Prague Spring," which led to a Russian invasion in August. At one point I was to be sent to Prague to cover that story but the idea was scotched because of the personnel shortage in London. I had a chance to do a little reporting on British reaction to the assassination of Bobby Kennedy, who was killed back home within two weeks of my arrival in London.

But it was an earlier assassination that diverted me from that story. On June 8, 1968, James Earl Ray, the suspected assassin of Dr. Martin Luther King was captured at London's Heathrow Airport as he was trying to leave the country on a phony Canadian passport. He had holed up in a London walk-up as part of his flight from the Memphis assassination in April. His capture came just three days after Robert Kennedy had been shot in a California hotel. That was still big news in London. This was bigger and blew the Bobby Kennedy story off of page one. In London it was a local story of international proportions.

I did an obligatory but routine piece about where he had stayed during his brief sojourn in London. It was an inexpensive, nondescript rooming house in an anonymous part of the city. I spoke with the landlady, and her comments would be repeated many times in my career in conjunction with other criminals who had "lived next door." They always seem to be "a quiet lad, nice enough, polite, kept to himself, caused no trouble, didn't bother anyone, was nice with neighborhood kids, came and went without much conversation, and paid his rent on time." Why is it that some of the most heinous criminals in history have been so described by those whose lives they touched as kids or adults, or by those whose paths they crossed on the run?

The extradition process was not very complicated nor was it prolonged. My Westinghouse colleague—Jerry Landay, the London Bureau chief—covered the legal proceedings. Landay attended the limited number of court appearances necessary to send Ray back to America. He said he never laid eyes on Ray in the courtroom. Ray was so completely surrounded by law enforcement security officers during those pro-forma court appearances that he was visible to very few other than the judge and lawyers. The order had come down from Britain's Home Secretary that nothing had better happen to Mr. Ray pending his extradition from British soil. The only thing that happened was the extradition itself.

After this brief association with a major historical event, my life returned to the routine of funneling important news stories from someplace else to someplace else. By August, I was back in Baltimore covering the kind of events that comprised local television news then . . . and now . . . crime and punishment. The country was jumping with the political conventions, including the so-called "police riot" in Chicago at the Democratic Convention. The Vietnam War, other seismic international events, and continued civil unrest at home filled the airwaves and the newspapers. The big stories were elsewhere rather than Baltimore, and someone else was covering them. I was also put in a position in which I was unable to cover stories closer to home. I was pulled from the ranks to become news director, a position I would hold for some two years and for the remainder of my time in Baltimore.

Strange as it may seem, my appointment as news director essentially took me out of the news business. Oddly enough, the chance to manage a staff of about forty and to determine the course and personality of our news coverage offered little real opportunity to do that. In that time and place, I reported to the station's program director. It was he who decided whom we hired and fired, what our news "look" would be, and our budget. I also had the disadvantage of having come out of the ranks. The staff knew me, my strengths and weaknesses. Those who had heard me complain about certain newsroom conditions now found me unresponsive to their same complaints. My hands were tied when it came to correcting them. I was left to deal with personnel problems, staff complaints, overtime, equipment maintenance, and technical issues over which I had no expertise and little understanding. I did get the chance to remodel the news room. It was not for me. I was the *Peter Principal* personified. Successful enough in one area to be bumped up beyond my capabilities.

We took a lengthy newspaper strike in Baltimore in the late 1960s and scheduled a lot of additional news production to help fill the void. I assigned myself to the least attractive shifts to produce news and occasionally anchor news briefs we had inserted into the schedule to fill the local information gap. I assigned myself to read a five-minute mid-afternoon obituary program, which happened to be one of the dullest yet one of the most popular news inserts on our air. I had no idea so many people relied as heavily as they did and do on obits. As management, I was entitled to both produce programs and appear on air. However, as management, I was not entitled to the union fees that went to performers for on-the-air appearances.

Those who were entitled to that extra money were furious that I was on the air at all and perceived it as an effort to save the company money. The shifts I covered were the least attractive and my involvement was simply to keep as much staff available as possible to cover the news and the major newscasts of the day. The union on-air employees still received lucrative fees for the additional programming, but none of them had to come in at three in the morning as I did to earn it, leaving them available during the day. But I understand the feeling. I didn't handle it well. I was still under thirty years of age, and I did not have the experience or the maturity to deal with the strike, the internal dissension it spawned, or any of the complicated issues a news director must negotiate. On the whole, I was just not very good at it, and any criticism of my tenure is justified. After two years of it I wanted out.

My personal reluctance to continue doing what I neither liked nor did well was exacerbated with the arrival of a new program director; a new boss for me. I was well along in my decision to return to reporting when he eliminated any doubt that might have remained. I'll not use his real name. Let's say it was Bill Jones. One of the things about most broadcast operations that I like is that it's relatively informal and almost universally so. With some rare exceptions, people interact on a first-name basis. I have never worked for a station manager whom I did not call by his or her first name; and so it has always been up and down the line. The only exception to this that I can recall? Bill Jones. During his first day, he met individually with staffers; kind of a get acquainted thing. We chatted and for me it was "Bill this and Bill that." After a few minutes of this, he told me in no uncertain terms that he preferred not to be called Bill. "It's Dr. Jones," he said. "I want to be called Dr. Jones by my department heads."

Well, what does one do? So, it was "Doctor Jones." I learned a short time later that Dr. Jones's advanced degree was in Theater Arts. Not to diminish any PhD's academic accomplishment, calling him "doctor" just didn't cut it.

If there was any self-doubt about getting "back into the real news business" as a working reporter, that conversation pretty much settled it. Goodbye Baltimore; hello St. Louis.

St. Louis

*O*kay, I admit it. When I was traveling to St. Louis for a job interview I was among those arrogant East Coasters who expected something close to teepees on the edge of town, steamboats puffing down the rivers, and stovepipe hats. While that is obviously an exaggeration, I was among those many who believed that the Midwest was America's backwater. There are many, apparently, who still have a distorted view of the Midwest. Think of that old *New Yorker* cartoon captioned something like "a New Yorker's View of the Country." It showed a map of New York divided from California by only the Hudson River. So much for the rest of the country.

I was surprised by St. Louis. Having grown up just a few miles from New York City, I was used to congestion and close quarters. The northeast in particular had a big head start in growth on the rest of the country. New York was already getting crowded when St. Louis began to spread its wings, even though St. Louis had a larger immigrant population than New York in the mid-nineteenth century. Cities had to make maximum use of space as they grew. The result was often a feeling of being squeezed as twentieth-century populations had to make do with nineteenth-century city planning. Space was no issue in the Midwest.

When I arrived in St. Louis I found wide boulevards and expansive parks, Mayberry-type suburbs, and a whole bunch of Fortune 500 companies headquartered in the city and its environs. It was also remarkably like Baltimore, a city that had grown on me and still has its pull. Baltimore and St. Louis have similar boundary growth limitations. The layout of each is strikingly similar; the roads, waterfront, zoo, big parks, downtown, and suburbs are configured very much alike.

One big difference is the pedestrian pace. In St. Louis, its measurably slower and more European than Baltimore, New York, and other big cities in the Northeast where everyone seems always in a hurry to get where they are going. Unfortunately, in Missouri, that pace is often extended to getting some important things done politically. The Show Me State did, indeed, need to be shown before taking action on important issues. In a way, that was part of its charm. That is, when it wasn't frustrating.

A case in point. When I left Baltimore in late 1971, a big part of the statewide debate was whether to have a Maryland state lottery. That debate was just beginning in Missouri. In Maryland, the legislature approved a lottery in 1972 and implemented it in 1973. Missouri's lottery was established in 1985. That's the way it goes in the "Show Me" State. Some say it should be "Missouri . . . Show Me . . . Tomorrow." That's the way the state works.

In one of those delicious bits of historic irony, George P. "Your Home Is Your Castle, Protect It" Mahoney was named the first Chairman of the Maryland State Lottery Commission. It was the same year Spiro Agnew resigned the vice presidency in disgrace.

I was offered the job of reporter/executive news editor at KTVI-TV, the ABC St. Louis affiliate. It was owned by the S.I. Newhouse newspaper and publishing empire, giving it a strong journalistic pedigree. I never quite understood what the executive news editor title really meant. However, beggars can't be choosers. I had had considerable difficulty selling myself as a reporter to other news directors by coming at them as a fellow news director who wanted to be a reporter, even though virtually all of my professional experience at home and abroad had been as a reporter. No news director fully understood why a news director would want to reduce his status and return to the streets. It was part of a lesson I learned over time, which is that many television news directors . . . many or most of whom have limited reportorial experience . . . often hold higher paid on-air personnel in some disdain even though they are the news department's bread and butter.

The general manager at KTVI got it, and I got the job, which meant a move from the twentieth or twenty-first market in the country to the tenth. That was pretty heady in and of itself (although St. Louis ultimately dropped to around twenty-second as populations exploded in Sunbelt states).

Getting back to reporting was the good news. The bad news was that KTVI was a joke in the market. It put on newscasts Monday through Friday only, and only the late evening version at 10:00 p.m. The staff was small, and the commitment to support-technology was limited. However, there were promises of better days to come and they did come, but slowly. It took almost a decade before the station became a competitive factor in the market.

At times it was extremely frustrating. However, that frustration was frequently tempered by opportunities to be a little more creative in coverage. And because staff size was small, the odds were better than ever that I would get the chance to cover the bigger stories. In the beginning, there was also the luxury of having more time to work on stories without having the interruption of multiple newscasts.

The dates of June 23–24 had coincidentally been the time frame for memorable news events I'd been a part of in Bonn and Baltimore. They were to prove so again in St. Louis in one of the more bizarre incidents I'd experienced before or since.

Skyjacking

*S*t. Louis's Lambert International Airport is a lot bigger and busier now than it was in the early 1970s. It was busy enough though. Because of its location in the center of the country it was served by most of the major airlines. It was a different time, and security considerations were not nearly as extensive or comprehensive as they would eventually become at all big-city airports. Lambert then was journalist-friendly. There was even a "media only" section of the airport parking garage for news vehicles, which reporters utilized when traveling out of town. We also used them when taking personal flights by putting an easy-to-acquire "media" sign in the window. Times were much simpler then.

High temperatures and smothering humidity arrive in St. Louis in June and stay the summer. Summer had arrived in all respects on the night of June 23, a Friday. A skyjacking was taking place over the skies of Oklahoma and Texas during the early evening. A young man had gotten aboard an American Airlines jetliner with a submachine gun and some explosives. He announced his intention to commandeer the plane and hold it and the passengers for ransom. As the story unfolded there was no hint in our newsroom that it would become a local story.

But police radio chatter in the newsroom soon brought that distant story to us. The plane was being diverted north, possibly to St. Louis, which proved enough for me and a cameraman to get moving. It was Friday. We were nearing the end of our shifts. The last thing we really wanted was a breaking story. Nonetheless, we were dispatched to Lambert "just in case." It turned out to be a good move and a long night. The plane had indeed landed in St. Louis and was on the ground when we arrived at the airport. It was shortly after 9:30 p.m.

Our vantage point for the unfolding drama was the roof of the airport parking garage from which we had an unobstructed view of the captive American Airlines 737 jetliner located about half a mile away. Radio, television, and newspaper reporters shared the space.

All eyes were fixed on the aircraft, which was bathed in bright light and standing well away from other traffic on the distant runway. The long lens of the camera was helpful in following the activity on the ground. We monitored half a dozen people moving around outside the aircraft and watched as vehicles moved to and from the area. The specifics of their activity was a mystery to us.

The information available to us was limited to what we could see and what little radio traffic was relayed to us from our offices where the story was being followed by the wire services. Occasionally, an airport police officer would come by and provide some information. Reporters had the impression these visits were not so much to be helpful with details but rather to make certain we stayed put. We were essentially waiting for something to happen; either police would storm the plane, it would remain there indefinitely, or it would take off. It was a waiting game.

What we knew at the time, or came to know later, was that a young man from suburban Detroit, armed with a submachine gun and at least one hand grenade, had taken over an American Airlines flight over Tulsa, Oklahoma, and forced it to fly to St. Louis. Upon landing, he specifically demanded $502,000 (why he specified the unusual amount was never explained), five parachutes, a shovel, and an unimpeded flight to Toronto. He held eleven passengers and a flight crew hostage onboard in St. Louis as the money was gathered from a local bank.

For two hours the situation seemed static to us observers on the roof. Certainly, negotiations of some sort were taking place. We were, however, unable to ascertain exactly what was going on. Speculation was fairly intense among those of us watching. It was based on nothing more than what little information we had and our active imaginations.

Shortly before midnight, however, we became aware of an increase in activity around the plane. We were able to see, and film with a long lens, a number of people leaving the plane. We thought at first the drama was playing out. As it happened, negotiations with the hijacker had produced a limited agreement. He had released the eleven passengers, who were whisked off to be debriefed by the FBI. The flight crew, including two stewardesses (what they were called at the time) were kept captive onboard. All told, there were six hostages still on the plane. Once again, activity shut down, and we were left to wonder what the next step would be.

Unbeknownst to us, a second drama was being played out a few hundred yards behind us in a penthouse bar in one of the several airport hotels just south of Lambert. Bar customers had a clear view of the hijacked plane in the distance and were listening to radio traffic from the airport tower, which was piped into the establishment as a novelty for added ambiance. Under most conditions, customer fascination was usually short-lived after a few moments of listening to those monotone conversations between anonymous pilots and listless controllers. This night was different.

Some of the conversations between the tower and the captive American Airlines jet were clearly audible to those at the bar. The chatter included early negotiations between the hijacker and the FBI as relayed by the pilot. They included hijacker demands and conditions for departure. The hijacker was impatient. Response to his demands was slow. Listeners at the bar might have heard, as he was eventually assured, that the money was being assembled. Coming up with half a million dollars on a Friday night was difficult, he was told. In fact, a local bank was getting the cash together to meet the young man's demands.

A thirty-something businessman in the bar was listening intently as he awaited the delayed arrival of a relative. The man was David Hanley. He was a successful law-abiding citizen and family man who became increasingly angry over the impasse playing out about a half mile away. He was drinking but not intoxicated.

When the plane had been on the ground for almost three hours, and about an hour after the eleven passengers had been released, Hanley had heard enough. He may or may not have known that the ransom money had been delivered, but he undoubtedly sensed that the plane was close to takeoff and that the hijacker was about to continue his odyssey.

Hanley announced loudly enough for anyone within earshot at the bar to hear, "Turn on the radio in a few minutes and you'll hear something that will rock the world." It's unknown whether anyone really thought his comment was anything more than idle braggadocio. Having finished his drink, Hanley calmly left the bar, took the elevator to the lobby, and with a determination apparent only to himself, walked to his car, a late-model Cadillac.

The distance between the hotel parking lot and the periphery of the airport was only a few dozen yards. It was approaching half-past midnight and there was finally some relief from the June heat and humidity thanks to a welcoming breeze. One can only speculate what Hanley might have been thinking as he started his car. Clearly, his resolve to accomplish what only he knew he wanted to do intensified as he put the car into gear. No one paid any attention as he steered the vehicle toward the airport. At first.

Those of us on the roof heard it before we saw it. What we heard was the screeching of rubber on the road. As one, we turned toward the noise and watched as the late-model vehicle below us smashed into the first of a pair of chain-link fences guarding the airport property. The car bounced back from the stubborn first fence. Tires squealed and spewed smoke as the vehicle got hung up briefly on a curb. They spun on the pavement then hurtled once again toward the fence. The car broke through, coming to rest against the second ten-foot barrier. Another attack. The second fence held. The car bounced back a few feet one more time, and once again Hanley accelerated in a cloud of smoke from the squealing, spinning tires. We watched incredulously. For an instant, the Cadillac remained stationary, wrapped in smoke and sound before jumping into the fence again. This time the fence gave, and a section flattened before the car. Hanley drove through the opening with a roaring engine and screeching tires. It had all happened so quickly that a small group of city police officers just a few yards away had no time to fully digest what was happening or react to what they were seeing. Not that they could have done anything to stop Hanley short of putting a few rounds into the car. They were as immobilized by surprise as were the rest of us. By the time they processed what was happening Hanley was streaming at right angles across airport runways.

The car was speeding toward the end of a runway at the western edge of the airport. It took only seconds to get there, and he remained in our full view. If there was anything said aside from a few "what the hells?" and "holy shits," I can't recall. We watched in disbelief as the scene unfolded before us, although it was increasingly clear what the driver had in mind. No one wanted to believe what could lie ahead.

The Cadillac turned on the western edge of the runway to face the fully fueled plane a thousand yards away. Hanley paused the car briefly. It was mindful of an animal pawing the ground before charging. Picture the bull about to charge a matador standing transfixed while awaiting the attack. In this case, it was a mismatch as a fully loaded, one hundred–ton 727 jetliner awaited the assault from a three thousand pound automobile.

Then, the charge. Even though we were probably half a mile from the car, we could hear those tires scream as Hanley aimed it at the parked plane.

There was no doubt now amongst any of us about what was about to happen. The driver of the car planned to stop the aircraft. Would he attempt to block it or crash into it? We knew the big plane had just been fueled and was probably ready for takeoff. By striking the plane, the impact would result in nothing short of a violent, powerful explosion followed by a gasoline-fueled, fiery certain loss of life for those in the plane, the car, and for anyone near the aircraft.

The car sped toward the waiting plane reaching speeds that we on the roof correctly estimated as approaching one hundred miles an hour. We filmed the blur of lights in the middle of the runway as it narrowed the gap with its target. The car closed on the plane. There was almost a slow-motion quality to the assault to those of us watching from a distance even though the car was moving at high speed. It took no longer than twenty seconds to reach the helpless jet.

No one will ever be able to fully explain why the worst of the scenarios did not play out as tragically as we anticipated. Fate trumped physics. The Cadillac smashed into the nose of the plane. It struck at just enough of an angle to deflect the car into the left landing gear where it became wedged against the wheel and its mount. It stopped within inches of the potentially lethal fuel tanks. There was no explosion. There was no fire. There was also very little left of the Cadillac. No one watching could believe what they'd just observed.

I have tried to imagine what might have been going through the minds of those aboard the plane in the seconds before impact as they awaited the four-wheeled missile coming at them. The cockpit crew knew what was coming. The pilot and co-pilot were advised by radio, and they could also see the oncoming lights from where they sat. There was no time to prepare, other than to utter a few words of prayer, brace themselves, and wait.

There was the additional concern, of course, that the hijacker would assume that the assault was the work of the FBI attempting some sort of attack on the plane. Would he unleash a volley of bullets in response? Would he kill the hostages?

The three thousand–pound David, the Cadillac, came out second best to the 150,000-pound Goliath. The plane was only jarred slightly. Impact was hardly noticed by those onboard. When told what had happened, the hijacker said, in a comment that is deliciously ironic, "That guy must be nuts!" That comment came from a fellow carrying a submachine gun, explosives, half a million in cash, five parachutes, and a shovel, preparing to fly a stolen jetliner to Canada with at least six hostages.

"That guy" may have been nuts, but his assault on the plane caused a dramatic shift in activity. First, emergency crews had to deal with Hanley. Remarkably, he was alive, but just barely. He had to be removed from the mangled wreckage now twisted around the left landing gear of the jet. Extrication was difficult enough, but Hanley's injuries were severe, making his removal from the vehicle extremely delicate. He had suffered multiple fractures including a broken jaw, broken ribs, and a broken back. The driver was ultimately and successfully pulled from the mangled wreckage and taken to a waiting ambulance for a life-saving run.

However, the jetliner was no longer airworthy, and officials were confronted with new demands from the increasingly impatient hijacker. He was more nervous than ever and had no intention of amending his basic plan. He demanded that he be provided with a new plane and that it be done quickly so he could be on his way.

In what may have been record time, a second American Airlines 727 was brought from the tarmac and put in place. The hijacker moved cautiously from one plane to the next, placing himself between captive crew members to reduce chances of sharpshooters dropping him on the runway. The transfer was made quickly and efficiently. About an hour after David Hanley's reckless assault, it was wheels up on the replacement plane. One mangled car and one damaged aircraft were left behind. Within seconds after takeoff, the second 727 was disappearing into the eastern sky.

It was a short flight for the hijacker. Less than an hour out of St. Louis, he donned a parachute, grabbed his weapon and his loot, and jumped from the speeding aircraft. Before the jump, he must have wondered about survival. He was over rural Indiana. Hundreds of square acres of darkness and farmland loomed below. It must have felt to him as if he were jumping into a deep, bottomless hole. In a sense, he was.

The transition from a pressurized jetliner cabin to the great void must have been a violent one. The hijacker went out with his weapon and the cash. A wall of wind stripped both from his grasp. The harness tore into his skin as he opened his chute. Now, he had to manage a landing in the pitch black darkness, a landing that would have been challenging to any trained chutist. It was before 3:00 a.m. on the morning of June 25 when the hijacker found himself floating to the earth over farmland in Peru, Indiana. He landed successfully, disappeared into the darkness, and to all intents and purposes vanished entirely. Well, not quite.

It was no trick to determine when the hijacker had bailed out, and therefore, no big mystery to extrapolate as to approximately where. But Howard County, Indiana, is a big piece of rural real estate. Search crews were out at first light. For two days, more than two hundred men searched the area looking for the suspect. They zeroed in fairly quickly on the spot where he'd landed. It was strewn with evidence. Almost all of the ransom money was found in packets or drifting loosely in the field. The weapon used to commandeer the plane was intact nearby. Bits of the hijacker's pants were also found. Portions had been ripped off by the same force that had torn the gun and money from his hands.

Three days later, federal agents and local police arrested a twenty-eight-year-old unemployed service station attendant in a Detroit suburb. He was identified as Martin J. McNally, a Vietnam veteran. He was taken into custody without incident. He had thirteen dollars in his pocket and bruises on his torso caused when the parachute straps twisted into his skin as the chute opened in the Indiana darkness. McNally was apprehended because his fingerprints were found on the plane he had commandeered and on the weapon found in the field. He never really had a chance to put his prints on the money. When all was said and done, the entire effort had gone for naught. Instead of walking away from the incident with half a million bucks, Martin McNally now had to pay the piper.

The Trial

Such was the speed of justice in 1972 that Martin Joseph McNally was on trial for his crime before the year was out. I covered the trial. It was an open-and-shut case but nonetheless lasted the better part of a week. Like the incident itself, it was not without its bizarre moments.

I must say that I found McNally to be a surprisingly personable, if misdirected, young man. He had an engaging manner and a certain charm that was not diminished by his position at the defense table or on the stand. He wore a bemused smile as if he were enjoying the proceedings. He reacted to developments during the week as if it were some kind of put-on. He was never disrespectful in court. He simply seemed like a friendly guy who wanted to be in on the fun. Were the charges against him less serious, I would have been rooting for him to be acquitted as we sometimes do at the movies when we secretly hope the bad guys get away with it. But that was not to be nor should it have been.

The nice-guy personality on display in the courtroom had worked well for him when he was on the run. He had apparently put it to good use within hours of his daring jump from the plane in an incident that proved to be an embarrassing episode for Peru, Indiana's police chief.

His name was Richard Blair. He was a giant of a man dressed in a lumpy suit. He wore his hair closely cropped. He was a cop on the stand and acted like one, all business, unsmiling, and somewhat nervous. Cops are used to being the ones in control, not controlled by others. And he was controlled by court officers, court procedure, and the knowledge that he was going to be subject to some ridicule. Unfortunately for him, his testimony would show that as an officer of the law he missed what might have been the biggest bust of his career. For, you see, Chief Blair had Martin McNally not only in his grasp but also in his car within hours after the hijacker had tumbled from the sky trailing cash and his weapon.

Blair testified that he was driving to breakfast with his wife in the area where search teams were looking for the hijacker. He saw McNally walking along the side of the road and offered him a lift. He noted that McNally, who gave a false name (his brother's) did have some bruises that Chief Blair inquired about. McNally told Blair that he was in the area visiting his brother, that the two had been drinking the night before and had gotten into a fight. That sort of thing happens from time to time in Peru, so the chief had no problem buying the story. He asked the young man where he was going. McNally gave him the name of a local hotel where the chief dropped him off.

On the stand, Blair was asked why he did not suspect that this stranger walking alone along the highway at 8:00 a.m. might have been the hijacker. Why was he not more suspicious when a massive manhunt involving several of his own officers was taking place nearby within hours of a suspect having bailed out of a plane in that area? Why was he not more curious about his passenger's bruises? Chief Blair could only say that while McNally was somewhat suspicious, "He did not fit the description of the man we were looking for." It must have been difficult for Chief Richard Blair, in retrospect, to have to admit that.

It certainly didn't hurt the case against McNally, which was never in dispute. A federal judge sentenced him to life in prison for his crime.

Postscript

$\mathcal{A}$ few new facts on the skyjacking incident came out after the capture of McNally. He was nothing if not gallant. He was so appreciative of the treatment afforded him by his two captive flight attendants that he tipped each of them with fifteen hundred dollars of his loot during the getaway flight. They turned it in upon landing.

It was clear the hijacker planned to bail out of the plane. No one knew when or where, perhaps not even McNally himself. During the time he was on the ground at the airport, he had demanded and received hasty instructions on the procedure from a member of the Air National Guard unit at Lambert. McNally had apparently chosen the 727 because of its rear door. He had had no experience in using a parachute but apparently knew that a rear-door exit was the safest means of bailing without risking a side-door jump and the possibility of being smashed against the side of a large, fast-moving jet.

The pilot of the aircraft had his own plan for dealing with McNally. Even with a rear-door exit, the aeronautical dynamics only favored a successful parachute jump up to a point. The pilot knew if he achieved a speed in excess of three hundred miles an hour, the likelihood of a parachutist's survival was small. Call it beginner's luck that McNally survived. His loot, his weapon, and even big chunks of his trousers did not. But he did.

Six years later, in 1978, while confined to the federal prison in Marion, Illinois, McNally was one of the prisoners implicated in a daring escape attempt. A helicopter was hired by a young woman in St. Louis ostensibly to do some aerial research for a real estate project. The woman was described as nervous and demanding. Once airborne, she pulled a gun on the pilot.

Once the gun was drawn, the woman announced her intention to fly to the medium-security institution, make a daring Rambo-like landing in the courtyard, where her boyfriend and McNally would be waiting. They were to leap aboard the chopper immediately upon landing to be whisked away before guards could react. It was a daring and implausible plot. It was all the more implausible because the plotters had not taken the measure of the pilot, Allen Barklage, who was well known to all local St. Louis television reporters.

Barklage was a Vietnam chopper veteran regarded as something of a daredevil. He had been shot down in Vietnam, had performed numerous high-risk river rescues in St. Louis, and he often acted as the eyes of police in dangerous chase situations. He flew for local radio and television stations doing traffic reports, and he transported news crews in and around the St. Louis area.

As Barklage told the story of his own hijacking, he was determined to stop the plot for many reasons, not the least of which was his own safety. He had no doubt that prison guards would fire on the helicopter before, during, and after it landed. Air space around the prison, not unsurprisingly, was a no fly zone. Even if they did land, Barklage knew they'd never take off.

The armed woman had insisted on flying in the rear seat of the helicopter rather than next to the pilot. That put her in a position that would make it difficult for Barklage to subdue her and gain control of the gun while still maintaining control of the chopper. He convinced her to open the door so the escapees would not have to waste time getting into the aircraft. She agreed. He turned to help her and made a grab for her gun. As the helicopter, with no one at the controls, began an erratic, dangerous descent, the two struggled for the weapon. With the helicopter twisting and turning as it plunged toward the ground, the pilot managed to wrest the weapon from her. As he did so, she reached to the floor for a second weapon, announcing, "I have another."

With no hesitation, Barklage fired over his shoulder. Unaware that he had struck the woman and killed her, he regained control of the helicopter just in time to make a safe landing on prison property where he radioed for help, still fearful that guards would pepper his aircraft with a lethal barrage of bullets. In all the confusion, prison personnel got the message and Barklage was spared a shoot first, ask questions later situation.

Ironically, this woman's daughter was arrested some two years later attempting to hire a fixed-wing plane for use in a similar plot. If the chances of a successful helicopter attempt were implausible, the probability of successfully landing a fixed-wing in a prison court-yard was impossible.

Sadly, Allen Barklage, cited for heroism for several daring rescues in the years after this incident, was killed in 1998 while piloting an experimental aircraft. In his career, he amassed thirty-two thousand hours of helicopter flight time. He was fifty years old.

David Hanley

$\mathcal{D}$avid Hanley was charged in a federal indictment with willfully damaging a commercial aircraft. He faced twenty years in prison and a ten thousand–dollar fine. For several years, scheduled court dates for Hanley were continued as a result of his very serious injuries. Few expected that he would ever go to trial. News reports indicated that he was likely to escape prosecution because of the serious nature of the injuries he had suffered.

The following item appeared in *Time* magazine a few months after the incident:

Expensive Samaritanism

Last June, apparently on a wild impulse, David J. Hanley, thirty, dashed out of a cocktail lounge near St. Louis' Lambert Airport. He got into his 1972 Cadillac convertible and crashed it into an American Airlines 727 jet airliner in a foolhardy attempt to stop a skyjacking then in progress. The skyjacker and his hostage crew merely switched to another plane and took off with $502,500 in ransom (he parachuted safely, but was later arrested). Even so, Hanley was seen by some as a courageous citizen acting boldly to stop a crime.

It now turns out that Hanley would have been much better off had he sat tight and let the proper officials worry about the skyjacking. As a result of his derring-do, he was charged by the Federal Government with interfering with an aircraft. He sustained severe injuries and is accumulating medical bills for which he has not yet been fully compensated by his medical insurance.

Moreover, his auto-insurance company is refusing to pay for any of the damages to his demolished car, the plane or the airport fences he drove through.

Hanley might well yearn for the simplicity of biblical days, when the Good Samaritan, reaching humanely to help a stricken traveler, had no need to fret about warrants, lawsuits, the high cost of medical care or the expensive frailties of Cadillacs and jet airliners.[8]

At some point, stories about David Hanley stopped appearing in the press. I never found any record indicating that he had been prosecuted or that charges had been dropped. Even the U.S. Attorney's Office in St. Louis said it had no records on this part of the case. People in the know just stopped talking about him. In a sense, David Hanley did a much better job of disappearing than Martin Joseph McNally had done.

Tom Eagleton

*F*ew Missouri politicians in recent history have been as respected as the late former Senator Thomas Eagleton. He was the Missouri Democratic Party's knight in shining armor for fifty years, holding local and state office before moving on to the U.S. Senate, where he served with distinction for two decades. The ten years his terms coincided with those of Republican Senator John Danforth were considered a model of bipartisan cooperation and collegiality that many feel has been sadly lacking since the Gingrich-led Republican Revolution in 1994.

Eagleton retired in 1987. He tired of the process of having to spend so much energy raising the money needed to fund re-election campaigns. He continued in private life as a respected attorney, educator, civic leader, columnist, and commentator. Once unleashed from the shackles of public office, he was a no-holds-barred critic of government and government officials he thought had gone astray, and he took full advantage of the bully pulpit offered by his senior statesman status. He was especially caustic in his criticism of President George W. Bush and the war in Iraq. There were times, as we have learned more recently, that he was not quite so publicly outspoken.

His most impressive résumé includes an eighteen-day period during which those Americans not familiar with Missouri politics came to know Tom Eagleton. Those were the eighteen days in 1972 during which he was Democratic presidential candidate George McGovern's running mate. Eagleton was the key player in what some pundits have called the "greatest campaign fiasco in modern times."

It was a surprise to many when McGovern selected Eagleton as his running mate. The Missouri senator was clearly elated that he had been chosen. It was a relatively rushed selection, and not all of the due diligence that might have been performed into Eagleton's background was, in fact, done. The story is outlined in detail in State University of New York Professor Bruce Miroff's excellent book on the McGovern campaign, *The McGovern Insurgency and the Identity Crisis of the Democratic Party,* portions of which I paraphrase below.

Word began to surface after the selection (of Eagleton) that there were some mental health issues and other skeletons in his closet. Rumors of mental health problems surfaced, accompanied by suggestions that Eagleton had issues with alcohol. Inch by inch over the following days, rumors, bolstered by an anonymous phone call, told of the Missouri senator's hospitalization several times for mental health problems, and that treatment had included controversial electroshock therapy. McGovern's closest aides questioned Eagleton about the reports. While he admitted to hospital stays, he was stingy with details. At first he did not admit to the controversial treatment, saying rest and some medication had helped him through what he called "a period of melancholia." He finally did admit to having undergone shock therapy but discounted its relevance.

McGovern's people, aware that the news was a potential disaster for the campaign, insisted on seeing the senator's medical records. Eagleton delayed and obfuscated, convincing McGovern for days that his health problems were behind him. Though requested to do so, he never made his hospital records available to the McGovern team. Despite an increasingly frantic concern among McGovern staffers that Eagleton had to go, McGovern stood by him "one thousand percent."

In retrospect, there is every reason to believe that McGovern had not only been intentionally misled by Eagleton, but also that he had been deceived outright. Eagleton never told McGovern the full truth. Adding fuel to the fire was a memo McGovern's staffers had in their possession indicating Eagleton suffered from manic depressive psychosis and suicidal tendencies. As Miroff tells it, psychiatrists were warning the McGovern people saying, "You can't have Eagleton in control of the bomb."

In the midst of all of this, columnist Jack Anderson wrote in his syndicated column that Eagleton had been arrested several times for drunk driving, an allegation for which Anderson had no proof and for which he later had to make a public apology. Ironically, this allegation, which came as the McGovern-Eagleton ticket was losing public support, actually worked in Eagleton's favor. While on the one hand the public was concerned about the possibility that a man with a history of mental problems might be one heartbeat away from the presidency if McGovern were elected, there was a wave of public sympathy for Eagleton after the Anderson story and apology. That made it more difficult for McGovern to dump him from the ticket as it was eventually abundantly clear he must do. Advantage Eagleton. Sensing the public support, Eagleton began to argue that he was an asset rather than a liability to the ticket. He pledged publicly to "irrevocably" remain on it. McGovern was in a box.

Nonetheless, McGovern, after consulting with doctors who had treated Eagleton for his mental health issues and receiving negative feedback from them, finally decided that the senator had to go. Eagleton, still appearing in the public eye as a victim, gave in. Or did he? The two appeared at a joint news conference with McGovern making the following statement:

I have consistently supported Senator Eagleton. He is a talented, able United States Senator whose ability will make him a prominent figure in American politics for many, many years. I am fully satisfied that his health is excellent. I base that conclusion upon my conversations with his doctors and my close personal and political association with him. In the joint decision that we have reached tonight, health was not a factor. But the public debate over Senator Eagleton's past medical history continues to divert attention from the great national issues that need to be discussed.[9]

This is how author Bruce Miroff analyzed it after extensive interviews with McGovern:

This statement nailed down the impression that Eagleton was capable of continuing on the ticket and had only been removed to serve McGovern's political interests. Its genesis was the fourth hidden dimension in the Eagleton affair. The words that McGovern read to the press were, he (McGovern) says, not his own; they had been drafted by Eagleton and his staff to ensure his (Eagleton's) political survival. It was Eagleton who was behind the claim that health was not a factor in McGovern's decision. McGovern argues that since he had no authority to fire Eagleton, who was the nominee selected by the Democratic convention, he had no option but to accept Eagleton's terms, even with their high cost to his own reputation. As McGovern puts it; "If I had said, 'Well Tom . . . I've got to explain to the country that you have an illness that is one that competent psychiatrists feel should keep you from occupying the highest office in the land,' he would not have stepped down." On the contrary, McGovern recalls, Eagleton threatened that if there was one word spoken by McGovern or his staff about the issue of mental health,

"I'll stay on this ticket and fight you all the way to November."

To the public, unaware of the hidden dimensions of the affair, Eagleton came out of it the victim and McGovern was viewed as the transgressor. The media was remarkably gentle with the senator from Missouri. . . ."[10]

We in the Missouri media were especially gentle. He came home as something of a wounded hero who'd been sacrificed on the altar of political expediency. I had the opportunity to do an extended televised interview with Senator Eagleton after he left the ticket. He was a guest on one of the first of more than twelve hundred public affairs programs I did at KTVI during my career there. I must confess we played softball, which must have been easy for him, coming as it did a few days after the hardball game he'd just finished with McGovern. I, along with most others who had followed the unfolding events during those eighteen days, had no idea of the behind-the-scenes maneuvering that had been going on. I approached the interview as if he had been a victim. While critics thought the interview was fair and tough enough, I wish I had been armed with the information provided in Miroff's excellent book. I like to believe the interview would have been conducted quite differently. As it was, he simply told his version of the episode, which only served to reinforce his role as victim.

An article in *Time* magazine in August of 1972 examined the so called "Eagleton Affair." One explanation of the Missouri senator's motives came from the then Democratic governor of Missouri.

Missouri Governor Warren Hearnes, no close friend of Eagleton's, had an explanation: "It is hard for people not in politics to understand Eagleton's position. Eagleton's lifelong ambition to be vice president overshadowed any rational consideration."[11]

Eagleton's selection never would have happened had the campaign known that the Missouri senator told columnist Robert Novak in the spring of 1972 that "The people don't know McGovern is for (Vietnam era) amnesty, abortion and the legalization of pot . . . Once middle America—Catholic middle America in particular . . . finds this out, he's dead." (This was before the senator was tapped as McGovern's running mate.)

Novak reported the anonymous quote in early 1972. Eagleton refused to allow him to reveal the source. It took thirty-five years and

Eagleton's death before Novak disclosed who had made the comment.

While some might look with criticism upon his handling of the vice presidential "fiasco" and Eagleton's refusal to admit to the Novak quote, his senate career was nothing short of distinguished. He was active, courageous, and influential on such issues as defense, the Vietnam War, civil liberties, limitations on presidential authority, environmental protection, and many more of the most important issues of his day. Few legislators of recent vintage are held in higher regard by Democrats and Republican colleagues than Tom Eagleton. It is widely held, and with dismay, that not many of his ilk are to be found serving in Congress today.

The senator and I maintained a cordial relationship in the years that followed. I traveled with him during his subsequent senate campaigns and was always impressed by his energy, wit, and intelligence. As his margins of victory reveal, his constituents loved him. The memorial service following his death was a tribute to his reputation and was attended by a veritable Who's Who of national and local political and civic leaders. McGovern was not among them.

Eagleton loved to write and remained active with the pen until the very end. At the conclusion of his memorial service, a two-page, single-space farewell letter he'd written shortly before his death was distributed to those in attendance. He took a final bitter shot at the George W. Bush administration for the war in Iraq but ended it with final words of advice:

"Go forth in love and peace—be kind to dogs—and vote Democratic!"[2]

I treasure a warm and flattering letter he wrote me upon my leaving KTVI in the mid-1990s.

Dear Don:
You are one of the finest, ablest journalists I have ever dealt with in my 30 years of public life. You know what questions to ask and how to ask them. You are determined to get the story, but you are never out to be a wanton character assassin.
I wish you every success in your future.
You have been a credit to your profession and your community.
Warm regards.
Thomas F. Eagleton
September 2, 1994

Ghost Story

*B*elieve in ghosts? I'm not going to say I do, but I'm not saying I don't either.

It was an irresistible invitation, the chance to film a paranormal hunting expedition. In this case, the quarry was a ghost. It came from a local psychic who was not easy to discount as a flake. Her name was Bevy Jaegers, a local woman who had had some success with her paranormal investigations and experiments and would ultimately receive a nice reward for her psychic talents.

I would not attempt to make anyone a believer in this strange world about which so many of us are at once both curious and skeptical. Jaegers had come to my attention as a result of what believers might call a "psychic home run" or what skeptics might call "luck or coincidence."

There had been a celebrated missing-person case that had captured the attention of the Midwest in the early 1970s. An attractive suburban housewife had gone missing, and authorities feared the worst. However, they were stymied in their search for the woman. Enter Bevy Jaegers and a fledgling group that came to be known as the PSI Squad. The squad billed itself as a band of psychic detectives and set out to put the talents of its members to the test in an attempt to locate the woman, Sally Lucas. Here is how the organization later described its efforts in the Lucas case. I have edited the excerpt to include the salient points.

The history of the PSI Squad began in 1971. Formed of senior PSI students in a class being taught by instructor Beverly C. "Bevy" Jaegers, this class had decided to try their developing skills on a real puzzle. Picking out the five-week-old case of a missing local socialite, Sally Lucas, initial work by Bevy and senior student Jim Mueller was done which eventually led to locating the exact spot at which the woman's murdered body had been deposited by her killer, and then inevitably to the formation of the Squad itself.

A nightgown and powder puff belonging to the missing Sally Lucas had been given to a member of the group, and proved to be the significant factor in solving the case . . .

. . . Mrs. Jaegers had been verified first when the victim's auto was found in Florida, and later, when she (Mrs. Jaegers) sat in the vehicle itself on Sat. Sept. 5, 1971, and vividly described the murder and disposal of the body in a place she identified, in writing, as having C and CC, as well as horses' heads, a small airport, a thick row of pillar mail boxes, an abandoned ancient and ruined-looking building that had been a church, a small bridge, and a creek bed.

Mrs. Jaegers, along with Mueller, had searched a particular area before going to the police garage to sit in the car and returned to that area afterwards. Weeds and undergrowth in this wild area were head high, impenetrable. They told Feustel (a newspaper editor) and Sgt. Kiriakos (of the highway patrol) where they had been all morning, describing it thoroughly.

At dusk the group disbanded, Mrs. Jaegers returning home to work a map of the area with a pendulum. This form of using remote viewing is commonly known as map 'dowsing'. The pendulum indicated the exact same place they had spent the afternoon. It was decided to return the next day and resume their search. On Sunday, Sept. 6, a torrential rainstorm prevented the return. Later that afternoon a couple walking their dog discovered the body in a creek bed, 15 yards from the small bridge. Spirit of St. Louis Airport was over a ridge less than a mile away. Ten yards from the bridge stood a thick cluster of pillar mailboxes, and the road itself was designated as Wild Horse Creek, County designation as Rt. C. An intersection a block or two away was the crossing of Rt. C and Rt. CC. Five hundred yards from the bridge was a ruined building which turned out to have been an Assembly of God church in earlier days. In addition to these facts, one of Jaegers' written comments involved the word "poker" and a crushing blow to the right side of Mrs. Lucas' head. When the body was examined, it was found that the right side of her head had been crushed by a brutal blow. Bordering the body site was a horse ranch known as "Poker Flats."[13]

There are other impressive reports of Jaegers' psychic prowess. She was, on a number of occasions, quietly brought in for consultations by law enforcement seeking her input in especially frustrating cases. Her involvement was usually kept confidential because police, fearing ridicule, were not eager to publicize the fact they would, or ever felt they had need to, turn to psychics in difficult cases. However, it goes on a lot all over the country.

I was personally involved in one of Bevy Jaegers' cases. A young black elementary school student was reported missing and became the subject of much police and press attention. There was no evidence of foul play; however, the youngster had seemingly vanished from the planet. Bevy took it upon herself to assist in the search for the child. I am not certain whether she had received any request from the police to help. Given the fact they did call upon her from time to time, that may have been the case. She was discrete about any such requests and helped keep them well below the radar. However, Bevy was not without her public relations instincts. She was always eager to lend credibility to her psychic work.

She called me to announce the effort to find the youngster, wondering if I was interested in it as a story. Being aware that she was not what police and some other circles regarded as a "nut case," I was interested in watching her do her thing.

Using the pendulum or "map dowsing" technique described previously, we filmed her going through the process. Dowsing involved making a pendulum by putting a weight on the end of a string. The resulting device was held over a local map. Bevy focused on the missing youngster. Eventually, the pendulum would move back and forth slightly. Once the direction of that movement was established, she drew a line on the map as dictated by the pendulum movement. Then she turned the map 90 degrees and repeated the process. She maintained that the spot where the lines intersected indicated the child's location. With the destination established, we hustled over. No child.

A day or two later, the child's body was found. He had apparently been climbing on a garage, fell from the roof, and died in the fall. No foul play was suggested. Here's the rub. The garage was no more than two blocks from the spot where Bevy's pendulum lines had intersected. The map we had used would account for a slight variation in the location, but not two blocks.

Here's Bevy's explanation for that. After the child's body was found, police investigated to determine if a crime had been committed. Had the child been abducted and died trying to escape his abductors? That was the question. It turns out the explanation was relatively simple. At the same time it addressed a rather sad commentary on the complexities of life in a poor community that few of those more fortunate can easily grasp.

While not an everyday occurrence, it was, and is, not necessarily uncommon for African American youngsters to be temporarily "adopted" by black families under certain sets of circumstances. A youngster might come home with a friend after school and wind up staying with the friend's family for a few days. The family, perhaps suspecting the child had problems at home, will allow the youngster to stay with no questions asked. In some cases, those problems might include that the youngster had come from a large family and was either not missed; that no one at home really cared where he was; or that the parent or parents were themselves absent from the home for a period of time. While it reflects a sad aspect of family life in some communities, white and black, there is something quite admirable about the willingness of families to care temporarily for young strangers.

Bevy would insist until the day she died twenty years later that her location for the child was accurate . . . at the time she worked her pendulum. She believes that at the moment she was putting the lines on the map, that IS where the child was at that time. As it happens, the lines intersected very close to the home where the youngster had been staying. No ten-year-old child is stationary very long. This one might very well have gone out to play and met his fate as part of a game or during a solitary climbing adventure.

So, a call from Bevy to "cover" her group's ghost hunt was intriguing and something I had no difficulty agreeing to. I did not expect that we would ever actually see a ghost or film one, but I thought a story on the process would be interesting.

A local couple had contacted Bevy complaining about a "presence" in their middle-class suburban home. It was manifested by unexplained footsteps on the second floor, the family dog's annoying barking at the bottom of the stairs, and its refusal to venture upstairs. Water was turned on and off in the kitchen sink when no one was in the room. Lights went on and off on their own. The door to the basement, which was perpetually stuck and required a two-handed yank to open, would open and slam shut on its own when no one was in the vicinity.

The activity was more than bothersome to the home owners. Their nerves were on edge. Apprehension and nervousness inside the house had reached a critical level. The two were unable to sleep and were increasingly uneasy. An uncharacteristic level of tension surfaced between the two as they found themselves discussing both divorce and the notion of abandoning their home. They were quite frantic and frazzled when they contacted Bevy to see if she could help.

She made an independent visit to the home and determined that there was, in fact, an unwanted and unwelcome "presence" there that should be removed. Bevy was convinced that while it was annoying there was nothing evil at work. She described a ghost, including this one, as an energy field (her explanation for ghosts) that was "lost or confused" or was unwilling to cross to "the other side." I've heard one psychic since explain such unwillingness this way: "If a mother of two were suddenly struck by a car, she would not want to leave. She would want to stay for the sake of the children." Bevy offered to bring in her team and attempt to remove the presence from the home. The home owners readily agreed.

The visit came in mid-September. The house was to be empty for the team's work with the air conditioner turned off. The explanation for the former was to avoid interference or distraction. Deactivating the air conditioner was necessary because ghosts, according to Bevy, are usually identified as incongruous cold single bubbles of air. The air conditioner could lead the ghost hunters astray and disguise the target.

Mid-September can be as hot as mid-summer in St. Louis. When we arrived and entered the house, it was more than 90 degrees outside, and stifling hot inside. The team consisted of half a dozen of Bevy's group, all of whom professed some psychic ability and were being trained in Bevy's techniques. They ranged from a young college student to an elderly widow. In all, it was an eclectic group. Its members did not appear out of the ordinary in any way and certainly did not present themselves as a band of loonies. My cameraman and I were uncertain as to what to expect. We could only wait for something to happen. We watched and filmed them doing their thing. Their "thing" was to wander through the house in groups of two. No incantations. No funny equipment. By the way, this pre-dated the film *Ghostbusters* by some ten years. Team members looked like prospective home buyers rather than as a band of psychics seeking contact with another dimension. All movement was slow. The house was oppressively hot, but we were assured again, necessarily so.

About twenty minutes into the inspection, we heard someone call from upstairs. "We've found something," they said. The rest of the group moved to them from their locations in other parts of the house until all of us were gathered in an upstairs bedroom. The team formed a loose circle in the center of the room. Bevy motioned me over and invited me to join her in the center of the circle. She asked me to thrust my hand to an area just beyond her shoulder. I did as directed. It was like sticking my arm out the window on a wintry day.

I don't mean it was cool or even chilly. It was the bubble of icy air of the type Bevy had described surrounded by the warmer air found throughout the rest of the house. The hair on my arm stood straight up as I plunged my arm into the bubble. As I slowly moved my arm I felt that the cold area was about the size of a beach ball and floated five or six feet above the floor. As I withdrew my arm, the cold vanished as if it had never been there. When I put my arm back into the "bubble" the icy chill was immediate.

Bevy advised that the icy spot was, in fact, "the presence," which again she described as an electric energy field that is as much a part of all of us as our skin and bones and blood. This field, she explained, can be released when we die. It can become "confused" and even "lost" when death is sudden such as when it occurs as a result of violence, accidental or otherwise. She had earlier advised me not to think of ghosts as something like the cartoon "Casper." They are not something, she would say, that are dressed in white sheets and go "boo."

She was quite serious in saying that a "presence" can have a diverse personality ranging from mischievous to malevolent, from friendly to frustrated. Seems our home owners had one that might be characterized as both mischievous and frustrated.

The task of the team was to guide the frosty sphere from up-stairs to downstairs and ultimately out of the house and to do it very carefully. They treated it as if it were a big and delicate soap bubble. They kept it surrounded and moved it gently with their hands as if they were afraid it might "pop." They guided it down the stairs and into the center of the living room. Once it was stabilized, Bevy spoke to it as if it were a living being, telling it simply that it did not belong in this place and that it was time to go. After delivering that friendly but firm admonition, she opened the front door, allowing the team to guide the "bubble" from inside the house to outside and on to the great beyond.

A few days later, I revisited the home to interview the couple. They had returned after getting the all clear from Bevy. The air conditioner was humming, and the house was cool. The dog was sleeping at the foot of the stairs. I was told that the puppy now happily visited the upstairs bedrooms from which there was no longer the eerie sound of unexplained footsteps. The couple said there was a different atmosphere in the house altogether. There had been no repetition of the water being turned off and on at the sink. The husband went to the basement door and showed me how difficult it was to open it.

I returned a week or two later to be told that nothing had changed and that the house had been completely normal since Bevy's visit. The relief they felt was obvious and evident. And whereas they had seemed tired and edgy during our first meeting, they were now happy, well rested, and relaxed.

So, you tell me. Is there any such thing as ghosts?

I recognize that skeptics say if professed psychics have such powers, why don't they win the lottery every week? Bevy Jaegers might say psychics can't direct their abilities in order to accomplish specific objectives. It can't be turned on and off like that. Rather, she would say, the ability is like a guide that takes its instrument, the psychic, where the guide wants to go. So, Bevy never won the lottery. But she did hit the jackpot years later.

She was contacted by a friend in the investment business who was considering putting a great deal of money into one of three investment possibilities. He was uncertain which way to go and asked Bevy for her input. She was reluctant, feeling it was too much like hocus-pocus. Nonetheless, at her direction he put a description of each opportunity into separate sealed envelopes and gave them to her. Bevy admitted having no financial expertise beyond balancing her check book. She was uncertain that she could be of much help.

Several days later she was contacted by her friend. She told him she had not opened the envelopes but had a very positive feeling about one of them. She could not explain her feeling beyond that and did not know what was inside the still-sealed envelope. But she said she was convinced that whatever was contained therein gave her good vibes. She received no impressions from the other two.

She heard nothing more from her friend for several months. When she did, he brought with him a special surprise. He had invested heavily in coffee futures in Brazil based on her response to the envelope containing that investment opportunity. Extreme weather conditions in Brazil had affected the crop dramatically, increasing the value of his investment many, many times over. So lucrative was the investment, he promised that as a reward he would build her a luxury home costing well into six figures. And he did!

Ozark Flight 809

$\mathcal{I}$t was a dark and stormy night—nothing unusual in St. Louis in the summertime. Dark clouds dash in from the west during the late afternoon and early evening propelled by strong winds partnered with lightning and thunder. Such summer storms are commonplace. They often do annoying damage, bringing down trees, tree limbs, power lines, and ripping shingles from rooftops. In July 1973, they brought down an airplane, an Ozark Airlines Fairchild FH 227-B with forty-four aboard, forty-one passengers and a crew of three. It was inbound from Nashville, Tennessee. Ozark was St. Louis's own homegrown airline.

Driving rain and heavy winds made the outdoors extremely in-hospitable this July 23 evening. It was the kind of day one could get soaked through just getting to and from the car. It was a night for excuses to stay inside. It was a night not to be out. Especially not to be outside covering a story.

The crackle of the police radio eliminated all excuses. An Ozark Airlines plane was down. Off we went.

The rain had not abated by the time we arrived at the scene. The plane had gone down two miles short of the Lambert runway, crashing in a wooded area between a row of residential backyards and the campus of the fledgling University of Missouri–St. Louis. It was just past 5:30 p.m. when the plane crashed. We arrived less than an hour later. It was prematurely dark because of the driving rain and heavy black cloud cover. The scene was made all the more eerie by the flashing red and blue lights of emergency vehicles. The lights reflected off of leaves, grass, soaked clothing, the raindrops themselves and the steaming wreckage of the plane.

Taking in the visual was difficult enough, but the horror of the scene was compounded by the still-audible, piercing screams of victims onboard the aircraft. Thirty-eight of the forty-four people aboard died, most of them apparently while trapped inside the wreckage with rescue crews trying to get to them. Fire and impact had left little of the plane intact making it even more difficult for the emergency responders. The wreckage among wiry brush and crushed trees was not easily accessible, which slowed rescue teams accordingly. We could not see much of the wreckage, but we could hear the screaming victims. It's a sound that remains with me to this day.

Settled as it had in the wooded area, television crews had difficulty getting pictures. We were pointedly advised not to get anywhere near the wreckage. Emergency crews did not want to have to work around clumsy reporters and cumbersome photographic equipment. There was also danger. Small fires were still burning amid the debris. The sudden detonation of pools of fuel remained a concern. We could get no closer than one hundred feet or so. It was dark, it was raining, and we were not welcome beyond a well-established point. We moved to establish what angles we could and to gather what limited information was available. However, our ability to successfully accomplish much of either was severly limited.

After about two hours on the scene, totally soaked by the still-driving rain and mindful of the looming deadline of our television newscast, I returned with what video and what facts we had. I was the sole reporter on staff that night and was also anchoring the ten-o-clock news. In the KTVI operation of those days, the anchor had principal production responsibility for the evening newscast. Simply put, it meant that I formatted, wrote, and presented the half-hour newscast. Our minimal staff that night consisted of my cameraman, an assignment editor, and a newsroom assistant.

When I returned around 8:00 p.m., I was astounded to find that neither of the two who had remained in the newsroom had done anything in the way of production assistance for the newscast. I was faced with processing our video (this was the day of film, not videotape.) Processing the sixteen millimeter film was time consuming and required the cameraman to make it happen. I was also faced with editing the processed film, meeting a network request for the latest information and video, and writing the story for our newscast. The local story required separate treatment because it included more local detail. In addition, the remainder of the newscast had to be structured and written.

I will not vouch for the quality of what finally made the air, but I can report that the newscast went on on time, and got off on time. Aside from the material on the tragedy, I can recollect none of the other stories in the newscast. Nor can I vouch for the overall quality of the presentation. I suspect it was well short of average. Perhaps even well short of below average.

Happiness Is a Warm Puppy

$\mathcal{A}$h, but what a difference a day makes. The sun shone brightly on the pile of rubble that was all that remained of the ill-fated Ozark airliner. The charred remains of the plane sat in the mud amid the trees in twisted testimony to the events of fourteen hours earlier. It was hard to comprehend the violence, death, and misery that had taken place just a few hours earlier in this now-silent spot. Now, songbirds and an early morning breeze supplanted the anguished screams of the dying and injured and the frantic shouts of emergency responders trying to save lives.

July's routine summer blast of heat was still an hour or two away, which helped draw reporters shortly after first light. Reporters from all media were there hoping to find a scrap of information to add to the story. This was the first real opportunity to get a close look at the plane, or what was left of it. Litter was everywhere and included pieces of the plane itself, bits of clothing and luggage, many shoes, soggy newspapers, and bits of stuff that defied identification. Standing there near the debris, it was difficult to believe that anyone could have been pulled alive from the mayhem of the night before. Only a few were.

Again, we were kept at arm's length as investigators poked around in the wreckage. It gave us something other than the static remains of the plane to photograph. Local fire officials, airline officials, federal investigators, and local police were scattered around the area, many conversing in small groups. A few desultory interviews did not bring much in the way of new information to us on the scene.

Overnight wire service reports filled in some of the blanks from the night before. Only six of the forty-four onboard survived. Two crew members were among those who lived. All survivors were badly injured. The cause of the tragedy was long from being determined. All that was available to us was speculation that the aircraft had been battered by the storm and that the pilot was unable to keep it aloft in the high winds. Lightning was considered a possible factor in the crash. At that moment, everyone was long on theory but short on facts. Although the investigation had started within hours of the crash, it would be months before any definitive conclusions were reached.

At about the time most of the news crews were packing up and preparing to leave the mess to the investigators we learned there was another survivor. Someone near the battered tail section of the plane was shouting something that, although unintelligible, drew the attention of all of us. There was excitement in the voice. Everyone turned toward the sound. At first, nothing. Then we watched as a firefighter emerged from behind the plane carrying a small dog.

Incredibly, the pup's eyes were bright, and its tail was wagging happily. The fireman held it for all to see. It was covered in dirty smudges of ash, but nothing could stop that tail. Clearly it was a brown and white puppy with some apparent beagle DNA, and perhaps some from a few other breeds too. It had been in the plane's cargo hold when the aircraft went down. The probing firefighter had been drawn to the area by the whimpering sound of the tiny animal. He pulled it from its restraints in the plane's underside. The puppy showed its gratitude with a few generous swipes of its tongue along the firefighter's face, its tail remained in full gear. It didn't stop for an instant as the photographers went to work with a new enthusiasm. They knew they had a story that would pluck heartstrings the way Les Paul strummed a Gibson.

Needless to say, the big story of the evening was "Another Survivor." The story detailing what had happened the night before began with a full description of the dog's discovery. The pictures brought tears. And while the survival of the dog was less important than the survival of six people, and certainly less important than the deaths of thirty-eight souls, it was a perfect follow-up to the tragedy of the night before. To this day, more people remember the recovery of that little dog than can tell you how many people died in that crash. Life trumps tragedy.

Animal stories do that. Some years later we had a story on a midwinter newscast about some abandoned horses found in an isolated field. They were nearly frozen and knee-deep in snow. In the same newscast, we carried a story about the death of a homeless man found in a cardboard box on a frozen downtown street. Viewers responded. Some 150 people called expressing concern about the animals. Many offered to adopt them. There were no calls expressing concern over circumstances of the man's death or the plight of the homeless.

Aftermath

*N*ine months later, the National Transportation Safety Board completed its investigation into the crash. The violence of the storm, including a powerful wind shear, pilot error, and misinformation from the tower were all cited by the NTSB, as indicated in the report synopsis below, which also cites lightning as having played a role in the crash.

NTSB SYNOPSIS

FH-227B (N4215) crashed 2.3 miles southeast of the Lambert-St. Louis International Airport, in St. Louis, Missouri about 1743 daylight saving time on July 23, 1973.

Of the 44 passengers onboard the aircraft, 38 were killed. The aircraft was destroyed by impact and fire.

While Flight 809 was making an ILS approach to runway 30L at Lambert-St. Louis a severe thunderstorm with heavy rain, strong winds, and roll clouds moved across the approach end of the runway and the localizer course from the southwest. After passing the outer marker, the aircraft descended below the glide slope, entered an area of heavy rain, was struck by lightning, and crashed.

There was no in-flight damage to, or malfunction of, the aircraft's structure power plants, or systems. There was no evidence that lightning had caused a malfunction of an essential system or structural damage.

The National Transportation Safety Board determines that the probable cause of the accident was the aircraft's encounter with a downdraft following the captain's decision to initiate and continue an instrument approach into a thunderstorm. The captain's decision probably was influenced by the lack of a timely issuance of a severe weather warning by the National Weather Service, and the improper assessment of the weather conditions in the terminal area by the flight crew and the flight dispatcher.[14]

There is no mention of the puppy in the NTSB forty-three-page report.

Golden Handcuffs

*I*t is in the nature of covering local news, especially for a local television station, that a reporter may be called upon to cover a wide variety of stories on any given day. Most reporters go to work having little idea of what the day will bring. You can cover a five-alarm fire in the morning then wish you had changed clothes before interviewing the governor or a movie star the same afternoon. Most of the colleagues I have worked with over the years have exhibited the ability to make these adjustments on a daily basis. The ongoing joke is that local television news reporters have an acre of knowledge about many things, but it is only an inch deep. I would agree with that, although I would like to think that some of us may have an inch or two more on at least some subjects.

There is another aspect of television news reporting that is not unlike many other professions. It's called "the desire to keep the job." In large part it's because people in television, at any level, generally make more money than those with comparable talents doing similar work in other media. A local television reporter, for instance, will likely make more money than a comparably educated and experienced reporter for a daily newspaper. Therefore, if there is an inclination to protest some of the assignments one is asked to do or object to the tack taken by a news department in its approach to news, there is an equal inclination not to get emotional and do something rash, like quit in protest. It's what's called the "golden handcuffs." You remain bound to the job because the pay is so good. You hope that continues and that those who make the offensive policy don't.

My handcuffs were securely in place in the mid-1970s when the film *Jaws* took the country by storm and almost took me with it. Our news director at that point was a gentleman who shall remain nameless. His name, however, is inscribed on an Emmy he won for his work as a writer on the old Smothers Brothers Comedy show in 1968. He shares the honor with nearly a dozen other writers, including comic Steve Martin. Martin became a star in his own right while many of the others went on to be associated with some of the most acclaimed television comedies in history. The award represents having reached the top of the entertainment mountain and should rightly be regarded as a major accomplishment. Our new colleague's slice of the award was largely the result of his contributions to the "Pat Paulson for President Campaign," which the *New York Times* called the "most successful put-on in recent years" comparing it to the satire of Will Rogers. Very funny stuff.

Our new boss liked to tell stories about his college days when he roomed with none other than Dan Rather. THE Dan Rather. Perhaps therein lies the otherwise elusive journalism connection. He did have some time at a Los Angeles radio station after CBS dumped the Smothers Brothers. He cited as his principal accomplishment there a system he devised for rigging rooftop television antennas in Los Angeles, enabling viewers to watch the locally blacked-out Super Bowl I.

One brief paragraph of the press release announcing his arrival in St. Louis alluded to a newspaper background with unspecified publications, one of which won a prestigious award. The remaining nine paragraphs focused on comedy writing and non-journalistic credentials.

It puzzled most of the staff when the announcement came. It soon became clear that the hire was based on his show business background rather than his journalistic credentials and signaled that our general manager was desperate to put our operation on the ratings map. I believe the new news director's arrival in St. Louis coincided with the first steps in a changing local and national approach to covering news on television. It was a harbinger of what was to come. Let's call it *"Infotainment!"* Everybody else does.

The seeds of "infotainment," which were being planted all over the country in the mid to late 1970s, were in full flower by the late 1980s and 1990s, and remain so today. Fifteen years later, another KTVI news director explained his approach to news coverage this way, "I'm not in the news business, I'm in the entertainment business." He also told me at one point, "I'm not a newsman, I'm a businessman." By then, no one would dispute the fact that the bottom line ruled. But the trend began in the mid-1970s.

In all fairness, it must be pointed out that the planting of those seeds was not isolated to KTVI in St. Louis during the mid-1970s. One of our local competitors was the CBS-owned station, KMOX-TV. It brought in an entire staff in what was a successful attempt to change the local television ratings landscape. The staffers were young, attractive, and hip. A lot of emphasis was put on pop culture, consumer news, and "coping" stories. I recall one investigative report in which a reporter counted the number of sheets in a role of name-brand toilet paper and "revealed" that the number fell short of the advertised and promised "500 sheets." Hold the presses.

KMOX was also moving toward the cutting edge of technology during this time and assisting in what would change news coverage for decades to come. It was the first CBS station in the country to use mini-cam video cameras for news coverage. It meant videotape would replace film, eliminating the cumbersome need to process film. The camera equipment was much smaller and more portable. It was a successful proving ground that led to the adoption of similar technology all over the country. The combination of youthful reporters and young technology yielded impressive audience growth at KMOX.

It paid off for the anchorman Patrick Emory. He was an attractive stud who admitted to colleagues that his ultimate goal was to become a network game-show host. He was so successful in St. Louis, that he was quickly promoted to the CBS-owned station in Los Angeles in an attempt to work similar ratings magic there. That was a big jump, and the stakes were big. The ratings success he had in St. Louis was not duplicated in L.A. He was ultimately fired with most of the news staff when a focus group responded poorly to the news on-air personnel and product. The focus group members were hooked to gadgets designed to measure their sweat. I've never been clear as to whether sweating too much or too little is favorable or unfavorable. Whatever it is, that's what they did, and it resulted in unemployment checks for a large number of news staffers. However, Emory was not out of work long. His looks and earlier ratings success ensured a long career, including a long stint with CNN, although I don't believe he ever achieved the measure of success he had in St. Louis.

When Emory transferred, and the process of finding a replacement was under way, the general manager of the station attempted to lure Ted Knight (Ted Baxter of *Mary Tyler Moore* fame) to anchor the news on an interim basis. It would have been a gig of about six weeks. Given the curiosity factor and the growing acceptance of entertainment as news, there's no question in my mind it would certainly have guaranteed a bigger audience share. It did not fit Baxter's *Mary Tyler Moore* shooting schedule, so he declined after apparently considering it seriously. The GM then called upon an old friend to fill the role, thereby inflicting Regis Philbin on the market. Regis, at that point in his struggling career . . . after being Joey Bishop's sidekick and before all the modern success . . . was happy to sign on and do the news for a limited period of time. For several months after that, he hosted a weekend variety show on the station. Then, as they say, he ultimately went on to bigger and better things.

Neil Sedaka

*B*ack at KTVI, the man from L.A. arrived in a dusty Mercedes carrying the Emmy, which he placed in a prominent place in his office. It was a daily reminder that he had the ability to make people laugh. The staff rarely got the joke. Instead of laughing *with*, we found ourselves being laughed *at*.

Internally, we snickered behind his back at what seemed to be something of an obsession with the Neil Sedaka hit song, "Laughter in the Rain." It surfaced every time it rained. He would invariably dispatch a cameraman to "cruise" looking for this:

Strolling along country roads with my baby
It starts to rain, it begins to pour
Without an umbrella we're soaked to the skin
I feel a shiver run up my spine

I feel the warmth of her hand in mine

Oh, I hear laughter in the rain
Walking hand in hand with the one I love
Oh, how I love the rainy days
And the happy way I feel inside

After a while we run under a tree
I turn to her and she kisses me
There with the beat of the rain on the leaves
Softly she breathes and I close my eyes
Sharing our love under stormy skies

Oh, I hear laughter in the rain
Walking hand in hand with the one I love
Oh, how I love the rainy days
And the happy way I feel inside . . .[15]

What he wanted the photographer to find was something relating to the lyrics of the hit song. Why? So he could run the video on a newscast and play the song along with it. It never worked out. Seems in St. Louis there aren't too many lovers who walk "hand in hand in the rain," or "run under a tree" for that matter. I'm not sure he ever grasped that St. Louisans were smart enough to come in out of the rain whether they were in love or not.

Miss Nude America

hen there was the time I was assigned to interview the recently crowned "Miss Nude America." She was a young woman who was very nice but who might have also laid claim to the title of "Miss Trailer Trash." She had been crowned in some sort of publicity stunt at a truck stop in Indiana. I don't recall why she was in town, but someone associated with her advised television stations that she was "available" for an interview. I got the assignment, which I received with enthusiasm, and was dispatched to a fairly high-end hotel.

My cameraman and I arrived at the appointed room at the appointed time and knocked on the door, not quite certain what to expect. We got what we should have expected, a nude woman. She wore nothing but that proverbial smile and, perhaps, a necklace. Of course we were taken aback, trying to appear as if it were the most normal thing in the world to be greeted by an attractive naked woman. I mean, what kind of small talk do you make? "Nice tits. Great job on the cellulite. What is that perfume?" We were more uneasy than she was, but we soon got over it as we got down to business, the interview.

She sat with her legs crossed and arms folded and answered all the questions I could muster. I don't remember any of the questions but do recall ending it by saying, "It was nice *seeing* you." Ha Ha. We then took our time getting cover video of her doing things like answering the phone, making a cup of coffee and so on. It was important to us that she walk, bend over, stretch, etc. We would not have shot as much cover video of Mother Teresa in Calcutta. Our queen never took off the smile . . . or put on any clothes.

The video was quite the hit back in the newsroom. I never expected it would make the air, but I underestimated our determined news leader. It went on the air all right, all two minutes of it on our early newscast. (Yes, by now the station had added an early evening newscast. And the news director also hired his brother to anchor it and the major newscast at ten o-clock.) Two minutes is a lot of time in television news, but those were the instructions. Those golden handcuffs chafed somewhat but not enough to cause me to protest or otherwise object to getting the piece ready for air.

The response from the audience was pretty much what you might expect. A few calls of "well done" and "let's see it again at ten." We also received several hundred calls of complaint. It was a clear indication that overall the story had met with a serious disapproval quotient. Mail over the next few days would confirm it, including one letter of protest signed by all of the nuns in a local convent. Taking a page out of P. T. Barnum's philosophy of, "I don't care what you say about me as long as you mention my name," the boss-man directed that I prepare a longer report for the late newscast. He was thinking ratings. Given the initial response, I was thinking, great, the ten-o-clock program had twice the audience of the earlier newscast. That meant there would be twice as many people to offend. Damn, those handcuffs could get tight.

The station was not the only beneficiary of audience animosity. The reporter also took his share of grief from a formerly supportive audience. Under different newsroom leadership, if that piece had aired with my name attached to it, those golden handcuffs would have been cut from my wrist and thrown at me as the door was closing behind me. We all survived the blitz of criticism on Miss Nude America. Little did I know, however, that I was going for the audience disapproval hat trick.

Mississippi Mud Monster

*I*n a period in which any notion of journalistic integrity was given a holiday, the personal nadir came with the success of *Jaws*. If you remember the movie's first scene and the attractive swimmer's demise, you can imagine what she might have been thinking. I *know* what she was thinking. I went down with the *Mississippi Mud Monster*. It has to be called a self-inflicted wound. That golden streak down my back was a pretty good match with the golden handcuffs. I just didn't take a stand.

Jaws was a monster success at the box office. Anyone with an entertainment background would try to capitalize on it. Our entertainment—I mean news—director was no exception. He decided to make up a news story just as easily as he had made up jokes for Tommy and Dick Smothers. I was to be the straight man. No pie in the face . . . just mud on my reputation.

The news director, who by now we all suspected had a pharmacological second mate, had hired a freelancer to help produce some of the local interest "stories" he favored in the newscast. The freelancer was something of a regional historian who came up with local color ideas, did the necessary research, wrote the appropriate script, then traveled with a cameraman and producer to the appropriate location to put the piece together. It was up to the producer to convert it from the written word to a television piece that would be fronted by a reporter or anchor.

For instance, Abraham Lincoln and Stephen A. Douglas held one of their famous debates in Alton, Illinois, which was in our viewing area. Putting together something was fairly simple. All that was required was some research on the actual debate, a trip to the location, and video showing anything related to the event. The components were put together and made into an interesting feature. That's the kind of thing he did. So far, so good. Some of the material was actually pretty interesting.

This time he was asked by the news director, whose creative juices were obviously flowing, to concoct a legend designed to capitalize on the *Jaws* success. He accepted the assignment with relish. His legend centered on the *Mississippi River Mud Monster*. Get it? It was a huge fish that lived in the deepest part of the river. It would rise from the depths from time to time and snatch a boater from a kayak or canoe, or a crewman from one of the scores of barges that plied the Mississippi every day. The monster fish had never been seen by anyone, although stories about it had been passed down for more than a century. The story was kept under wraps to prevent public panic. Yadda-yadda-yadda.

To produce this "story," all we had to do was find a fearsome-looking fish, shoot video of it in such a way that its real size was distorted while making it appear uglier, more dangerous, and above all, larger, than it really was.

We found the creature in a local fish market. It was about a ten pounder that we had to transform into something resembling a great white! A generous use of extreme close-ups, tight shots of the jaw line and the eyes, as well as some other tricks of the trade, and Spielberg's "Bruce," looked like Nemo in comparison. All that was left was for me to take his script and turn it into television.

I had enormous reservations about it. I insisted on some sort of disclaimer and was assured there would be one. The piece aired with appropriate *Jaws* music played in the background. Of course, there was no disclaimer at the end of the piece. And it scared the hell out of a whole bunch of people. It proved to be too believable. People bought it. Parents called for more information because they fished with their kids on the river. Boaters called in panic. People who parked their cars along the levee wondered if they were at risk. "When was the 'monster' last seen and where?" On and on it went suggesting a low-grade panic. It is one thing to simply offend as we had done with "Miss Nude America." Mongering fear is different and more serious. This time it was not aired a second time. The damage had been done. We had gone too far. Even news management knew it. The station and our news department were severely criticized. We had people talking about us all right, but that was not being translated into ratings. We were a local joke. The comedy writer had scored another success.

I can blame the news director. I can blame the freelancer. I can blame the station management. I can find any number of people to fault for the fiasco. However, it is I who must assume a lion's share of the blame. I never should have done it. I should have quit. I should have protested. I should have gone to the station manager. I should have done any number of things to prevent that lousy piece from seeing the light of day. It was not news. It was just a piece of concocted tripe put on the air to entertain. It didn't even qualify for that. Any criticism that came my way for being a part of it is justified. Perhaps I could not have stopped it, but I could have taken a stand. I probably would have been fired, and I knew that. That is precisely why I flopped like that damn fish probably did when someone hauled it into the boat. It makes me blush even today to recall that day and that story and my lack of backbone. Local television news was changing, and I was changing with it. Those golden handcuffs not only bound me to my job. They made me mute.

Just a quick postscript. At one point during this period, Tommy Smothers showed up at the station for an appearance on the noon news program that I anchored. Smothers was appearing in a local production of some sort. He arrived just before air time so there was no time to chat off the air. When the interview was over and we went to commercial break, I mentioned that one of his old writers was our news director and would he like to stop in the newsroom and say hello? He asked who it was. When I told him he just nodded, said, "No thanks," and left without passing Go. Hmmm.

Death, Live at 10:00

A s a rule, television is fairly careful about showing the dead and the dying. As a rule.

One of the medium's finest moments may have involved the decision to stop the repetitive airing of planes slamming into the World Trade Center on 9/11 and more particularly, to refrain early on from showing trapped victims in upper levels of the Twin Towers as they plummeted to their deaths one hundred floors below rather than face the heat and flames stalking them.

Natural disasters and wars are something of an exception, although for the most part, news organizations do a fairly good job of policing themselves on the issue of overindulging in gore. A pool of blood here and there, a smashed up car, or a bloody toy can tell the story quite clearly. It is a challenge for local news organizations that seem to thrive on crime news, fires, and accidents. Although it can be tempting at times, there is something of an unwritten rule to keep from stepping over the line when it comes to showing bodies or body parts.

The KTVI news management philosophy of the mid-1970s seemed to be that anything shocking enough to get people talking was a plus and would ultimately translate into higher ratings. In this station's case, however, the theory was proved flawed time and time again. As you may have surmised by now, stepping over the line was the *modus operandi*. There are those who might question whether there even was a line.

The incident in question involved a young black man who was either mentally unbalanced, under the influence, or both. This young man in his late teens or early twenties, armed with a pistol, attempted a holdup at a convenience store early one summer evening. A silent alarm was sounded during the process and police were outside the establishment before the holdup man had left the building. His options were limited. He grabbed a young female clerk, put his pistol to her head, and stood at the door demanding that police officers allow him an unimpeded departure with the hostage in return for her safety. That was not going to happen. Thus began a negotiation that was to last several hours.

Alerted by police radio traffic, television news teams and print reporters were on the scene quickly to watch the proceedings and wait out the outcome, which, if this were a typical situation, would likely drag on for a good long time. Police were never in a rush to bring such situations to a conclusion, preferring them to play out at a pace that would not cause anxiety levels to escalate suddenly, forcing the subject to act even more irrationally or rashly. The objective was a successful conclusion regardless of how long it took.

Nonetheless, sharpshooters were in place, and there was a cordon of police officers around the building. The gunman, by accident or design, never presented himself as a real target to sharpshooters who were not likely to fire in any case unless the situation escalated, especially with the frightened hostage being used as a shield. Dropping the gunman with a high-powered rifle might have ended one situation, but it could have created another that was worse. This was a rough neighborhood and a lot of people were drawn to the scene. Scores of neighborhood residents crowded around the front of the building. Many of those outside the store seemed as concerned over the well being of the robber as they were for the hostage, creating a tension all of its own.

Aside from periodic episodes of agitation, the gunman maintained an otherwise casual posture holding the gun loosely in his hand or waving it erratically as he spoke with officers. Initially, the hostage was understandably terrified. Tears streamed down her face, although, as the situation evolved, she appeared to be less anxious. She said nothing. He put his face close to her head from time to time to say something to her. Perhaps he was reassuring her that he meant no harm. She never seemed to react to the words and maintained a fixed expression as the evening wore on.

When the negotiation continued into a second hour, the TV stations decided to make it a "made for television" event. This was relatively early in the days of live, remote coverage for local news departments. This standoff was tailor made for just such coverage. There was plenty of time to set up as the negotiations droned on. If anything, aside from the potential for dramatics, it was monotonous.

Television cameras had to be set well back from the front of the shop. However, there is no question that the young man with the gun was aware of them. The local stations broke into regular programming with irritating frequency to show live updates of the proceedings. What viewers saw in each case was a static shot showing a good portion of the predominantly black crowd and several police officers near the front of the store. The officers were predominantly white, which helped the onlookers appear to take sides. Some of the cops were negotiators talking with the gunman. The young man was alternately animated and impassive. At times he put his weapon to his own head threatening to kill himself if his demands were not accepted. This gave the situation a new dimension and represented a more urgent challenge for the negotiators while, ironically, making it all the more necessary that they not rush the process.

Viewers at home were most likely upset at the number of interruptions. I was one of them, and I found it extremely irritating even though I fully understood what the stations were doing with all of them on the scene, playing with their new technology, and training their cameras on the man and his hostage. For more than three hours, the scenario played itself out with little change in the status quo from the moment the police arrived until well into prime-time programming.

Murphy's law proved itself alive and well during the course of the evening. Despite the number of interruptions during regular programming, the incident also continued "off camera" in the sense that it climaxed at a time when there was no live coverage. Crews were still recording the incident on videotape. It should be pointed out that interruptions in live coverage were usually timed to return to programming in time to carry the commercials.

During one of these breaks and after several hours of discussions between the gunman and the police, the young man once again turned the gun toward his own head. This time, however, he was not bluffing. As video cameras were recording, he suddenly and calmly pulled the trigger. Just as quickly as it had begun, the incident was over. Stations broke in one final time to report the outcome and promise viewers "full details at ten." My station was going to do that one better.

I was at home when the news came on. The first thing I saw was video of the holdup man moving the gun from the ear of his hostage, pointing it to the side of his head, pulling the trigger, and dropping out of the picture. It was the first of three times this gruesome scene was shown during the newscast. Showing it violated all of the unwritten rules, yet it was shown again and again and again. It is extraordinarily uncommon to have video of an actual death. Common practice in a situation involving violence, its aftermath, or any scene that might be considered too gory to air, was to cover the objectionable material with cutaways. The cutaway was a video editing technique in which editors covered the objectionable video at the critical moment, showing instead a shot of onlookers or a street sign. While viewers might still hear the shot, as in this case, the audience would not see it being fired. That's the way other stations handled it.

I stood from my chair in disbelief as I watched the first showing on my station. I was convinced it had been a mistake and that some editor had forgotten to cut away from the actual shooting. It was unbelievable to watch and horrifying even to someone who had had more than a little exposure to the urban violence that comprised so much of our news. Even with all the graphic violence available on television and the movies, watching the real thing was offensive. I called the station after the second showing and one of the staffers told me it was no mistake, that in fact it was a news management decision to "go with it," so the audience could appreciate what violence was like on the "mean streets." In other words, it was a disingenuous act wrapped in altruism on news management's part.

I was among those staffers protesting the decision the following morning. Our voices joined the very negative audience reaction. The plan was to show the video again during later newscasts. I was assigned to go to the gunman's neighborhood and do a background piece on the shooter. Who was he? What kind of family did he come from? What might have driven him to his final actions? Having watched the incident and knowing the neighborhood in which it had taken place I, and everyone else in the news department, already knew the answers to the questions.

I knew the proposed story was merely an excuse to justify showing the video again. I objected, not to the assignment, but to the notion that the objectionable scene would be used again. I made it clear that I would have no part of using that unedited video in any piece that I prepared for later newscasts. My objections were not received well by news management. Partly, I suppose, because of my concerns, and largely because the internal and external reaction was so pronounced, the decision was finally made to show the video in any subsequent newscast only with appropriate cutaways.

I was particularly uncomfortable going to the young man's neighborhood. There had been a highly negative reaction to the incident in the black community. Residents were blaming the police for having allowed the situation to deteriorate to the point it had. When we arrived, my cameraman and I were the only white faces for blocks. We were viewed with conspicuous hostility. Groups of young men, photocopies of the gunman, stood sullenly on street corners or sat on the hoods of rusted cars watching us with undisguised contempt. As Shakespeare might say, "there was malice in the air."

Half the houses in the area were vacant. One or two had been burned out. Debris littered the sidewalks and what passed for front lawns. Long orange extension cords draped from windows of some houses to windows of others as electricity was shared among those who had it with neighbors who did not.

Stores on the corners were plastered with signs selling cigarettes, beer, and hair treatments. It was grim and yet typical of the poorest sections of the ghetto where hapless, desperate people had little money, no jobs, and no pride of ownership. It was a place where people lived from day to day, often at the mercy of absent landlords and anonymous utility companies who had no patience for late payment.

I had to go door to door looking for people who might have known the gunman. Door after door was shut in my face as I made my inquiries. All except one. A woman who could have been forty or sixty years of age, wiped her hands uneasily on a plain blue apron as she listened to my request for information. Though nervous, she presented a sense of nobility and somehow seemed out of place in this setting and circumstance.

Surprisingly, she invited us in. We were guided into a small living room furnished with a sofa and some worn upholstered chairs. Most of them were occupied. It was tidy but sparsely furnished except for a large television against one wall. A dozen smiling black faces watched us from photos on the walls: young people, old people, people in uniform, and people of past generations in flowered hats. I could see that some of the people in the room were among those in the photographs. There were eight or ten of them crowded into the space. Some were seated in the few available seats while the others stood. There was nothing one could call friendly about this gathering, at least as far as its response to us was concerned.

I asked if anyone in the room knew anything about the young man who had killed himself. A few heads nodded affirmatively in mute response. I had found what I wanted and needed and asked if they would mind talking to me "on camera" to tell us something about the gunman. Glances were exchanged, but initially, nothing was said in response. Finally, the woman who had answered the door spoke up. Central casting might have given the role to Della Reese.

She was a pleasant-looking slightly plump lady whose hair was grey and framed a face that exuded authority. She was more than in charge of this group. She was in command of it. Her voice was soft but precise as if she knew that when she spoke, one would listen. "You from Channel 2?" she asked. When I said "yes," subtle glances were exchanged among those in the room, the meaning of which escaped me at that moment.

What she had to say to me explained everything. "No, there would be no interviews." While I cannot remember the exact words, the message was quite dramatic. Yes, they knew the young man. In fact, everyone in the room was related to him. Aunts, uncles, and cousins were there. He was a good boy, a high school dropout who could not find work. His girlfriend was pregnant, but he wanted to "do the right thing." He was desperate. He took matters into his own hands. That is undoubtedly what drove him to that store. It was a variation on a neighborhood theme.

She, as it turns out, was the young man's aunt. Her brother was his father. She then explained in measured sentences what could only be interpreted as a heartbreaking part of the story. I learned that the family had no idea what had been playing out at the convenience store during the previous evening. There was some sort of family get-together, and most of those in the room had gathered in the kitchen, the boy's father among them. One of the guests was watching the news on our station at ten o'clock and watched that first video in stunned disbelief. Whoever it was called to the kitchen and the others came into the living room, where the boy's father, unaware of the drama that had been unfolding all evening, watched his son kill himself. That was the last image of his boy, placing that gun to his head, pulling the trigger, and dropping out of the scene like a bag of sand.

She stopped as she related the story as if waiting for me to fully digest the moment. Then she said, "Why did you have to show it? Why?" The same question was in the eyes of the others in the room. They remained silent. I was stunned. We had stumbled into the very heart of a family's grief. And we were a large part of the cause of it. It was bad enough that the young man had done what he had done. Our station's blithe disregard for these people on the other end of the telecast had brought them even more pain. And we had inflicted it. That pain was clearly expressed in that single word, "Why?" So much emotion in a syllable.

I had no answer. All I could do was apologize and say it never should have happened. "I'm sorry," I said.

There was no reaction other than cold, hard stares that showed no hint of forgiveness. There was nothing left for us to do but leave, and we did so as quickly as we could.

It was a lesson that everyone in the news business should take to heart. Every word that is written, every picture that is shown, has someone reacting to it on the other end. It may be a favorable reaction, or it may be one of hurt and pain or even painful recollection. Every time a murder scene is shown, friends and relatives of both the victim and the killer re-live the crime and the anguish. Television stations are notorious for doing this. When a suspect is captured, when a trial begins, when a trial ends, the scene of the original crime is shown again and again, awakening the grief and pain of those directly involved. It may be a body on a gurney, the wreckage of an auto, or a burned-out house. In any scenario when there is pain and loss, a retelling of the story in word or pictures revives the anguish. I will never forget those people in that room and what we had done to them. We did not improve ratings by showing that video. In fact, I am quite certain our station lost viewers in that tortured household forever. And who could blame them?

Fired

My complaints about the incident just described and others led to a strange move on the part of the news director. I was taking a few days vacation at home when my doorbell rang. My visitor was a co-worker from the mail room. He had a letter for me from the news director that basically said I was fired. It was a rambling letter that contained numerous misspellings and words that had been scratched out or written over. It reinforced my belief in the possibility that there was a pharmacological aspect to the man's behavior. No specific reason for my termination was given. It basically said that I should not return to work.

To make a long story short, I took a page from John Kennedy's book when Nikita Khrushchev sent a highly provocative, bellicose, and threatening letter to him in the midst of the Cuban Missile Crisis. Kennedy merely ignored the letter and continued the behind-the-scenes diplomacy that finally resolved the highly volatile dispute that had put the world on the brink of nuclear conflict. Though nothing like World War III was at stake, I ignored my letter, returned to work when my vacation was over, and the matter was never mentioned again. Either he had forgotten what he had done or, for reasons that I cannot decipher, chose not to pursue the issue.

Some months later, the news director was fired for deceiving the general manager on a personal issue, and I was named interim news director. It was a sweet moment when he had to turn over the keys to his office and to the company-supplied car to me. It marked the beginning of a new era for me, the news department, and the station.

New Era

*O*ut with the old, in with the new. And it was welcome news to those of us who had hung on through the previous era. The new news director was someone with actual credentials. His name was Rabun Matthews. He had a long history with the CBS network and highly respected stations on both ends of the country. His message upon arrival was simple: "I don't want to see the morning newspaper on our evening newscasts. I want to see our evening newscasts in the next morning's newspaper." The message was loud and clear. We were going to do news, not create or copy it.

The first days of our personal relationship were somewhat cool. Because I had been "interim" news director in the weeks prior to his arrival, he assumed my ambitions lay in that direction and that I might have been put off by his having gotten the job. It was another example of the assumption that everyone would rather be a chief than an Indian. In actuality, I had had my fill of news directing in Baltimore and was as eager as anyone for a full-time news director to be named. I had never seen my position as anything but keeping the seat warm for the next guy or gal (though in this time frame, precious few "gals" were likely candidates.) When that was made clear, the relationship became as strong as the previous one had been tenuous.

Matthews hit the ground running. Making key personnel changes and establishing beats for reporters, he eliminated those on the staff who had been disciples of his predecessor. He added experienced journalists, producers, and photographers, many of whom he had come to know in previous markets. The changing atmosphere was further reinforced when, coincidentally, Newhouse sold the station to the Times Mirror Corporation not long after Matthews' arrival. It was beginning to feel like the big leagues.

Matthews changed my role and put me on a full-time political beat, which was exciting in the 1980 election year. I was assigned a full-time producer to cover local and national politics, and we were given free reign to do our thing, as long as we generated material of our own and didn't report "yesterday's political news."

The Political Beat

$\mathcal{I}$t was a great run that led me to cover ten national political conventions in a row, as well as some interesting, complicated, and sometimes Byzantine local politics. That first year took the team to Detroit for the Republican Convention and the launching of the Ronald Reagan era. Then it was on to New York for the Democratic Party conclave. It was here that I had a chance to reflect on my first meeting with Ted Kennedy back in Bonn. He was engaged in a very tough and animated battle for the nomination with incumbent Jimmy Carter. It was to fall short, of course, as did the ultimate Carter/Mondale race against Reagan and George H.W. Bush.

Kennedy fought for the nomination right up to the end at the convention. Although he won a few battles, he ultimately lost the war. Nonetheless, he stole the show in New York. Too little too late. His strategy was an attempt to pull the nomination rabbit out of a hat at the convention itself. It was the last convention of either party in which a prominent candidate tried to lure delegates away from the candidate to whom they had been committed. When it was over and he knew it, he exited with grace, dignity, and as most old-school professional politicians do, with a bow to the party itself.

Well, things worked out a little different from the way I thought, but let me tell you, I still love New York.

My fellow Democrats and my fellow Americans, I have come here tonight not to argue as a candidate but to affirm a cause.

I'm asking you—I am asking you to renew the commitment of the Democratic Party to economic justice.

I am asking you to renew our commitment to a fair and lasting prosperity that can put America back to work.

This is the cause that brought me into the campaign and that sustained me for nine months across one hundred thousand miles in forty different states. We had our losses, but the pain of our defeats is far, far less than the pain of the people that I have met.

We have learned that it is important to take issues seriously but never to take ourselves too seriously.

The serious issue before us tonight is the cause for which the Democratic Party has stood in its finest hours, the cause that keeps our Party young and makes it, in the second century of its age, the largest political party in this republic and the longest lasting political party on this planet. . . .[16]

And so it continued with loud approval from the delegates. This was as far from the Edward Kennedy I had met so briefly in Bonn sixteen years earlier as Homer Simpson is from Ned Flanders. He went on to extol the virtue of the party and its practitioners and to make the obligatory but flawed prediction of party victory in November. He brought it to a close with words and phrases that made MacArthur's "old soldiers never die" speech sound like something from a high school yearbook.

And someday, long after this convention, long after the signs come down and the crowds stop cheering, and the bands stop playing, may it be said of our campaign that we kept the faith.

May it be said of our Party in 1980 that we found our faith again.

And may it be said of us, both in dark passages and in bright days, in the words of Tennyson that my brothers quoted and loved, and that have special meaning for me now:

"I am a part of all that I have met
To [Tho] much is taken, much abides
That which we are, we are—
One equal temper of heroic hearts
Strong in will
To strive, to seek, to find, and not to yield."

For me, a few hours ago, this campaign came to an end.

For all those whose cares have been our concern, the work goes on, the cause endures, the hope still lives, and the dream shall never die.

Thank you, and let's proceed with the Convention.[17]

Aside from the nomination itself, the best that Mr. Carter could manage at the same convention was to misidentify Hubert Horatio Humphrey as "Hubert Horatio Hornblower." Oh, well, it got a laugh.

The Republican Convention a month earlier in Detroit had its own intra-party drama. Ronald Reagan was considering the notion of asking Gerald Ford to be his running mate, but Ford was reportedly holding out for expanding the vice presidency into something the pundits were calling a "co-presidency." Ronald Reagan might not have objected to a co-star in Hollywood. He was not inclined the same way with Washington in his sights. So, he selected George H.W. Bush. Unknown at the time, their election was also the first step in putting this Bush and his son, George W., into the history books as the first father-son presidents since the Adamses almost two centuries earlier.

The GOP convention may also have helped the religious right further establish its roots as a political factor in the country. It would achieve its apogee in the political process in the younger Bush's election in 2000. Evangelical Christians flocked to his candidacy. Could Reagan's final words at the convention have helped inspire them to dig in, fight the long fight, and make their presence indelible two decades later? You decide.

I have thought of something that is not part of my speech and I'm worried over whether I should do it.

Can we doubt that only a Divine Providence placed this land, this island of freedom, here as a refuge for all those people in the world who yearn to breathe freely: Jews and Christians enduring persecution behind the Iron Curtain, the boat people of Southeast Asia, of Cuba and Haiti, the victims of drought and famine in Africa, the freedom fighters of Afghanistan and our own countrymen held in savage captivity.

I'll confess that I've been a little afraid to suggest what I'm going to suggest—I'm more afraid not to—that we begin our crusade joined together in a moment of silent prayer. God bless America.[18]

That button was pushed. The major theme for Ronald Reagan was *"Make America Great Again."* It was a theme that was to resonate as Americans had watched the economy waffle. They'd also watched dozens of their countrymen languish in captivity in Iran and waited for someone to resolve the crises. The nation did not have to wait long for the 444-day Iran hostage crisis to end. It was resolved at the moment of Reagan's inauguration the following January when Iran released the American hostages.

There was a third national convention in 1980. It was held in Cleveland. Our political team attended because there was a St. Louis connection. Washington University biologist and eco-socialist Dr. Barry Commoner was the presidential candidate of the Citizens Party. It was a well-intentioned gathering of liberals whose green platform was loaded with wide-ranging environmental programs and socialist initiatives. The party championed something called economic democracy. This is how it is described in Wikipedia:

Economic Democracy is a philosophy that suggests a transfer of socio-economic decision-making from a small minority of corporate shareholders to the much larger majority of public stakeholders. As monopoly structures progressively restrict labor from access to the universe of natural opportunities, the ability of modern society to purchase its own output production tends to diminish. Assuming that full political rights cannot be won without full economic rights, workers manage production democratically to distribute the surplus generated by labor more equitably, thus restoring legal and political control to the majority. With some variance of approach, all models of Economic Democracy tend to support democratic regionalization as the most viable alternative to the central-planning tendencies of state and corporate imperialism. Suggested catalysts include monetary reform, democratic cooperatives, and regionalization of currency and food production.[19]

Whew! Little wonder the party was extinct eight years later.

Nearly three hundred delegates from thirty states attended the convention, which looked more like a hippie reunion than a political gathering. But these delegates weren't smoking "mellow yellow" and chillin'. They came to Cleveland armed with scores of proposed platform planks that quickly transformed the gathering from a commune-like-happening into a loud, argumentative, and unwieldy free-for-all. The result was a hodgepodge of a platform that was undecipherable even to some of those in attendance, not to mention a majority of the American public.

The convention was held in a downtown hotel, the Cleveland Plaza, which was destined to become a municipal jail when the convention ended. It was as in need of repair as the party's prospects of victory and was as threadbare as the delegates themselves. Producer Randy Wolfe painted a word-picture of the attendees with the phrase, "The Citizens Party Convention was attended by the ragtag remnants of the radical sixties. . . ."

1984 Campaign

*T*he 1984 conventions were as different as a field goal is from a fumble. The Reagan-Bush train rolled into Dallas as a well-choreographed production. The Democrats hoped their San Francisco convention would derail the GOP. On the one hand, the choice of Geraldine Ferraro as Walter Mondale's running mate seemed a good start. She was the first female of either party ever put on the national ticket. But Mondale needed more than this historic first to catapult him past Reagan and Bush. He stumbled badly at the gate. Words he uttered during his acceptance speech signaled his doom.

Whoever is inaugurated in January, the American people will have to pay Mr. Reagan's bills. The budget will be squeezed. Taxes will go up. And anyone who says they won't is not telling the truth to the American people.

I mean business. By the end of my first term, I will reduce the Reagan budget deficit by two-thirds.

Let's tell the truth. It must be done, it must be done. Mr. Reagan will raise taxes, and so will I. He won't tell you. I just did.[20]

Telegraphing a punch can do less harm than "telegraphing" a tax increase in an election year. It didn't work. Veterans like Missouri Congressman Dick Gephardt knew it before the ink had dried on news reports of Mondale's speech. Gephardt was good at rallying the troops and he was convincing as he told a gathering of the Missouri delegation with enthusiasm and apparent confidence that Mondale was "going to win." He seemed excited about the prospect of Democrats taking the initiative for the rest of the campaign with the objective of sending Ronald Reagan back to Hollywood and George Bush to Houston or Kennebunkport.

After the gathering, Gephardt was overheard telling confidants that the campaign was over, that Mondale had lost it with the speech. Ever the good party man, however, Gephardt worked hard for the ticket for the remainder of the campaign, knowing in his

heart there was no chance for victory. Four years later, he learned
that about his own presidential ambitions, but in his case, it was
long before convention time.

The thing that I found most striking about the Mondale campaign during my coverage of it was his dry sense of humor. He was
a somewhat understated, but funny guy, and typically he had audiences, particularly the smaller groups, enjoying belly laughs and in
a good mood wherever he appeared. The larger the group the less
likely he was to try humor. Mondale might have thought that over-
doing the use of the light touch was too risky, especially given the
fact that he was running against the "great communicator." When it
came to delivering a line, Reagan was hard to beat. Mondale's quips
rarely made the evening news. Reagan's did invariably.

Frankly, while my recollection of Mondale was that of an ami-
able, good-natured candidate who could be funny when he wanted
to be, I can't remember specific examples, with the exception of his
"where's the beef?"

It was Reagan who came up with the memorable lines, often at
Mondale's expense. In fact, the former actor often turned Mondale's
wit against him. Reagan was not afraid to crack a joke, usually self-
deprecating, and that clearly delighted voters. During the early stages
of the campaign, when Mondale seemed to be holding his own, the
fifty-six-year-old Democrat attempted to make an issue of Reagan's
age. During their second debate, the seventy-three-year-old former
actor found an effective counterpunch. As he put it, "I will not make
age an issue of this campaign. I am not going to exploit, for political purposes, my opponent's youth and inexperience." The audience
laughed from coast to coast. Mondale himself was among them.

Mondale, however, did not fully learn a lesson from it. There
was another time when he accused Reagan of "government by amnesia." Reagan pulled another rabbit out of the bag when he coun-
tered, "I thought that remark accusing me of amnesia was uncalled
for. I just wish I could remember who said it."

Reagan's one liners that year were great. At one time he said that
he had asked his aides to waken him if a crisis erupted anywhere in
the world . . . "even if I'm in a cabinet meeting." Another time he
talked about burning the "mid-day oil" at a busy White House.

One cannot necessarily say that the real Walter Mondale was

not revealed to the nation in 1984. Nor, can one conclude that had the man who was effective in small groups surfaced on the national level he might have done better against Reagan. The bottom line is that it was the "real" Mondale that the nation got to know, just as it was the "real" Reagan. Regardless, for the former Minnesota senator, the election outcome was no laughing matter. He won only the District of Columbia and his native Minnesota on election day.

The fact that Mondale would lose was a foregone conclusion to most analysts across the country almost from the moment of his "raising taxes" comment in San Francisco. Nonetheless, Mondale waged a tireless campaign. On those occasions when I was with him, the crowds were always good-sized and enthusiastic. Even the most cynical reporters, who were among the most certain that Mondale could not win, agreed that the candidate himself did not share that pessimism. In city after city, gathering after gathering, he exuded confidence and optimism.

I never had the impression at any stage in the campaign that his optimism was an act. I was convinced that he really believed he could win! Candidates can act. Jimmy Carter stopped in St. Louis hours before the 1980 election. The incumbent gave no indication he was anything but confident that he would win even though his campaign advisers, reading the latest polling data, had quietly told him three days before the election that it was lost and beyond any last-minute repair. Carter lost in a landslide, 489 electoral votes to 49.

During the Mondale campaign, I had a sit-down interview with Phyllis Schlafly, the conservative anti-feminist activist. She was very much at home supporting Ronald Reagan against Walter Mondale for many reasons, not the least of which was Mondale's historic support for the Equal Rights Amendment. The St. Louis–based Schlafly led the national campaign against it.

I was chatting with her about my impression that Mondale actually seemed to think he could win the election, even when the polls and all the analysts were nearly unanimous that he neither could nor would win. Ms. Schlafly had a very cogent explanation that was as simple as it was obvious.

Candidates, she said, are typically fairly isolated from the negative. They read the papers and watch the news as best they can as they scurry from one campaign stop to another across the country and rely on campaign staff to keep them informed.

She pointed out that candidates are rarely exposed to people who don't support them. It is supporters who advise them, travel with them, and who, of course, attend their political rallies. Those who oppose them are attending rallies for *their* candidate. Couple this with the fact that campaign stops are often selected to ensure good turnouts and with the fact that those closest to candidates are paid to be cheerleaders, the negative inclinations are therefore few and far between. It is a form of isolation within a crowd. Therefore, they face only the most positive response to their message. Because of that, Schlafly said, they see a partisan-charged landscape that distorts reality and convinces trailing candidates that the media and the polls have it wrong. I think Phyllis Schlafly had it right and that the same holds true now, although to a lesser degree because of the twenty-four-hour news cycle and *You Tube*.

Dick Gephardt

$\mathcal{D}$ick Gephardt was a good soldier during the Mondale campaign, even though he knew it was a lost cause. He may have been building some IOUs for 1988; however, the Missouri congressman, then as later, was always extremely generous in helping fellow Democrats in their campaigns and in helping raise money for those campaigns. In his years as house majority leader, and later minority leader, he was tireless in those efforts which paid off in reciprocal support as he was trying to build consensus on legislation close to him and the party. While he was extremely effective at raising money, he would learn that even a lot of money is not necessarily enough when it comes to going for the big prize, the White House.

If 1600 Pennsylvania Avenue was ever an objective of his, it was not obvious when our paths first crossed in the mid-1970s. He was then a young attorney and member of the St. Louis Board of Aldermen who had come up through traditional party ranks. It was the beginning of an era of change for the board. Older, more traditional ward politicians, primarily saloon keepers and ward heelers, dominated the board. They were being replaced by a younger, more aggressive, and better educated breed. These young aldermen, called the Young Turks, were advancing more progressive legislation in a city that had always found change to be a tediously slow process. They were often frustrated and impatient. They were also insufficient in number to change city government quickly.

In 1976, Gephardt's own impatience to advance his political career became a matter of public record when he announced his intention to run for a vacant congressional seat. Then, as later, Gephardt was an energetic, attractive, and intelligent young man who clearly had the potential to go on to bigger and better things. I put together a lengthy piece on that potential when I got word that he was planning to announce for Congress. That may have helped me later. I always enjoyed access to Gephardt even when he was prominent on the national stage. He won the seat going away in 1976, and continued to win until he retired in 2004.

On January 23, 1987, two full years before the next inauguration day, Gephardt went for the brass ring when he announced
his candidacy for the Democratic presidential nomination. Before a
packed house in the recently renovated and historic Union Station
in downtown St. Louis, he formally tossed his hat into the ring. It
started a journey that would cover thousands of miles, cost millions
of dollars, and end in frustration. Along the way a soap opera scandal gave his campaign a mighty shove forward.

In early May, the media played "gotcha" with Colorado Senator
Gary Hart, the man who many pundits felt was in a position to lap
the field in the presidential race. He had run George McGovern's
campaign in 1972, was smart, attractive, and well known. And he
was cocky. He had challenged reporters to find a flaw. They did, in
the person of Donna Rice . . . a model, actress, and beauty queen,
who had had a "relationship" with Hart. Once a liaison aboard
a yacht called *Monkey Business* was revealed, the married Hart
bowed out of the race. For the Gephardt campaign, it was a shot
in the arm. He was in Jacksonville, Florida, at the time. I hopped
on a plane with a cameraman and went looking for him to get his
reaction to the Hart downfall. We found him and had a deliciously
successful competitive moment that evening.

We had arranged to interview him in the early evening live on
our six-o-clock newscast when he was to be at a Jacksonville hotel
to meet with local media. As it happens, the news conference was
still in progress at the time of our arranged meeting. That news
conference was being televised live back to St. Louis by one of our
local competitors. I give them credit for getting that set up and taking him "live" at the time. However, when we arrived and I made
our presence known to Gephardt, he excused himself from the local
media, stepped away from the podium, and came over to us. We
were set up to broadcast live. The end result was we got the one-on-
one interview (one on one is always a competitive plus), which was
also being broadcast live on the competing station. For us, it was a
two-fer. Two stations for the price of one and an embarrassing few
moments for the competitor. The other station was locked into its
live coverage and had to take us along for the ride, including my
interruption of the news conference. That was followed by a moment or two of dead air for them as I waited for cues from St. Louis

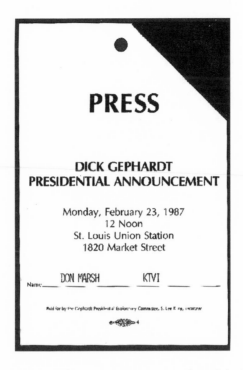

PRESS

DICK GEPHARDT
PRESIDENTIAL ANNOUNCEMENT

Monday, February 23, 1987
12 Noon
St. Louis Union Station
1820 Market Street

Name: DON MARSH   KTVI

Paid for by the Gephardt Presidential Exploratory Committee, S. Lee King, treasurer

to begin my interview. Then my interview played in its entirety on both stations.

While that was a nice moment for our team, there was a personal "better" moment on the way home. We had traveled a long way on short notice from St. Louis to Jacksonville. There had been little time for the amenities, such as eating. The return home late that night was via Atlanta on a last flight out. Of course, even then there was nothing beyond peanuts offered on the plane trip from Jacksonville to Atlanta.

We had some time on the ground in Atlanta, so I went off to forage for food. As busy as the Atlanta airport is, this section was remarkably quiet as midnight approached. I found signs pointing to an area that promised vending machines. As I walked down a long hallway to the promised land, I noticed a man walking alone ahead of me. The walk was unmistakable and could only have belonged to one man. Or, in this case, one I considered something of a superhuman. Having lived in Baltimore during some of the glory years of the then Baltimore Colts, the bandy-legged stride of the man ahead of me could only belong to one person, Johnny Unitas. There was no one else in sight. He was apparently hungry too. He took a sharp right at the welcome signs and colorful machines that signaled food and beverage. I was right behind him.

Parenthetically, I should note that on my way to the St. Louis airport some sixteen hours earlier to catch the flight to Jacksonville, I had listened to local icon Jack Buck on one of his regular morning radio feature programs discussing events linked to this date in history. He ended the segment wishing a happy birthday to his friend, Johnny Unitas. Had I not been such a Unitas fan, I might not have paid any attention.

In any case, Unitas was seated alone at a plastic table eating an equally plastic hot dog. We were the only two people in the area. I approached him and could tell he was wary of the intrusion from the moment he sensed my shadow. His shoulders came up to his ears as if he were trying to ward off an attack. I was either undaunted or insensitive or both, but I said to him, "You're John Unitas aren't you?" Inasmuch as I knew very well who it was, it amounted to nothing less than a dolt's attempt at small talk, and it was received as such. There was nothing in his expression or body language that invited more conversation. Here's a guy who had had a life of celebrity, intrusions, and inane requests from strangers, who could not even find refuge behind a tasteless hot dog in a deserted airport cafeteria. To say that it was clear this was a one-sided "big moment" would be an understatement. Even I recognized it. I apologized and said that I didn't want to bother him but just wanted to "wish you a happy birthday."

I had thrown the touchdown pass. His entire demeanor changed. Hunched shoulders relaxed, and a smile erased the look of pain. "How did you know it was my birthday?"

I said, "Jack Buck told me." He laughed. "Jack Buck told you. How is that old dog?" I explained that I had heard it on the radio that morning. I also told him that I had lived in Baltimore during the late 1960s and was most appreciative for all the thrills he provided. He seemed appreciative and I left the moment right there, leaving him to his nasty-looking hot dog, and me with the hope that I could find one just like it in one of those machines guarding the wall.

Back to the campaign. Gephardt's early strategy was to focus on the Iowa caucuses. Again and again he visited the state. The principal opposition for the nomination would be Senator Paul Simon of

Illinois and Massachusetts Governor Michael Dukakis. Gephardt had something of an advantage over the two, especially Dukakis, because the congressman was able to shuttle supporters from neighboring Missouri to work for him in Iowa. He always enjoyed strong labor support, and union men and women, not to mention Missouri Democrats not affiliated with labor, flocked north to help him. Simon, also an Iowa neighbor, did not have the troops at his disposal that Gephardt did.

As a result, Gephardt became an early front runner in Iowa and was asked to keynote the Iowa party's biggest fund-raiser, the Jefferson-Jackson Day Dinner in the fall of 1987. I could see, and later confirmed, that the audience was impressed with his speech, which focused on trade and the economy. Gephardt has never displayed much in the way of oratorical skills, but as this campaign was advancing he was becoming much better at it as a result of some expert coaching from consultants who specialized in such matters.

His Jefferson-Jackson Day success was blunted somewhat by his inability to pull off a back-door stunt designed to further bolster his reputation among Democrats in Iowa and elsewhere. In past years, the Jefferson-Jackson Day event had featured a straw poll. A good showing in that poll gave candidates even more traction for the forthcoming winter caucus and primary season while giving those who did poorly the opportunity to reconsider their political future and strategies.

By 1987, the Iowa Democratic Party had outlawed such polls. Nonetheless, Gephardt's supporters came up with a plan in which college students would pose as journalists and conduct an independent poll of the some eight thousand Democrats attending the event. When officials got wind of it, and even though it was billed as "independent," the scheme was stopped. Gephardt's campaign, which had earlier announced its desire for a poll, distanced itself from the staffer who had arranged this one.

In any case, the poll that counted—the Iowa Caucuses—was the following February. Dick Gephardt won, and his campaign was off and running.

There was a slight setback later in February in New Hampshire when Gephardt came in second to Dukakis. Just as Gephardt, and to a lesser degree, Simon had had an advantage in Iowa, the Massachusetts governor had the same advantage in his neighboring state, New Hampshire.

Gephardt wanted it, however, and had spent a lot of time in New Hampshire. I traveled with him, when he and his wife Jane (yes, it was Dick and Jane) and their kids brought a band of Missourians to New Hampshire months before the primary. They were an attractive family, and they were welcomed wherever they went. They crisscrossed the state attending any meeting that would have them. They became fixtures in living rooms, meeting halls, and churches, spreading the Gephardt populist gospel. The Gephardt presidential campaign show was playing well in the Granite State.

Gephardt was a man I had observed for more than ten years at this point. If there was any one thing about his physical appearance that was predictable, aside from the fact he did not have discernable eyebrows, it was that he always wore conservative suits and ties along with crisply starched shirts, all of which looked as if they had just been put on. No matter what the conditions, how hectic the pace, his uniform was always intact. One of the things that helped him maintain that freshly pressed look was the fact he did not sweat. At least he never seemed to. On this campaign trip, New Hampshire was experiencing abnormally hot weather. Nonetheless, no bead of sweat ever showed on him whether he was climbing porches or podiums or shaking hundreds of hands on a sunny parking lot. In the even more sweltering environment of St. Louis the man did not perspire.

But the biggest shock in New Hampshire was when he invited his summertime campaign entourage to a picnic toward the end of the trip. He wanted to thank supporters for their hard work on his behalf during the week. Lo and behold, he showed up in white Bermuda shorts, tennis shoes, and a golf shirt. It was an image that did not fit. His clothes looked as if they had just come off the rack. I could imagine Jane having jumped off the campaign bus to "get me something to wear at the picnic." It was Billy Graham in a Speedo, George Hamilton without a tan, Mother Teresa in high heels. I was mesmerized by the transformation. Although it was an ensemble not unlike ones seen at every backyard barbecue in the country, it seemed somehow comic on him.

He was, of course, showing no signs of perspiration as he moved around the picnic area. His skinny legs were on display appearing as hairless as his brow as he made small talk with the guests, most of whom were fellow Missourians. He looked so remarkably unlike the buttoned-down Richard Gephardt I had observed over the years. I was reminded of a famous photograph of Richard Nixon trying to look casual while walking on a California beach in a suit and tie. Now, that was in character but out of place. With Gephardt's garb, it was appropriate and in place, but out of character.

During the months before primary season, candidates then as now spent a good deal of their time priming the pump; that is, looking for money to fund the campaign. It was as necessary an evil then as it is now, although the number of dollars was measured in the millions rather than the tens of millions necessary to stalk today's presidential nominations. Gephardt was good at it. He was an attractive candidate who already had an influential job, and he was able to do fairly well raising campaign money. He would break away from the campaign on a daily basis and hit the phones. I remember seeing him often crouched over the phone, his hat figuratively in his hand.

A significant treasury was going to be especially necessary early in 1988 when a new term was to be indelibly stamped into the U.S. political lexicon: "Super Tuesday." That was March 8, 1988, when primaries in fourteen Southern and border states selected almost one third of the delegates to national political conventions. It was going to take a lot of cash to survive Super Tuesday with a campaign that was still intact, much less one that was still financially viable. Gephardt had pretty much held his own in that regard, having raised some $10 million from donors. He was also putting many thousands on his personal gold credit card.

Gephardt had used his political clout at home to get Missouri's primary moved up several weeks from its traditional mid-spring date to Super Tuesday. He knew he would win Missouri. He needed it in March when it meant something rather than weeks later. The Democratic legislature granted him his wish and moved up the primary date. The early March date had a double advantage for Gephardt. It not only put his "secure" state into the Super Tuesday pack, but also left him a little wiggle room. If his candidacy imploded, he would also have time, though not much, to meet a March deadline for filing to rerun for his congressional seat.

Good thing. The only state Gephardt won was Missouri. He had hopes that his strong labor background would give him a jumpstart in Michigan. He had just enough gas in the tank to give it a whirl after the Super Tuesday disappointment. Again, he fell short, receiving only 13 percent of the vote in a state in which he had expected to do much better. So, after twenty-six months, all that work and expended energy, all that strategizing, all those dinners and speeches, and after spending $10 million, it was over. But it was not the end.

Dick Gephardt, the following year, was one of the post powerful men in Washington when he became the house majority leader, a position he would hold until the "Gingrich Revolution" six years later, at which point he became minority leader until 2003. The following year brought with it another bid for the presidency. It did not have the gusto of the earlier campaign, and this time it ended in Iowa. He was mentioned more than once as a potential vice presidential candidate, but it never came to anything more than Sunday morning talk show speculation.

There are many factors that go into a losing political campaign, but often one can be cited as a "tipping point." Just as that goofy TV campaign ad showing Michael Dukakis smiling from a tank while looking silly in a protective helmet had people laughing rather than taking him seriously, a campaign ad put out by the Dukakis camp did in Gephardt. It should be noted, however, that it was the result of Gephardt's own doing.

That was the famous flip-flop ad that showed a man resembling the candidate doing acrobatic forward and backward flips while Gephardt's changing position on several issues was cited, including abortion. He had modified his long-standing and outspoken opposition to abortion when the political winds indicated a pro-life stance could hurt his presidential campaign. It was an awkward adjustment and brought with it harsh criticism from the pro-life forces. Although national polls showed most people favored abortion, the pro-life movement was anything but impotent. People may have had trouble understanding altered positions on taxes and other issues, but they had no trouble understanding this one. Some people even got to calling him "Tricky Dick," a nickname with obvious unflattering connotations that haunted one earlier president and helped keep the Missouri congressman from becoming one.

The 1988 Convention

*T*he nomination went to Michael Dukakis. The presidency didn't. Dukakis left the Atlanta conclave to take a few weeks, and ultimately his political career, off, blowing a seventeen-point lead in the polls. Remarkably, Dukakis felt that the best way to begin a post-convention campaign was to go on vacation from the presidential campaign. That left the late summer political stage to George H. W. Bush, who left steamy New Orleans with Dan Quayle in tow. Though behind initially, once they moved ahead in the polls, they were never headed. In New Orleans Bush had set the stage for his rout of Dukakis with the famous convention phrase, "Read my lips, no new taxes." He also pronounced his "thousand points of light" approach to harnessing America's greatest natural resource, its people.

> *I am speaking of a new engagement in the lives of others, a new activism, hands-on and involved, that gets the job done. We must bring in the generations, harnessing the unused talent of the elderly and the unfocused energy of the young. For not only leadership is passed from generation to generation, but so is stewardship. And the generation born after the Second World War has come of age.*
>
> *I have spoken of a thousand points of light, of all the community organizations that are spread like stars throughout the Nation, doing good. We will work hand in hand, encouraging, sometimes leading, sometimes being led, rewarding. We will work on this in the White House, in the Cabinet agencies. I will go to the people and the programs that are the brighter points of light, and I will ask every member of my government to become involved. The old ideas are new again because they are not old, they are timeless: duty, sacrifice, commitment, and a patriotism that finds its expression in taking part and pitching in.[21]*

The most famous convention line of that season did not belong to Bush, nor to Ronald Reagan who also addressed the Republicans, nor to Jesse Jackson nor to Ted Kennedy on the Democratic side. It went to soon-to-become Texas governor, Anne Richards, who pronounced that "Poor George" was "born with a silver foot in his mouth."

The most famous speech belonged to none of the above. That honor went to Arkansas Governor Bill Clinton and put him in a prominent spot on the national political stage. His speech was noteworthy, not for its content but rather for its length. Dukakis had decided that he would ignore tradition and be introduced in nomination by a single speaker rather than by a more traditional parade of high-profile supporters. Clinton, who had a relatively low national profile, got the nod.

A relatively short fifteen-minute speech was scheduled. Clinton, presumably aware of the high visibility of stage he held, refused to yield it. His tedious speech went beyond twice the allotted time. As I thought back on it, it seemed to me that he had spoken for more than an hour. My research puts the actual length of the speech at thirty-two minutes. It seemed much longer than that. As the minutes ticked by, impatient convention delegates grew weary of the rhetoric. They didn't want Clinton. They wanted the man they had come to coronate, Dukakis. Clinton was hardly halfway through when delegates began to call for his exit. I listened to some very unflattering comments from the floor as Clinton droned on. "Get the hook" was mild in comparison. Great cheers went up from the thousands of Democrats when the Arkansas governor finally finished. If he thought the cheering was for him or for his words, he was wrong. The cheers were cheers of relief that it was finally over. I was reminded of the old joke when a newcomer joined a political rally. He asked, "Is the speech over?" The man to whom he had put the questions answered, "It was over twenty minutes ago, but he's still talking."

In typical fashion, Clinton showed the political savvy that would take him from a role so roundly criticized by those at the convention to his coming out of nowhere four years later to receive the nomination himself. He did that in part by taking the wave of criticism directed at him and making it work for him. He made the round of television talk shows, gaining more publicity and attention primarily through his self-deprecating approach. With lines like, "It wasn't my finest hour. It wasn't even my finest hour and a half," Bill Clinton was on his way.

Paula Sims and the Death Poll

$\mathcal{T}$he 1980s proved an era for my television station's finest hours, and for a gradual return to the bad old days. News Director Matthews left after a couple of years, having finally brought ratings success and respectability to the news department. He went on to bigger and better things in Atlanta, Louisville, and Cincinnati. In the hands of Times Mirror the station did little to continue the advances of the early 1980s as the corporation yielded to stockholder demands for higher profits. Ultimately, Times Mirror sold the station at a tidy profit to a much smaller organization which had neither the desire nor the wherewithal to maintain earlier momentum. So it went nationally and locally in the 1980s as properties all over the country were bought and sold, each time carrying ever-higher price tags. The higher the cost of the property, the less the inclination to put even more money into it in terms of staff and technology.

A low point was reached late in the decade when a woman in nearby Illinois was convicted to murdering two of her children. In 1986, Paula Sims reported the abduction of her thirteen-day-old daughter by a masked gunman. She told police he broke into her Brighton, Illinois, home while her husband was at work and threatened to kill her unless she turned over her child. He took the baby, she said, and fled. The reported abduction led to a massive manhunt and investigation. Paula and her husband were questioned repeatedly by police. Needless to say, the media were all over it.

Less than two weeks later, the skeletal remains of a child were found in the woods some fifty yards from the Sims' home. The remains were never definitively identified as those of little Lorelei Sims, although authorities were all but certain it was the infant. Authorities hinted that they suspected Paula and her husband, but there was never enough evidence to file charges. A year and a half later, Paula gave birth to a son. A second daughter was born about a year after that.

By then the Sims had moved and were now living several miles from the earlier home in Brighton when tragedy struck again. The second child, tiny Heather Sims, born only weeks earlier, was reported missing. Again, Paula claimed a masked gunman had approached her outside her home, knocked her out, and stole her baby while her husband was at work. The young Sims son was asleep inside the house. Again, police responded, more incredulous this time than the last. Although the jurisdiction and investigators were different, everyone knew the details of this crime were a perfect match with the first. And for those who didn't get it, the media was there to fill in the blanks.

Heather's body was found some days later in a trash bin not far from where she had been abducted. Paula and her husband were now even more obvious suspects than they had been the first time around.

She was ultimately charged with murder, convicted, and sentenced to life in prison. Her husband was never charged. Paula Sims confessed to killing the girls after her conviction. Fifteen years later, she was seeking to have that conviction overturned claiming postpartum depression.

As it happens, I was anchoring the station's major newscasts during this period. However, at the end of the trial, I was on assignment in Mount Kisco, New York, interviewing Carl Icahn. He is now and was then the billionaire-financier-corporate raider who specialized in taking over struggling companies, bleeding them dry, taking huge profits for himself, then walking away. He was then in the process of ravaging Trans World Airlines, whose hub presence in St. Louis was an important part of the local economy. Icahn was selling off lucrative pieces of TWA. It cost the airline thousands of jobs and millions in assets. He was an important guy to talk to at this, the mid-way point of his "stewardship" of one of the nation's most historic airlines.

The climax to the Paula Sims trial was unfolding on the day I traveled to Mount Kisco. The trial was ending and the case was on the verge of going to the jury. I was in New York when our newscast reported the story during the early evening newscasts that night. Our news director, who began her career as a wardrobe consultant and had somehow stumbled into television news, was relatively new to the market. She had found a new way to exploit the Paula Sims story, which had been sensational enough to have long since satisfied most people's blood-lust.

Her idea was to do a viewer poll reminiscent of the days of the Roman Coliseum. Her question to the audience: "Should Paula Sims live or die? Tonight, you have the chance to be the jury." Thumbs up? Thumbs down? It was that simple. Forget the Sims tragedy. Forget the court system. Forget the fact jurors could be influenced by such a poll. Forget any sense of ethical propriety. Let the audience decide!

An infuriated prosecutor got wind of the poll and raised the issue in court. He demanded a recess. "I have just gotten word that Channel 2 (KTVI) is conducting a poll asking if Paula Sims should live or die. I have never heard of anything so low and callous." He called the station, and to his credit General Manager Wayne Thomas killed any further mention of the poll on the spot. Nonetheless, the mere announcement of the poll also prompted another public and media outcry. One media critic called it "smarmy."

The news director defended the poll by saying the station's signal did not reach Peoria where the trial was being held and therefore could not influence jury members. If there was any audience response to the poll, no results were ever made public. Nothing aired beyond the initial "live or die" question. Regardless of what the audience might have "decided," the jury gave Paula Sims life.

I was back the following day. The job fell to me to do the apologizing for the poll question, which I did on the ten o-clock newscast. It was a straight up *mea culpa* for the news department written by the general manager. "It was a bad idea, ill conceived, and never should have happened. We apologize to all who were offended." The simple words were obvious; however, I had several conversations with the general manager about exactly which words to use. Although there were several changes, I think we finally found the right ones.

Ironically, such polls were relatively rare in those days. One of the innovators in this audience-interactivity stunt was actually a station in Baltimore. In the late 1960s, it used to pose *"Tonight's Big Question."* It was a straight-up yes-or-no question. *Tonight's Big Question* was put to the audience every evening after the early news. Usually, it was pretty innocuous. The result was to be broadcast on the late evening newscast. There were certainly no life or death polls. It was a stunt, designed purely and simply to draw audience to the later newscast. In that regard, it was hardly successful because this particular station languished well behind the others in local ratings. One evening, however, the system broke down and no question was broadcast. Nonetheless, some seven hundred people responded with either the yes votes outpolling the no votes by a healthy margin or the other way around, in spite of the fact there had been no question posed that night.

This technique, and other attempts such as the infamous Paula Sims poll might have had a chilling effect on using similar surveys as a part of a news promotion campaign. However, they are now in common use. Networks, local stations, and other media use them almost daily with stupid and unimportant questions that usually demand impossible prescience on the part of viewers, listeners, and readers. "Will the Rams win the Super Bowl?" . . . "Will tomorrow's temperature set a new record?" . . . "Will Hugo Chavez be assassinated?"

The motive has always been to help promote the news and stimulate interactivity, the new darling of the consultants. The polls were also further justified for the most important of all reasons, they generated bucks. Not only were the brief segments sponsored, there was a kickback from the various telephone companies involved for generating the calls to those special numbers. No bad idea, I guess, is ever totally bad if you can make money from it. Now, the polls are still usually sponsored but conducted primarily through the Internet.

The Paula Sims incident did not cost our incumbent news director her job. She was around long enough to drag our product down from past successes. I recall one battle, which I lost. Politics and elections were my thing. We had a local springtime election that typically produced low turnouts. The most important elections we conduct may be those local elections in which we decide issues that are closest to us. Regional tax issues, school board elections, municipal and county political races, etc., have a more direct impact on our lives than most national elections. Yet, typically, Americans vote in extraordinarily low numbers in these elections. Turnouts of 20 percent are often considered high. So, that 20 percent of the electorate determines if the remaining 80 percent will pay higher property taxes or close down a school or elect a Klansman to the city council.

On this occasion, a significant increase in a local utility rate was put before voters. The outcome would affect a quarter of a million households. As we met to go over the stories to be included in our major late evening newscast, the producers wanted to make a local crime story the lead. The election result was slated to be the top story of the newscast's second section following the first commercial break. That put it about ten minutes into the program. Arguments against that position got a little sticky, bringing the news director in as the final arbiter. She went with the producers. When faced with the argument that the rate increase affected virtually every household in our viewing area, she was unpersuaded. Her argument; "Only 14 percent of eligible voters went to the polls. People don't care. So, I'm not leading with it." So much for giving people what they ought to know. Give them instead what it is believed they want to know. Some of us dinosaurs believe that the two are not mutually exclusive.

Flash Frames

Honduras and Father Carney

$\mathcal{I}$t was not all politics. There were diversions—sometimes with international ramifications. One took me and a crew to Honduras in the early 1980s. It all began with a Jesuit priest, Father John Carney, who was missing in Honduras where he had been serving for two decades. His St. Louis relatives were frantic with concern about his safety. Father Carney's sister Eileen Connolly and her husband Joe were leading a long-distance campaign from St. Louis for information as to his whereabouts and fate. There had been disturbing rumors from friends in Honduras that he might have been the victim of foul play. In many ways, he was a prime candidate for it.

Central America in 1983 was rife with political unrest that was of major concern to official Washington. The Reagan administration had decided to draw a line in the sand in Honduras. Cuban-trained insurgents were causing significant problems in neighboring El Salvador. There was concern that a Castro-type government was also taking hold in the neighborhood . . . in Nicaragua. The brutal Nicaraguan strongman Antastasio Samoza had been overthrown by a rebel organization known as the Sandinistas. The drums of civil war were beating as a rival organization known as the Contras showed early strength in an effort to sweep the Sandinistas from power. The Contras initially had help from several Latin American nations. Ultimately, the United States muscled in to provide financial support to the Contra rebels.

The United States was also putting millions of dollars in military assistance into Honduras in 1983, the year of Father Carney's disappearance. Honduras was a staging area for the forces rebelling against the regimes in Nicaragua and El Salvador. This safe haven strategy worried governments in both Tegucigalpa and Washington who feared that the Sandinistas would invade Honduras to hunt down Contras in their Honduran refuge. It was the subject of much controversy and later, scandal in the United States.

Honduras was not without its own internal tension. There was a large and restive population in Honduras that was hungry for economic and agrarian reform. It was much needed. Seventy percent of the nation was poor. There were no social agencies to turn to. Infant mortality was high. At this moment in time, leftist guerrillas were being trained in Cuba possibly to mount a campaign against the Honduran government. In fact, there was already some rebel activity in rural parts of that country. Everyone was nervous, especially in Washington and Tegucigalpa. This is where Father Carney came in.

Though primarily a rural priest, Father Carney had become well known throughout much of the country and had become a champion of the poor. He had authored a book, *To Be a Revolutionary*, that left little doubt as to his sympathies. He was considered a subversive, an agitator, and a communist by official Honduras. Clearly, he would have made officials in Washington and Tegucigalpa uneasy. The following text from a Catholic publication best explains Father Carney. His was a theology of liberation.

Already a missionary in Honduras in 1961, Carney was enlivened by the Second Vatican Council's ideal of radical service to the poor. In this poor Central America country, Carney reasoned that, just as the Son of God became fully human as one of us, so he had to truly become one with the Honduran campesinos. As Saul became Paul to signify his new life in Christ, Carney took the Spanish name Guadalupe to symbolize his total identification with the Honduran people. Eventually, and after years of working on it, he became a citizen of Honduras and renounced his U.S. birthright.

In his book To Be a Revolutionary, *he elaborated on his ideas about spiritual formation. Traditional theological studies, Carney believed, seemed to train priests in the service of the status quo, the comfortable middle-class lives most lived within the capitalist system and hidden imperialist ideals of the United States. Carney maintained that it was the poor campesinos of Honduras who really taught him the Gospel, the Good News that Jesus brought, and that we who have a more middle class outlook cannot really understand what it means "to bring Good News to the poor." The story of his life is titled* To Be a Revolutionary, *because Fr. Carney firmly believed that one had to be a revolutionary to live a full Christian life. The Gospel is revolutionary.*

Guadalupe saw and understood the problems of the poor. He

Hillside homes around Tegucigalpa

*saw how American fruit companies had taken over the best lands
and plantations. They and a few wealthy Hondurans controlled 95
percent of the wealth. The rest of the people lived in dire poverty.
Attempts to organize unions often led to the deaths and disappear-
ances of the leaders.*[22]

And then the priest disappeared. Father Carney's St. Louis relatives were receiving conflicting reports as to his fate. One said that
he had been shot by government troops while traveling in the jungle
with rebel troops. Another said he had died of starvation while in
custody. Frustrated by their inability to get answers long distance,
Joe and Eileen Connolly decided to travel to Honduras to find out
for themselves. They wanted answers as to whether he was indeed
dead and if so, answers as to how he had died. If he was dead, they
wanted to recover his remains and arrange a proper burial for him
in his adopted country. If he had been in custody, they wanted to
determine if he had been charged with crimes or had received a fair
trial. Their greatest hope was that none of the rumors were true,
that he was alive and, if not in custody, perhaps still in the jungle.
They wanted reunion or closure.

They were not naïve as to his political inclinations and were

Poor Honduran women wash clothes in city river

convinced that the priest was likely involved in revolutionary activities. It was their strong conviction that the ultimate outcome of their investigations would not be good. Regardless of his fate, they wanted to find out. Given the military-political situation in the region, you can be sure no one in the Honduran government, nor any U.S. officer in the country, was eager to deal with Eileen and Joe Connolly, especially with a television crew in tow.

We arrived together at Tegucigalpa aboard a commercial airliner. The airport looked more like a military installation than a commercial facility. Row after row of military helicopters lined the periphery. All had been freshly painted in the traditional olive green. Even a casual observer could see the U.S. insignias beneath a thin coat of paint on every chopper. It was either carelessness or a rushed attempt at concealment. If any of these machines met a bad end and fell into enemy hands, it would be difficult to deny their country of origin.

The city itself was picturesque in its own disturbing way. It had been settled in a topographical saucer. The main sections of the city sat in the middle. Decrepit buildings in various stages of deterioration dotted the hillsides. Most were ramshackle shacks made of scraps of wood, cardboard, galvanized metal, or anything useful that could be scavenged for the purpose. We would learn later that most were oc cupied by large families of squatters living in obvious squalor.

The women washed clothes in the river at the bottom of the hills. These rivers were fed by heavy rains in the hills that would sometimes sweep fragile dwellings down the hillside on a sled of mud. The remnants were gathered, if they could be found, and the homes reassembled. It was poverty at a level unknown even in the most impoverished parts of the United States.

Children begged in the streets. It was extraordinarily sad and depressing. Dirty, ragged kids dressed in scraps of clothing filled the streets like insects. Their eyes held no joy. Their tiny, dirty hands were thrust at pedestrians, pulling at the sleeves of passers-by in what was more often than not an unrealized appeal for handouts. It was impossible to resist them and at the same time imperative to do so. Even a few coins to one child would bring a swarm of others. Their sheer numbers made it impossible to meet their heartbreaking requests. The poorest of the poor back home seemed "advantaged" in comparison.

One had to wonder what the effect would be on these kids if they ever watched American television or movies and saw how people lived in the United States. Was there any way they could not wonder why this world was being denied them, any way they could not aspire to become revolutionaries? And there were American movies and television programs available in the capital. What would they think seeing attractive men and women, with no visible means of support, living in million-dollar homes and driving expensive cars? What would they think watching Americans devouring Big Macs?

Our trip to the hotel presented a series of images that were to become a staple of our stay in the city. Armed military personnel were on every corner. They carried automatic weapons, bayonets, and bored expressions during what must have been numbingly boring, clock-stopping duty. They were Hispanic clones of their American counterparts. The weapons, uniforms, and insignia were identical to those of Americans around the world.

They seemed to have no specific role in the midst of pedestrian or vehicular traffic other than to maintain an intimidating presence and quiet surveillance. The government was exceedingly jumpy about revolution and/or terror. Suspicious Hondurans were arrested by the thousands. Rarely was there more than one soldier on any given corner, but every intersection seemed to include at least one. It was not something someone from our society got used to easily. There is something different about an armed soldier with unspecified orders stationed on a corner compared to an American policeman directing traffic or lifting apples while walking the beat.

Once settled in our hotels and having confirmed arrangements for satellite transmissions of our reports, we began what ultimately became a ten-day odyssey that took us to numerous visits with American and Honduran officials. For them, it was an exercise in

Joe Connolly chats with one of omnipresent Honduran soldiers in Tegucigalpa

Eileen and Joe Connolly interview political "prisoners" in Honduras

stonewalling. For us, an exercise in frustration.

Producer Ian MacBryde, photographer Chris Michelswirth, and I had no idea what to expect.

The Connollys shuttled back and forth in their quest for information. They were told repeatedly that there was no information to be had. Honduran officials sent them to the Americans. The Connollys met with various American intelligence officers and some lower level U.S. diplomats. We were excluded. The Americans sent them to the Hondurans. In all but a few instances, the Hondurans with whom they met were high ranking military officers. We also met a few of them as Joe and Eileen were welcomed. In fact, the Hondurans were more inclined to let us take video of the official welcome, though not of the actual conversations, than were the Americans. The American embassy was off limits to us altogether, ostensibly for security reasons because of the threat of local terrorists. Our passports meant nothing. The consulate across the street was a little more accessible, though we had to jump through the looking glass and undergo a rigorous inspection process on every visit.

In almost every case, the Honduran officers the Connollys met were impressive. They were all spit and polish. Brass dazzled. Uniforms were starched and creased, boots and shoes spit-shined to a mirror gloss. Interestingly, almost all of them wore big, gold Rolex watches. It seemed to be a required part of the uniform for officers ranking colonel or above. Most spoke reasonably good English. The English, we were told, was acquired during training with Americans in Texas and Panama. A lot of that was going on. The expensive watches, worth thousands of dollars, had been acquired at post exchanges at the military bases where they had "trained."

Our television cameras were prohibited at any of the actual conversations either with the Hondurans or Americans. We were generally reduced to accompanying Joe and Eileen from location to location. We'd take pictures of them entering a building then leaving it, at which point they would tell us on camera what went on. Time after time they told us no one knew anything about Father Carney's fate. The story was usually the same. Father Carney was well known, and there were concerns he had some undesirable friends. There was no news as to his whereabouts or well-being. There were a few instances where Joe and Eileen were told of "intelligence" as to places he had been seen in recent weeks and from which he had apparently moved on. Most of those places were not readily accessible. Father Carney was described as a shadow on the move.

The military put on a great show of making some two dozen political prisoners available to the couple allowing Joe and Eileen to question them about her brother. "Show" may be the operative word. The prisoners were assembled at a local soccer field where they waited for us under heavy guard. They were seated in the stands when we arrived. There was something about this group that didn't add up from the start, and we all sensed it. These men were just a little too well-groomed, dressed too well, and just a little too well-fed to have spent any significant time in the infamous Honduran dungeons. None of us was under the mistaken impression that Honduran rebels or sympathizers were treated well in Honduran prisons. Everyone had heard stories of torture, starvation, and humiliation. These were all alleged enemies of the state, yet they all wore shoes. The footwear, if not of choice but of necessity among the peasants, was sandals. We had no proof that these were ringers, but we all later agreed that we had likely met soldiers recruited for a "performance." Developments years later tended to corroborate our suspicions.

During a half hour or so of pointed questions and answers without substance, the "prisoners" merely echoed everything we had already been told. Father Carney was well-known to all. Some had seen and met him. Some had not. Some had heard he was here or there or that he was sick or well. The only encouragement for Joe and Eileen was that no one had said they had heard that Padre Guadalupe was dead. That was some comfort to the deeply religious couple whose prayers for his safety never ceased.

Of course they turned to the church. The St. Louis couple was somewhat less frustrated following meetings with several church representatives. Priests and nuns seemed to have a better feel for where Padre Guadalupe had been, might have been, or might be. He, of course, posed some risk to church people. As a suspected revolutionary, he could put those close to him at some risk. Nonetheless, those with whom Joe and Eileen met seemed to open their arms to them not only as people of faith but also quite probably because Eileen resembled her brother so closely. He was a hero to a great many Hondurans, including many who would not dare admit it. The couple had been given numerous locations where Padre Guadalupe was known to have been and the names of various people and priests in distant villages who might have more recent information about him. They decided to visit as many of these places as time would allow.

We traveled by van to some of the places that we had been referred to. Several of them were rural farm co-ops that had been established by Father Carney himself as many as fifteen years earlier. No one at these co-ops could provide the Connollys with any useful information. The Connollys were always treated with respect and compassion. Padre Guadalupe still maintained an emotional and spiritual hold on the *campesinos*.

At one point during our trek along alternately dusty and muddy roads, we drove from a heavily forested area into a huge section of meadowland that seemed to have emerged out of nowhere. As we drove along the road we unexpectedly found ourselves flanked on one side by a huge military installation. Every imaginable kind of military vehicle was in view behind a very permanent-looking chain-link and barbed-wire fence. There were tanks, jeeps, and big trucks as well as earth-moving equipment as far as the eye could see. A small plane was taking off on a runway behind a row of vehicles.

Comayagua

Tents, dozens of them, dotted the landscape as we drove along. This, we would learn, was Comayagua. It was one of two tent cities established by the American military during extended "maneuvers" that were designed to discourage a possible invasion from Nicaragua. It was believed that as many as five thousand U.S. troops were in Honduras at that time. As to the extent and exact mission of those U.S. troops, I can't say. I can only imagine this was more likely a force less to engage in war games than to "engage" an invading force or homegrown rebels.

Everyone thought there might be some prospect for optimism in a small town called El Progresso. There was a priest there who was a close friend of Father Carney, and there was also a small radio station. Eileen, who spoke some passable Spanish, wanted to broadcast a message in the hope that her brother would hear it, or hear of it, or that the *campesinos* in the area could provide useful information.

The priest, a young Jesuit ironically enough from St. Louis, was a kind and thoughtful man who revered his friend Guadalupe. However, he knew nothing of his whereabouts or fate. We all suspected later that this priest might have known more than he was telling but that he might also have feared jeopardizing the campesinos or himself if word got out that he knew "too much." He was of little help beyond being of great comfort to the Connollys because of his friendship with, and the high regard in which he held, the missing priest.

With the Connollys drawing blanks, it appeared the proposed radio broadcast was a final, albeit slim opportunity. The visit to "Radio Progresso" was a surprise for everyone. The building was about the size of a garage and covered in rough white but yellowing plaster. It was at the end of a dirt path, quite literally in the middle of nowhere. It was hard to imagine this was a working radio station and even more difficult to believe that there were many radios within a hundred miles to receive its signal.

We were incredulous when we stepped inside and thought in a sense that we were back home. The console, the turntables, the microphones and all of the other equipment bore logos with the call letters "KMOX." KMOX is a St. Louis radio station owned then by CBS. What in the world was this stuff doing here? We learned that the St. Louis radio station, run by a man with well-publicized and close ties to the Catholic church, was responsible. Robert Hyland, a civic leader of enormous reputation, also had strong instincts to serve his religious community. He had responded to a request, no one knew from whom, for vintage equipment that was otherwise going to be destroyed or shelved. He complied. Equipment destined for the junk pile became a radio station in the middle of Central America.

Eileen's broadcast went well. It was also recorded with promises from the engineer of frequent repeat broadcasts. There was never any evidence that her appeal in the Honduran hinterlands was ever heard by anyone. There was never a whisper of response.

During the final days of the trip, Joe and Eileen were joined by Eileen's sister and another brother who had come to Honduras to lend moral support and to help in the investigation. They were hopeful of finally getting a long-requested meeting with U.S. Ambassador John Negroponte (Yes, that John Negroponte who has played several administrative and diplomatic roles in the George W. Bush administration). Such a meeting had been requested from day one, but Negroponte, who had been ambassador to Honduras for four years, was unable to find time for the couple.

Another visit with a local military commander provided a small ray of hope. Of the various rumors concerning Father Carney's fate, one said he had died of starvation in a remote jungle area while traveling with insurgents. The officer offered to facilitate a Connolly visit to the area along the treacherous Patuca River. There, they could speak with his troops who manned a scouting outpost in the region. He couched his offer in terms that offered both hope and some reason for concern. It was an area, he warned repeatedly, that was suspected of being hospitable to rebels where armed conflict was always a threat. However, it was also a place where information about Father Carney might be known.

The commander, in a gesture that seemed as generous as it was unexpected, said he would make a helicopter available to the Connollys. Only one member of our three-man crew would be allowed to travel along. No camera. There would be no pictures of any of the officers involved before or after the flight. Seems the nervousness about rebel terrorist action against local commanders and their families had everyone on edge. As the reporter on our team, it fell to me to accompany the priest's family on the flight deep into the jungle.

We were strapped into the helicopter for a flight we were told would be about an hour. Everything about the helicopter was American including the omnipresent U.S. insignia. It, too, had been recently painted over just like those planes at the airport in Tegucigalpa. The pilots spoke English and advised us almost too matter-of-factly that we were going over territory in which rebels were known to operate and that we could take fire from the ground. It was not comforting to note that the pilot and co-pilot sat on cushions of lead and that armored panels protected their heads, while no such protection was available to us passengers. The large door along one side of the chopper was left open, giving us a view of the terrain below. Of course, at lower altitudes, rebels might be able to see us, and that was unsettling.

The Patuca is a long, winding, muddy river that is the second largest in Central America. It runs fast and brown through triple canopy jungle that comes right to the river's edge, making the river invisible unless one flies directly over it. The thickness of the vegetation offered some comfort because it suggested that not much might be expected in the way of gunfire from the ground. That was certainly the hope. However, one need only remember that the terrain we were seeing from the air was not unlike what chopper pilots traversed

Women demonstrate demanding information about "the disappeared" in Tegucigalpa

over in the jungles of Vietnam. And many of those pilots never came home because they were shot out of the sky from those jungles.

We reached our destination at what was essentially a nameless village populated by sullen peasants and children fascinated by the helicopter and the strangers it carried. Also present was a small unit of what appeared to be hardened veteran Honduran soldiers who used the village as a base camp for their operations against rebels. Discussions with villagers and soldiers proved fruitless. Again, we sensed another setup. On the one hand, this entire effort indicated the military was cooperating fully with the missing priest's family, even allowing a reporter to tag along. However, as had been the case at every stop along the way during the entire stay, no useful information was obtained. More frustration for all involved. The return to Tegucigalpa was solemn in the knowledge that virtually all cards had been played.

Eileen had become aware that relatives of the so-called "disappeared" met routinely in the capital to protest and demand information about missing loved ones. "The disappeared" was the name given to those countless thousands of Hondurans who had run afoul of the government and who had simply vanished. Some had been gone for years, others for days, weeks, or months. Few on the list ever reappeared. Those who did only returned years later.

The government, suffering from homicidal paranoia, gobbled up anyone who was perceived as any kind of a threat. They were killed, tortured, or imprisoned and their relatives were left to wonder which. Every week, the demonstrators, who were mostly women, gathered in Tegucigalpa carrying posters with names, pictures, and appeals for information. They got nothing but the comfort they afforded each other. The government wasn't listening and didn't care. Eileen Connolly wanted to let these women, the wives, mothers, and sisters of the "disappeared," know she was one of them and supported them. She too marched. She too demanded information. She too was denied it.

The trip was almost in its final hours when Ambassador Negroponte's schedule was suddenly able to accommodate that long-requested meeting with the Connollys. We, of course, were excluded. Ground rules stipulated it was to be an off-the-record meeting. Little of what was discussed could be made available to us by the Connollys other than that Negroponte assured them that the embassy was "doing all it could" in the Carney case. The Connollys didn't believe it. To them, it was clear that Negroponte had done nothing more than put the candle on this cake of innocence, misinformation, disinformation, and deception that everyone felt had characterized the entire visit. By meeting with the Connollys, Negroponte left them little to complain about as far as cooperation from the embassy was concerned.

As a group we had not been welcomed by the American diplomatic/military community. We had only been tolerated and fed a few bones to keep us at bay. Anyone knowing the relationship between America and Honduras at that point in time would know that the Hondurans did nothing without the advice and consent of the embassy.

The trip was essentially over, and as we prepared to leave, we knew virtually nothing more than we did when we arrived. From our point of view the trip was a failure. We had to assume that from the American, and therefore the Honduran, point of view, it was considered a success. For the Connollys, the only consolation was the persistent reaffirmation from so many of the people they encountered of the immense regard in which Father Carney was held by all who knew him or knew of his work.

The return to St. Louis was anything but a celebration. The Connolly's tried to keep the story of Padre Guadalupe alive. But essentially, the story did not change. News editors lost interest. There was nothing new to report. Within weeks, it was forgotten except by those closest to it, which included those of us who had traveled to Honduras with Eileen and Joe. I tried to revive it over the course of the next few years. But as they say, it lost its legs.

I learned with sadness more than a decade later that Eileen had died. But she went to her grave thinking she knew at last what had happened, or most likely happened to her brother, and that she had been correct in her suspicions of American duplicity.

Information began to filter out from various sources including the release of some previously classified CIA documents. New information also came to light as a result of an investigative report by the Canadian Broadcasting Corporation. Details from various sources were reported later by the *Catholic New Times* in an extensive report about Father Carney.

In the United States, his brother, sister, and a Jesuit friend have been seeking information on his death from the government for over twenty years. The Honduran government has come up with about six different stories, while in the United States Carney's supporters have now obtained about one hundred pages of declassified documents on their friend and relative; unfortunately, almost half of the information has been blacked out as not available to the public. The CIA seems to have been implicated somehow.

In a striking addendum to the above, the CBC in its Man Alive series did a show on Carney's life and the persistence of the Connollys (Jim's brother-in-law and sister) to find answers and some closure. They had become absolutely disgusted with the patent cover up by the U.S. embassy in Honduras at the time. In a remarkable geopolitical irony, the American proconsul believed to be leading the attack on liberation theology and justice movements in Latin America at that time was the ambassador to Honduras (1981–1985), John Negroponte, the present U.S. ambassador to the UN and recently named as the new proconsul in Iraq. The Man Alive show depicts

Negroponte as telling the Connollys that the embassy was doing all it could in the matter.

According to a 1997 CIA inspector general's report, US officials in Honduras were fully aware of human rights abuses by the army but did not report this as it "reflects negatively on Honduras and not to be beneficial in carrying out U.S. policy." In a handwritten declassified memo of August 19, 1985, proof of official obfuscation seemed obvious: "The Fr. Carney case is dead. Front office does not want the case active. We aren't telling the family."

In the CBC show, the Connollys were introduced to Senor Caballeros, a Honduran refugee and a former member of the Honduran death squads. He confirmed CIA involvement and said that he had heard from others that Padre Guadalupe had been murdered and thrown out of a plane into the jungle. As well, Caballeros stated that his final gesture was to hold out his arms like Jesus on the cross and forgive his captors. Caballeros later killed himself. With tears in their eyes, the Connollys stated that they knew they were right. They had been consistently lied to.[23]

Negroponte certainly did not come out of this episode looking good, though it did not seem to impede his career. In the George W. Busch administration, he has served as U.S. permanent representative to the United Nations, director of National Intelligence, and most recently as deputy secretary of state. He has never publicly addressed the Carney issue. News reports indicate that the Honduran general who gave the order to kill Father Carney was close to Negroponte. It is hard to imagine the incident was never discussed between the two. Twenty years after he met with the Connollys, and as bits and pieces of the story on the fate of Father Carney were being put together, the *National Catholic Reporter* wrote that Negroponte had maintained that he knew nothing about the circumstances of Father Carney's death nor of the activities of the unit that killed him. For that, he was described by the *National Catholic Reporter* in 2003 as being "duplicitous" and "the most uncaring official" the Carney family dealt with during its investigation.

Vignettes

$\mathcal{L}$et's change the pace. During the late 1970s and early 1980s, I anchored, at various times, weekend newscasts and a noon newscast that were typical for the time slots. There was a modicum of news and a maximum of soft features and interviews, some of which offered a call-in opportunity for viewers. Subject matter focused generally on pop culture staples such as entertainment, diet, and health news. St. Louis is an active university and theatrical town so there were a lot of visits by writers, authors, actors, musicians, politicians, and other national as well as local celebrities. Over the years, I interviewed scores of them, including some of the biggest names in all of the above-mentioned fields. It was always great fun and served no other real purpose than to promote the occasion of their being in town. It was good for them, and good for us because celebrities always helped draw an audience.

But a local lady trumped them all. Clearly the most popular feature at noon was the appearance of a local astrologer. Her name was Rose Cosentino. People would call, give her their birth dates, and she would glibly provide a quickie horoscope. The audience loved her. Rosie was only on the set for six or seven minutes, but once the fact she was going to be on was promoted early in the day, people would begin calling in. Some callers waited on the line for hours just for a chance to talk to her. She was very personable, pretty, and obviously popular. Why she was never offered her own program I will never know. Rosie was the most popular feature on any program I was ever associated with. She could have done an hour a day and still turned people away. Alas, for management it was not in the stars. She died at a very young age of breast cancer.

Two in-studio interviews come to mind with bona fide celebrities.

Henry Fonda

I can't imagine that anyone reading this page does not know Henry Fonda. He was an outstanding Academy Award–winning film star and stage actor whose career spanned half a century. For all of his accolades, and there were many, he may be best known in the collective mind of many as the father of actress Jane Fonda, who doubled her famous Dad's Oscar wins with two. He proved more prolific at the marriage game; he had five wives, while she had a mere three husbands.

Jane Fonda is acknowledged as an actress of great capability. In fact, her career survived a period in her life which might have easily, and most probably would have, derailed most celebrities. Jane Fonda had an established reputation for her role in liberal and activist causes by the early 1970s. That was the minor leagues compared to her anti-war activism.

There are millions of Americans who have abandoned her famous Fonda name in favor of "Hanoi Jane." In 1972, she visited Hanoi, the capital of then North Vietnam. She was quoted making comments critical of the American war effort in general and of the Nixon administration in particular. A photo was widely distributed showing a smiling Jane Fonda sitting at an anti-aircraft battery. It was a weapon that was used day after day and night after night to fire on American planes on missions over Hanoi. It created a firestorm of controversy and seriously jeopardized her career because many in this country considered her actions nothing less than treason. To this day, she is held in contempt by many Americans who fought in that war and those who supported it. It would be unfair not to suggest that there were also many in each group who thought she was heroic.

Several years after the incident, but with it still fresh in the minds of many, Henry Fonda came to St. Louis to appear in the biographical drama *Clarence Darrow*. He had been nominated for a Tony Award in New York for his run there with the play. He was still very much a star in spite of health problems and several film roles that were well short of his best work of earlier years.

Fonda was a guest for one of the in-studio interviews. I was eager to meet this icon who had won the praise and respect of two generations. I must confess that even after all the celebrity interviews, I still got excited about them. He was escorted into the studio before airtime by a coterie of colleagues and publicists who played a variety of rolls in ensuring his comfort and well being. Such attention was not unusual for celebrities of high status.

One of the publicity people sidled up to me as I was clipping a microphone to my tie and affixing my ear-piece (used by the director to communicate). The young man said something like, "I just wanted you to know that Mr. Fonda wants to talk primarily about the show tonight. He is willing to take some other questions. Only his daughter, Jane, is off limits."

"Off limits?" I asked.

"Yeah, no questions about Jane. He doesn't like to talk about her trip to Hanoi and that stuff." It reminded me of my days in Germany when second lieutenant aides would list what soon-to-be interviewed general officers would and would not discuss. Generals did not get there by accident and typically, regardless of the warnings from aides, they would discuss anything that wasn't classified. They were intelligent, practiced in the art of communicating, and could handle mere reporters. Celebrities with a few decades of dealing with media under their belts were the same.

Within a few seconds, the on-the-air light went on and we were off and running. The Fonda interview came up about ten minutes into the broadcast.

I began the interview by saying that I was told that he did not like to talk about his daughter, Jane. I wondered why. It was an interviewer's device to get him to talk about what he supposedly didn't want to talk about. He looked at me with incredulity and asked where I had gotten that idea. I told him. I suspect the publicist in question ultimately got a good chewing out. While Fonda's exact words in response are beyond my abilities of exact recall, his answer went pretty much like this.

"I don't know why anyone would have an idea like that," he said. "I am willing to talk about Jane any time, any place, to anyone. She's my daughter. I am her father. I could not be more proud of her. I always have been and always will be. She is a great person and a wonderful actress. I'm her father. I stand with her and support her. When kids go through some rough waters, that's what fathers do. She is entitled to her views, and I am not entirely sure she is off the mark with all of them. Mistakes? Yes, at times. But I'm her father. Does a father abandon a child when others are critical? I don't, and I stand by her, and with her, 100 percent."

I was blown away by the intensity of his comments and what seemed to me to be his obvious sincerity. This was not an actor playing a role about a make-believe daughter. This was a man who very clearly loved, and was proud of, a woman many Americans had come to revile. There was nothing phony about the response. If he were acting, he was better at his craft than even I believed. And I knew he was a fine actor. It was a great television moment and an insightful glimpse into the human side of the celebrity world stripped of the usually protective veneer applied by press agents and hangers-on.

Susan Anton

Susan Anton was stunning in 1980, and she is stunning now. The nearly six-foot-tall beauty queen, model, and actress was on her way to stardom quickly after winning the Miss California contest in 1969. She was beautiful, tall, blonde, and talented. That is not a bad combination for success. Movies and television beckoned. She responded with a lot of charisma, and audiences responded to her. Her beauty was a gift that opened the door for her in the entertainment world. By the same token, some found it difficult to get past her looks to see the gifts of talent that have shown through the years. And Susan Anton was successful. A film called *Goldengirl* was but another lap on a successful track. She was a beauty queen at nineteen and never looked back.

To say that I would be happy to welcome this stunningly attractive lady to the interview set would be an understatement. She was a scheduled guest on our noon news program. However, by the time we went on the air, she had not arrived at the station. Disappointed, I was concerned about what the producer might have in mind if

Ms. Anton failed to appear altogether. Hey, it happens! A no-show scenario would have left a lengthy hole in the newscast, and it had to be filled with something. But once we were on the air, it would be a problem for the producer to solve.

A few minutes into the newscast, I was advised that Ms. Anton was "in the building." Welcome words for a lot of reasons. All was on course. At least in the studio. I did not know at the time that this beautiful creature was, at the moment I was advised of her arrival, puking her guts out in the ladies room. She was sick as a dog.

Seems she had arrived in St. Louis to promote *Goldengirl* directly from the Cannes Film Festival. She had been traveling for many hours and had picked up a dose of food poisoning somewhere along the way. As I said, I was unaware of any of this until she was long gone.

At the appointed time, I went to the pre-interview break. As the commercials rolled, this beautiful, leggy Amazon of a woman stepped into the studio looking as gorgeous as advertised. She was radiant and offered no clue as to what had been going on only moments earlier. She was laughing and personable and charming on air, and a few minutes later she was gone.

Throughout the interview . . . and don't ask me what was said beyond talking about her movie . . . I had been struck by her resemblance to my old friend in Munich, Ingrid Gallmeister, the gal who had undoubtedly been done in by the anti-Gaullist generals. Anton was her twin. It was an eerie experience chatting with this ghost of memories past. It was apparently an experience of another sort for Ms. Anton.

I learned after the newscast that she had left the studio and assaulted the ladies room once again. According to those in there with her she threw up from the moment she entered the bathroom until there was nothing left to throw up. Then, it was off to the limo to head for the next public appearance. The show must go on.

Flash Frames

The Great Flood of 1993

*N*atural calamity is nothing new to St. Louis and Missouri. In 1811–12, the most severe earthquake the nation has ever known rattled windows in New Orleans, rang church bells in Boston, and caused the mighty Mississippi River to flow backwards. The epicenter was south of St. Louis. The quake's source was the New Madrid fault, a fault line that rivals San Andreas in California and still records measurable tremors every day of the year. Some experts say that's good and keeps pressure from building to a disastrous climax. Every now and then—even today—residents in St. Louis get a gentle reminder of the fault's existence.

Tornadoes are an annual threat, and have been known to strike in the city of St. Louis itself. Great swaths of Missouri and neighboring states have been mangled by twisters.

Summer thunderstorms roll in carrying green-hued clouds ripping out trees, tearing off roofs, and crippling power lines. Capistrano has its swallows in springtime. The Midwest has its thunderstorms each summer.

Since the city is located between America's two great rivers, the Missouri and Mississippi which meet in confluence north of the city, flooding is a frequent problem. There have been several in the last generation. In the early 1970s, back to back one-hundred-year floods struck the area. Hundred-year floods are *supposed* to happen every hundred years or so. St. Louis got them two years in a row.

But when it comes to flooding, the great flood of 1993 was the biggie. It was a five-hundred-year flood. Snowmelt in the north, accompanied by heavy springtime rains, collaborated to send billions of gallons of water southward repeating a process that had gone on for millennia. Gone were the wetlands that had historically absorbed the overflow as man and machines attempted to bring Mother Nature under their control with levees and flood walls. From time to time, it proved a mismatch. Nineteen ninety-three was a case in point, and much of the central part of the country paid the price. Nothing like it had happened since records were kept. Thousands of acres of

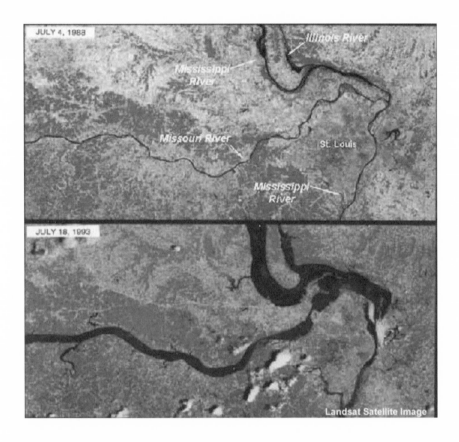

land—rural and urban-residential—were lost, as farms, farmhouses, livestock, urban homes, businesses, and lives were swept away. Fifty people died in the floods. In some cases, entire towns were lost and forced later to rebuild on higher ground. Damage was put at $15 billion. However, no price tag can be put on the emotional cost.

The area affected by the flooding surpassed forty thousand square miles. In St. Louis, the Mississippi River was fifty feet above flood stage for one hundred days. It was the biggest story for the St. Louis media in decades. Not only in terms of its impact, but also in terms of its duration.

Months later, when the land was dry once again, I was asked to write about the St. Louis flooding from my perspective as a television journalist for *The Flood of 1993: Stories from a Midwestern Disaster,* published by Patrice Press. It was available in 1994, a few months after the last of the floodwaters had receded. Rather than test my recall abilities fifteen years after the event, perhaps it would be best to excerpt and paraphrase what I wrote then, when memory of the event was a lot more vivid.

The rivers surged southward toward St. Louis with a message that was unmistakable. It read: "Made for Television."

We in the media licked our lips. We knew the dog days of July and August were approaching and that they were as capable of wiping out journalistic enterprise as the waters were of wiping out a cornfield. The flood promised what we seldom find in the summer: A big story. There was an impending sense of drama, and all the emotion that comes with it, including misery, heroism, futility and compassion. Those of us in television knew that nature's as predictable as a meteorologist's forecast. While no one could have forecast the scope of the disaster there was no doubt significant flooding was on the way.

We covered nuisance flooding all spring. Communities along the rivers got their feet wet in April and May. Then we watched the water rise in the tourist town of Grafton, Illinois, near St. Louis. The "Great River Road," which normally guided carloads of sightseers through the picturesque and historic area, was becoming a part of the river. Across the Missouri, West Alton, Missouri, started taking on water, as it does whenever the river rises. The "river rats" . . . those who lived along the river . . . were on the move, bailing out. As usual, they were judged harshly. Some said they got what they deserved for choosing to live riverside. Critics didn't understand the river's draw among those who loved it.

"Nothing like '73" some of us who'd been there said to rookie reporters. "Now, that was a flood."

Then, in the first days of summer, everything changed. At Winfield, Missouri, a community forty miles north of St. Louis that few of us had heard of, the levee broke, pouring water into suburban St. Charles County. Who among us might have predicted then that 45 percent of the state's fastest-growing county would eventually rest under water, or that one old community, Portage Des Sioux, would become an island for sixty-two days?

Winfield was the starter's gun for the main event, and journalists broke from the blocks. Helicopters whirled in the sky; reporters bought waders. The pictures were fantastic. The flood seemed less a danger than a picturesque happening customized for the six-o-clock and ten-o-clock news. For weeks, everywhere we looked and everyplace we went, there was a story. And as a news story, like the rivers, it got bigger and bigger.

Reporters patrolled the skies, scouting for new levee breaks, new misery and the chance to wade knee-deep in some unfortunate farmer's field while the cows and pigs were taken to higher ground. We used words like "corral" and "round-up." Then we commiserated as river families began hauling furniture to the second floor, content to wait it out. Early on, it was for them, a periodic bother. And those who were most honest told us that high water now and again was "good for the land" keeping it rich and fertile. They would suffer the inconvenience, and put up with the nuisance. At first they were confident that the crop, or most of it, could still be harvested, and that the yield would be abundant. At first.

We reporters danced in from the clouds as new levees broke and the forecasts promised more rain and then more rain, and incredibly, even more rain along the river basin. Constant downpours sent new and higher levels of water southward. Each day, the rivers inched higher. True to the television credo of "reporter involvement," we bobbed in john boats, canoes, and rowboats. In some ways during the last weeks in June covering the flood was still fun. Reporters posed in water up to their knees, then up to their waists and finally, by mid-summer, up to their chests and on to their armpits. They issued dire warnings of the danger posed by the water in which they themselves splashed.

Soon a new element was added to the story as the water spread from the farmers' fields toward more populated areas. Sandbaggers. Calls for help became increasingly urgent from communities which once seemed far removed from the rivers. Little rivers and streams joined their big cousins on the rampage. More and more sandbaggers were needed to hold off the growing menace. They became the new focus of the stories. It seemed heroic and made the drama even more compelling.

My first look at the flooding was from a helicopter over the Missouri River. On the ground the flood was impressive enough. We could hear the water and sense its restlessness and power at the river level. It pushed like defensive linemen putting their shoulders to the opposing line. But from the ground, we could not see how it meandered across the countryside. From the air, all we could hear was the trumpeting of the chopper, but we could see clearly how the river's course was dictated by the contour of the terrain. By early July, there were places in suburban areas only a few miles from downtown St. Louis, where I could see nothing but water from low flying helicopters.

Familiar terrain disappeared. Small bridges that had carried commuter traffic over once-benign rivers and streams now shimmered under water like figments of our imagination. One golf course was flooded, with only a few elevated greens spared. Ironically, an automatic sprinkler system robotically watered one surrounded green. Then a Little League complex slid into view. Ball fields were distinguishable only by the tops of scoreboards and grandstands poking above the waterline. I reported that thousands of youngsters were being denied the chance to play baseball, making them flood victims once removed. With half a season to go, the diamonds were covered by eight feet of water with more on the way.

One viewer thought my reference to these youngsters was frivolous. He asked me, "How can you call them 'victims' when there are people out there losing everything?" I told him that to some children, summer baseball is everything.

One small river's flood was not being fed from the north. It spilled over its banks because the swollen Mississippi acted as a dam. The smaller river's waters had no place to go and were pushed backwards and over its banks for seven miles upstream.

Storm water was routed to the Mississippi by a man-made storm water channel generously called a river, the River Des Peres. The big river, now approaching record depths, refused to accept what the River Des Peres threw at it, forcing its waters back through modest neighborhoods inundating walls of sandbags along the way. Two hundred homes were damaged before waters began to recede much later. Ironically, during the worst days of the flooding and only a few miles from the Mississippi, the River Des Peres was dry because water downstream had spilled into the neighborhoods. It was like a Fellini movie. And it was great television.

The grim, daily reportage was occasionally broken by stories that were uplifting. There was the marriage ceremony in which the bride and groom arrived by rowboat while friends sandbagged outside the church to keep the uninvited guest, the river, from crashing the ceremony.

Pictures of heroic rescues of farm animals were changing. As high ground was lost, the video now showed bloated corpses of animals bobbing in the dirty water. Farmers and others who lived near the rivers were watching television waiting for good news while keeping one eye upriver where it was still raining.

Then the big levee at Quincy, Illinois, to the north of St. Louis broke. We watched on television as the water bullied aside an earthen levee and devoured the fields. Hundreds of acres of young corn and soybeans were under water in seconds. Within hours, thousands of acres were inundated. It was a defining moment. Now there was no denying that the flood story was more than anyone had bargained for or that it was going to last longer than anyone had imagined. It was a sharp reminder that restless bloated rivers have minds of their own, and when they choose to show it, have power unmatched by anything we know.

Those downstream took a little comfort in Quincy's misfortune because it took some of the pressure off the water's march southward. The story was different now as we were reporting as much from rescue centers as we were from broken levees and sandbag lines. The wupeta-wupeta of television helicopter rotors was a constant sound in the sky as the choppers traveled north, south east and west from one story to another, from one tragedy to another.

With few exceptions, newscasts were devoted to the flood and viewers responded. Not everyone was touched directly by the flood. The number of acres flooded was only a fraction of those that were dry. But few people were untouched by the story in the sense that everyone knew someone who was suffering. Thousands were inconvenienced as routes were changed for once-routine trips. Some commuters were forced to add miles to their travels. Then the new routes were struck by floodwater and even newer paths to old destinations had to be found. People left early for work and they got home late. It was human drama. As much emotion could come from the rescue of a cat as from a farmer weeping at the loss of five thousand acres. Viewers watched closely because of it. Ratings soared.

In mid-July, there was a collective gasp in the community in what for the St. Louis area was the worst moment of the flood. Four youngsters from a school for troubled children along with two of their adult counselors were reported missing on an incomprehensibly ill-considered class day trip. At a time when three rivers in the immediate vicinity were approaching record flood crests, the group had undertaken an excursion into a park which was known for its underground caves. In a reckless rush to explore, members of the group ignored barriers forbidding entrance to the park and set out for the caves. It was a rainy day and for six of the group, that proved a death sentence. The rains had been falling on saturated land. Water had sought and found the lowest terrain, flooding the caverns. The six had ventured too far and the water came after them. Less adventurous classmates survived while the six who were trapped did not.

People now called the flood a scourge of Biblical proportions. "God is punishing us," said some. Others pointed to a brand new gambling casino boat on the Mississippi and wondered why, then, was God ignoring the boat which continued to do a thriving business in spite of the flooding by gerry-rigging access.

In mid-July the swollen Missouri and Mississippi rivers found each other sixteen miles north of their normal confluence. From the air, it looked like the middle of an ocean. We watched luminous green and yellow waters swirl around what had once been barns. Fertilizers and pesticides had been claimed too, mixing a toxic cocktail that spread out for hundreds of acres. The sluggish muddy waters of the Missouri waited patiently for the cleaner Mississippi to find them, then they merged until there was no distinction between the two.

Historic Kaskaskia Island, Illinois, downriver from St. Louis was claimed a few days later. The island had a history as rich as its fifteen thousand acres of fertile farmland. It had been explored and settled three hundred years earlier by Father Jacques Marquette. Kaskaskia had been isolated two centuries later when the Mississippi cut a channel separating it from the Illinois mainland.

In 1993, the old channel was a Mississippi backwash which separated the island from Missouri on the western side of the island. The channel waters were three feet lower than those of the river itself. The higher water was held back by a section of levee that had failed twenty years earlier. The two sections of water were normally hundreds of yards apart. Only ten feet separated them in late July.

Kaskaskia had been flooded before. However, even though the bridge connecting it to St. Mary, Missouri to the east was under water, a new, fifty-foot earthen levee was expected to protect the island. It didn't. A sand boil, a flaw that allowed water to burrow through, had formed under the new levee. Witnesses say that when it broke through, water exploded onto the island with the force and sound of a freight train. Within hours, and less than a week after we had visited the island, Kaskaskia and its some sixty buildings were under twelve feet of water. Only six homes were salvageable when the waters receded.

Throughout the summer, residents of the affluent St. Louis suburb of Chesterfield had remained high and dry. They were twenty-five miles west of the Mississippi River but a lot closer to the Missouri. Residents lived in upscale homes on relatively high ground. Even though the Missouri was just a few miles to their west, they felt secure. The lower Chesterfield valley was protected by a modern levee guaranteed to withstand a hundred year flood. Scores of businesses had established themselves in the lowland flood plain, many of them owned by people who lived on the surrounding hillside. A small regional airport that was home to dozens of corporate jets was thriving in the valley.

Then, on a Friday night at the end of July, late evening news bulletins sent shock waves through residents of Chesterfield's six and seven figure homes, as well as through owners of businesses located in the valley. The levee was not holding. Within a few hours, the valley was under 15 feet of water. The residents looked down on a lake. The interstate highway which brought them to and from their homes from the city and the valley was under water for a mile or more and impassible. Owners of flooded-out businesses returned to them by rowboat to salvage what they could above the waterline. They stepped into their buildings through second floor windows to be greeted with scenes reminiscent of Indiana Jones. Floors were covered with writhing snakes that had sought refuge there. The flood the people of Chesterfield had watched in the comfort of their living rooms had now found them.

Thirty miles to the east the people of Dupo, Illinois, were facing more than water. Dupo sits directly across the river from St. Louis which is about a thousand yards to the west. The poverty-stricken town of East St. Louis is Dupo's northern neighbor. Dupo is basted by humidity in the hot summers and wind-whipped in the winter. It's always dusty and colorless except for the blue collars of those who live there. An industrial levee protects the gritty community from the river; constant vigilance protects the white people of Dupo from what they fear is a greater danger posed by the blacks of East St. Louis. Experts had told them that if the levee broke, they would have only twenty seconds to evacuate. Opting to "protect" their homes, they put their faith in the levee, fearing what they perceived as a greater danger to their homes and belongings from their neighbors to the immediate north.

No levee, however, could hold in the face of an emerging threat from across the river in St. Louis where the river was now climbing well above flood stage and just three feet below the tops of downtown flood walls. And it was still rising. The southern end of the city had levee, but no flood wall protection. The levee protected real estate comprised of light industrial properties. The city flinched as a propane tank farm located in that area was assaulted by the floodwaters.

Fifty-one tanks that were fully loaded with propane, each one the size of a small car, were lifted from their wooden cradles by the rising water. They floated precariously in the rising water. The St. Louis fire chief proclaimed it "The most dangerous situation this fire department has ever faced. A single spark or lightning would incinerate the southern part of the city."

Everyone living up to half a mile from the bobbing tanks was endangered and ordered to evacuate. Grudgingly, a staggering 12 thousand residents from St. Louis, St. Louis County and across the river in Illinois, complied, including residents in Dupo. A monster propane explosion across the river would decimate the levee protecting them. Many of those forced to leave had believed until the moment they left that they had beaten the flood. Reporters too were prohibited from the danger zone. Though the tanks floated freely for days, occasionally slapping into each other, none blew.

Whenever television stations could, they covered events live either from the air or from the ground. On the first Sunday in August, the show was spectacular. It was hot, hazy and humid. On this day, it seemed even more so as the atmosphere was fed by waters that by now in many places roamed as far as the eye could see.

Virgil Gummersheimer and his family had a close-up view. He had a large farm not far from the Mississippi in Columbia, Illinois, south of St. Louis. Floodwaters were held at bay by an earthen levee. When it became clear that a portion of the levee was vulnerable and that a break was imminent, reporters scrambled like the Royal Air Force during the blitz. Gummersheimer's farm was at the most vulnerable point and at risk. The family could only ask "when?" rather than "if?" Helicopters circled like vultures, which, in a sense they were. Stations went "live" as the inevitability of what was to happen increased. The Gummersheimer farm was to become ground zero.

As people returned from church or other Sunday morning activities, they watched in horror as the levee broke and the farmhouse was simply swept away. The television video showed it all as rampaging water rushed through windows at the front of the house then poured out of those in the rear. Within minutes, the water was above the windows and minutes after that, the house was lifted from its foundation and swept away. It could be seen breaking apart in the flooded fields. The barn and silos went with it, crashing and splintering among helpless agricultural levees along the way.

A year later I visited the Gummersheimer farm. It was like the surface of the moon. Mounds of sand and gravel covered the area where the house and outbuildings had once stood. Debris from the destroyed buildings remained sprawled over several acres. Gummersheimer, who was on the south side of middle age, was still undecided whether to build on the property again. It was questionable whether the land could again be made arable in what remained of his lifetime.

He was bitter and complained without restraint about the network of levees that stretched from Minnesota to Columbia and beyond. He reasoned that he lost his farm because of the levees. They restricted the river from taking its natural course when waters rose. Levees held high water in a tight rein. The water was controlled only as long as levees were not breached. "Nature intended for the waters to spread during floods," he said. "That's God's way of feeding the land." He went on, "If the water had been allowed to take its natural course up north, the pressure would have been off us. And you city folks," he said with clear contempt, "if you didn't cover everything with so much damned asphalt and concrete, the land would absorb the rain instead of channeling it through the sewers and into the river." Gummesheimer was disconsolate and who could blame him.

The breached levee at Columbia only fed the river's appetite for destruction. The nearby town of Valmeyer was under water by dusk. It would ultimately relocate permanently on higher ground.

The historic community of Prairie du Rocher, with its celebrated fort, was threatened. The town had been settled by the French centuries earlier. The gutsy people of the late twentieth century weren't about to give it to the floods. They decided to fight the river on their own terms. Instead of fleeing, or hoping for the best, they *invited* the river in as part of a daring plan to save their town.

Engineers had a bold strategy to open the protective levee intentionally after building a second, diversionary sandbag levee. They believed they could control the floodwaters by guiding them around the town. As they awaited the river's crest only hours away, engineers and volunteers frantically set about the task of making it work. It was an enormous, long-shot challenge as workers set up a sandbagging line nearly a half mile long to get the job done. They were placing themselves at risk in doing so. If the main levee were breached before it was intentionally opened, those people, scores of them, would have been trapped. Reporters were told to leave and take their helicopters with them. The situation was so delicate and the floodwater so close to the top of the main levee, it was feared the downwash from the chopper rotor blades could create waves capable of breaching either levee before the one under construction was ready.

For a day and a half the resolute townspeople went about their work, fighting fatigue and the clock. They watched over their shoulders as the flood crest approached. Just before it did, prayers were said and fingers were crossed as the main levee was intentionally breached. The entire region cheered as the water spilled toward town, only to be turned aside and sent back to the river downstream. The flood had been successfully diverted past Prairie du Rocher just as all had both planned and hoped. The engineers and townspeople had won. It was one of the few victories over the flood that summer.

It was a summer in which the entire nation turned its attention to the waterlogged Midwest. The president and cabinet members came for first hand looks. The importance of what was going on was confirmed though, not when the politicians came, but when the top news names of the day, Jennings, Brokaw and Rather came to St. Louis to anchor their evening newscasts and show the waters and their destructive power to the entire country.

It was television in particular, and the media overall at their best. Television excels when covering unscripted events as they happen. Whether it be a Super Bowl, a political debate, or a breaking news story such as a flood, it gives the medium a chance to shine. There have been exceptions to this general rule, but when given a chance to do it right, and when it's done right, it can be extraordinary, as it was that summer.

As summer was drawing to a close and floodwaters were finally receding, autumn held the prospect of relief. However, mother nature was not finished yet. Torrential rains in September sent rivers rising once again. It was not nearly as devastating nor as long-lasting as the summer flooding. Nonetheless, many people who had only recently returned to their homes found themselves packing again and preparing for another siege. Brand new drywall was once again ruined. New carpeting was suddenly under water. This time, waters receded fairly quickly. The exhausted news media were as relieved as anyone. News organizations were far less eager for the second round than they had been to cover the first.

Finally, in early fall, the water was gone at last, but the story wasn't over. Yet to come were the assessments of damage, the tearful homecomings, the clean-up, the post-mortems from the engineers and the decisions about what should happen next. Rebuild homes? Rebuild levees? Let the rivers take back what rightfully belonged to them along the flood plain? Re-designate floodplains altogether? Buyouts? Bailouts? More government? Less government? It would remain a story for months. In many ways, the story that came after the flood was as important as the flood itself.

However, when the pictures are gone, so is the coverage. The debate about these issues was tougher to photograph. Predictably, like a wayward river, journalistic nature took its course. Reportage fell off. It stacked up poorly against what everyone had just gone through.

Except for those directly affected by the flood, the aftermath was a bore. Pictures of people standing in line with envelopes full of paperwork didn't cut it. The audience looked elsewhere to satiate its appetite for crisis and drama. And so did local television news.

That having been said, the flood proved that local media are capable of doing an exemplary job. News coverage during the weeks of the floods was at its very best by all media, especially local television. Unlike ongoing trends to trivialize the news, coverage of the flood provided information people needed to know rather than what some people cloistered in windowless newsrooms decided people *ought* to know. The coverage also provided the audience with what people wanted to know. Everyone wanted to know what areas were at risk or where the danger was lessening, what routes were available or not available for getting to and from work. It told heroic volunteers where they were needed and painted flattering pictures of people coping, fighting and winning against tough odds.

It was there when people needed it and was rewarded by higher ratings and higher circulation, the coveted Holy Grail for the media. In spite of that success, and the obvious lesson that quality journalism can beget ratings, the broadcast media returned to old ways.

Words of Wisdom from News Directors, Producers, Reporters, and Others

$\mathcal{T}$hese comments speak for themselves:

"The key to this business is honesty and integrity. Once you've learned to fake those two things, you've got it made." (Attributed to Sandor Vanocur when with NBC News)

"I want to create a 'reality-based' newscast." (News director)

"Good evening, I'm Larry Badders." (News anchorman inadvertently giving the name of a vacationing weatherman as his own at the beginning of the newscast)

"Good evening, I'm Larry Badders." (Same anchorman making same mistake the following night)

"Who says there has to be two sides to a story?" (News director)

"Who the hell is Scotty Reston?" (News producer)

"Which came first, the Great Depression or World War II?" (News reporter)

"Was the Korean War before or after World War II?" (Same news reporter)

"Who was James Michener?" (News reporter)

"Our job is to give people what they want." (News director)

"We don't do news, we do stories." (News producer)

"Who cares?" (By news producer on the death of Frank Sinatra)

"Everyone cares." (Managing editor on news the Rolling Stones would play St. Louis)

"I'm not in the news business, I'm in the entertainment business." (News director)

"I'm not a newsman, I'm a businessman." (News director)

"If people don't vote, they are not interested in election results." (News director)

"What's the big deal?" (Asked by a news producer when the Berlin Wall came down)

"Police said the victim's hands had been decapitated." (News reporter)

"Who is Lana Turner?" (Assignment editor)

"Wasn't it named after Marilyn Monroe?" (Statement by a news anchor after three years in the market about a city called Maryland Heights)

"Oh well, maybe I can go next year." (News anchor's response when told she would not be sent to cover a quadrennial national political convention)

"Let's have the meeting after the Simpsons." (10 p.m. news producer delaying prime time newscast editorial meeting)

"This is _____ _____ reporting from the scene of a devastation." (News reporter signing off after a fire partially damaged a vacant house)

"Nothing fills a television screen like a house fire. I don't care if the house is vacant." (Assistant news director)

"You're the kind who gives the homeless a bad name." (Photographer covering the Democratic convention in New York to pesky homeless panhandler)

"Television is not content, it's motion." (David Letterman)

Somalia

*D*epending on one's perspective, it was either good luck or bad luck that I found myself heading for Somalia in 1992. I think it was good luck now. At one point then, I feared for my life. Life was cheap there in those days for a lot of reasons. Somalia in the early 1990s was a country roiling with political, economic, and military tension and violence. It still is.

The sun-baked land shapes the horn on the Horn of Africa, marking the direct center of the African continent. The silvery waters of the Indian Ocean shimmer tantalizingly to the east while much of the nation is perpetually parched to the west. Sub-Saharan Africa lies beyond, including Somalia's neighbors Ethiopia and Kenya. Somalia's population is comprised primarily of pastoral nomads who move with the seasons guiding their small herds of goats, sheep, and camels to water and feeding grounds.

The Somali political situation was deteriorating and undecipherable to most Americans at this time. Rival political factions were in violent opposition. They chose sides by affiliation with one or the other of the half-dozen tribal clans that dominated the population. Each had its own militia, which might more accurately be described as gangs, and each played by its own rules. American forces would ultimately play a role, only to withdraw after the famous *Blackhawk Down* episode. The American public was drawn into the equation through heartbreaking video of starving Somalis, just as they had been years before in Biafra, and as they are at the time of this writing in Darfur. Famine and starvation are a staple of African history. The television pictures come and go. Famine in Africa remains, somewhere, always running in place.

It is as far from St. Louis as anyplace in the world and about the last place on the planet I might have expected to find myself. Yet, within a matter of hours in 1992, that is exactly where I found myself heading. If the country itself seemed in the middle of nowhere, I was soon to be moving by plane and truck in the middle of nowhere's "middle of nowhere."

My co-anchor in those days was a smart, personable, and pretty woman who was destined for bigger and better things in the world of television. She had been contacted . . . or maybe it was the other way around . . . by the ABC morning program *Good Morning America*, apparently as part of a network audition, to do some satellite reports from Somalia at the height of a famine there. I say "a" famine, because famine was an ongoing phenomenon in that part of the world then, as it is now. American television dropped in from time to time to tell the world, initiate a public outcry and a quick hit

Somali refugees

of aid, then depart, leaving the people to return to empty bowls.

The situation in Somalia was dire. Rival political factions were killing each other by the hundreds in the capital at Mogadishu. The political infrastructure was in shambles and any meaningful form of government no longer existed. A combination of natural factors

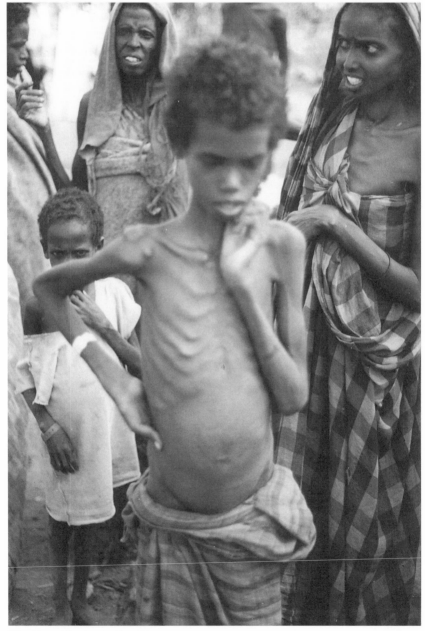

The face of famine in Somalia

conspired to make a bad situation worse. Early flooding followed by drought devastated Somali agricultural output. Food supplies dwindled. The fractured government was incapable of helping. For months the world largely ignored the crisis. Ultimately, the United States could watch no longer and initiated a relief campaign. Hundreds of thousands of tons of food were flown in and distributed in rural centers. Much of it never got where it was intended. Bands of thugs hijacked supplies and destroyed them rather than see them reach political rivals. Mogadishu was so unsettled it was off limits to any relief effort. The country was a chaotic, violent mess, and the normally placid people were paying the price. They had no place to turn and were dying by the thousands in makeshift camps and along the sides of roads.

My colleague was well aware of the danger in that part of the world. She insisted that if she went, she had to be equipped with body armor. She wanted a bullet-proof vest. Station management recused itself from the request. The torch was passed to me—not by *Good Morning America*, but by our news management, which had completed complicated arrangements for a reporter, cameraman, and producer to make the long trip to Africa's Horn to report on the relief effort. Her name was erased from the manifest. Mine was penciled in.

The hook for the entire enterprise was the fact that the Military Airlift Command, now Air Mobility Command based at Scott Air Force Base in nearby Belleville, Illinois, was running a humanitarian operation to Somalia. Local media were offered the chance to hitchhike, take a look, and spread the word. It was less about the famine than about the military's humanitarian involvement. My station signed on. We had three seats. I was now going to fill one of them. I had the passport. All I needed was a series of exotic inoculations, and I would be airborne. The next day, I was. We took a quick flight to Charleston where some fifty journalists from around the country had come together to travel to the African Horn in the huge C-130 Hercules.

Twenty hours after takeoff, our team landed in Mombasa, Kenya. Mombasa is an Indian Ocean coastal city. It's about one hundred miles south of the Somali border. It was in Mombasa that the U.S. maintained an airfield from which relief supplies were ferried into the Somali desert. Within an hour after checking into our hotel, we were advised that one such relief plane was about to make

a run. We were invited to go along for something of an indoctrina-
tion flight. It would give us an idea of what the trips were like and
what conditions were on the ground. We could go if we chose, and
our team did, along with a handful of our companions who'd come
in with us from Charleston.

A huge, olive green military cargo plane was waiting for us. An
American flag and red cross were stenciled in bold colors on the tail.
Twenty more of the cargo transports were within sight on the airfield. We anticipated a quick hop into Somalia, but in fact, the first
and subsequent daily flights deep into Somalia took two-and-a-half
hours or longer one way.

Once over Somali territory the terrain turned bleak. There was
little definition to the desert below from twenty thousand feet. A
few scrubby bushes came into view as we descended to land on an
airfield left over from the days prior to World War II, when Italy had
its hooks into that part of Africa. If anything, the terrain seemed
even more stark as we hit the ground trailing a cloud of dust. The
bleak landscape invited inevitable comparisons to the lunar surface.
There was no early evidence of a local population. We had seen no
signs of life coming in, neither people nor villages.

The rocky, sandy soil was as colorless and the heat was oppres-
sive. The scrubby bushes turned out to be miniature trees. Their
flimsy foliage extended downward from the treetops to some six or
seven feet from the sand where the branches were bare. I was later
told that foliage extended only from a point at which goats could
feed on it. They were hungry too and would literally jump at the
foliage to get to the higher levels.

The plane rolled to a stop in the middle of this bleak and arid
landscape. Skinny laborers with blue-black skin shining from their
sweat appeared as if from nowhere. They were dressed in khaki shorts
and shirts stained from their perspiration. They went right to work
as if they had gone through the routine many times before, which,
undoubtedly, they had. They had been hired by various relief agencies
on the ground designated to pick up and distribute the cargo to the villages and villagers who needed it most.

Plump burlap bags of grain were hauled from the gaping hatch
at the rear of the plane while the engines roared. There was no wasted motion as the men hauled their heavy cargo to waiting trucks

U.S. relief in Somalia

where the bags were stacked in rows that mirrored the pallets from which they had been taken from the plane. Clearly, the process was not going to take long.

Through the whirling dust we watched as a few of the local children . . . perhaps belonging to the stevedores . . . emerged tentatively and almost without notice on the fringe of the activity. They crouched at separate intervals to watch from the far edge of the runway. I was curious and wanted to get a closer look.

The noise at our landing site had not abated since our landing. The planes were in the practice of keeping engines running during the unloading process. This was to enable a rapid departure if necessary. It was another reminder that the political situation in Somalia was tenuous. Although we were in remote country, there were a number of heavily armed and increasingly brazen Somali gangs who were known to attack loaded convoys after planes had left. They stole grain and sold it elsewhere, not to starving villagers, but rather to the highest bidder. If the shipment were destined for a rival faction, they destroyed it. Their political loyalties were to themselves or to local warlords. Life *was* cheap in Somalia. Throughout the country these various gangs were given to indiscriminate murder if it would serve their interests. Given the international relief nature of the mission, and Washington's unwillingness to get involved in local politics, the American pilots were under strict orders to get airborne at the slightest indication of trouble on the ground.

Because of the noise, I continued to wear the tiny foam-rubber earplugs that had been given us as we boarded the plane. These tiny yellow plugs were remarkably proficient at reducing the noise inside the planes to bearable levels. While engines roared on the ground they were as necessary as they were in the air. I was wearing mine as I approached a skinny youngster crouching in the shadow of a tree that was struggling to survive in the dry, sandy soil.

The little boy was like so many I would come to see in the desert. He was more colorfully dressed than those unloading the plane. He wore a blue T-shirt and ragged denim shorts. Fashion was not a priority in Somalia and sometimes not a necessity. Color was. Children and adults wore a wide variety of multicolored garments. Shorts, T-shirts, and colorful fabrics wrapped sarong-like from the waist were favored. Sometimes the children wore nothing at all below the waist.

But if the omnipresent and vivid use of color impressed, there was a quality that had even more impact on strangers to this society. Somalis smiled. A lot. It seemed a part of their DNA. In Kenya in general, and in Somalia in particular, where conditions were so grim, everyone seemed to smile at the least incentive. Especially the children. They were wide, warm, friendly, innocent, and welcoming smiles that invited them into your heart.

That welcoming feature was obvious in that first youngster I met amid the noise and dust of that remote airfield. Chicklets-like teeth filled his wide grin. Communication was limited to gestures. This handsome and skinny kid with the broad smile motioned to me as if somehow beckoning. He pointed to my head. I could not make out what he was trying to say. He was muttering something I could not quite hear and would not have understood if I had. Nonetheless, I removed one of my little ear pieces which was about the size of the end of my finger. He seemed excited. His smile broadened. He extended his hand toward me as if he wanted to examine my curious accessory more closely. I could imagine him asking himself, "What is this colorful thing these white strangers have in their ears?" I handed him the one I had just taken from my ear. He promptly put it in his mouth and swallowed it.

Before making this trip to Kenya and Somalia, I had been told about a television news anchor in Dallas (who ultimately and briefly became a colleague of mine in St. Louis) who had been invited on a similar famine relief mission to Biafra a few years earlier. A monster famine there on the opposite side of Africa had captured the world's sympathy. As the story went, she had spent considerable time thinking about what she might bring as gifts for Biafran children. It was an admirable goal. She finally decided on bringing a case of lipsticks, thinking presumably, that the starving urchins might find some comfort in applying and wearing the colorful cosmetic.

She distributed the tiny golden tubes to a dozen or so of the first children she encountered at the initial village she visited, cheerfully showing each how to apply the lipstick. Their bony frames and distended bellies were a clear indication that they were indeed malnourished at best, actually starving, or at some intermediate level of deprivation. Each of the children proved adept at opening the lipsticks and twisting the base revealing the colorful makeup. To her horror as if on cue, the children began eating the lipstick. Within seconds, the crimson color adorned their lips and teeth, coloring them as they bit into the waxy makeup.

To them it was food, candy perhaps, something to eat, something to help them survive. It was gone, consumed, before she could stop them. I'm afraid the story, as it was told, subjected the newswoman to a lot of ridicule from colleagues who told the story.

Little did I know when I first heard that incident recounted that I could also be a candidate for that kind of ridicule. Fortunately, there was only the child as a witness.

Our nearly two weeks in Africa was a study in contrast: a resort hotel overlooking the Indian Ocean by night, five hours a day in the air to and from Somalia. It started with a daily pre-dawn takeoff. The mid-morning landings took place at remote airfields, a different one each day. The landing was followed by the routine unloading and loading of the plane's cargo. A wide variety of vehicles were always waiting to haul it away. Big trucks, little trucks, even some personal vehicles were used to transport the near-bursting burlap bags into the desert. The human cargo, we journalists, were shepherded from the landing field to the villages to see how the famine was be-

Somali air strip

ing managed. After unloading, the planes took off, maintaining the practice of staying on the ground no longer than necessary.

They left behind a few tough-looking men in civilian clothes lugging suitcases filled with electronic gear. They remained at the air strip after the planes departed to act as observers and to assure returning transports that it was safe to land, or to wave them off if bandits were spotted or reported in the area. It caused more than one of us on the ground to wonder what would happen to us if the planes were waved off.

The villages we visited were little more than tiny oases sheltered by a few of the desert shrubs that passed for trees. The typical village itself was usually no more than a few rows of ramshackle huts made of twigs, grasses, in some cases canvas, scraps of wood, or anything that had been scrounged for the purpose.

These camps had swelled in population over much of the southern part of the country as victims of famine came out of the desert seeking food or medical attention. Some had walked scores of miles hoping to find some respite from their desperation after they had eaten all the animals in their small herds or seen them stolen by bandits. They were left to forage in their stingy environment and eat what little they could find. Their situation was often worsened by the fact that they did not take to the road until all hope of survival was lost and they were already starving. Those who reached villages seeking help were often in the advanced stages of starvation and beyond help by the time they arrived. They had often buried family members along the way.

Given the hospitable nature of Somalis, the newcomers were welcomed by villagers who were generally in better shape because relief supplies had reached them or because they had more natural resources available to them. The more prosperous villagers kept camels near their huts, perhaps as insurance against potential starvation or to secure them from attack by bandits or those who were starving. Sometimes the starving wanderers found villages in which the population was also starving. These villagers often abandoned their homes and joined the nomadic survivors, adding to the pathetic procession in the desert.

The lucky ones found relief camps that were established just for the purpose of assisting the Somali refugees. They grew in size and number, and it was to these camps that the relief supplies we ferried were primarily directed. Some of these camps housed thousands of refugees. It was from these camps in particular that the images of starving Somalis came to America. Lethargic children rested near death in their mothers' arms as flies swarmed about them. Their fragile bones could be counted through their skin. Expressionless eyes bulging from shrunken sockets seemed larger than normal, giving the children the appearance of an alien or E.T. look. These images of children prompted the world to finally, although belatedly, address the famine.

The condition of many of the adults was at least as bad as that of the children. Day after day villagers and refugees watched new strangers who came into the camps with bodies too weak to respond and eyes that were too weak to plead, too resigned to show any hope. These, the medically worst of the refugees, would likely die in spite of the influx of grain from our planes.

Those who were stronger waited in lines to be served a form of edible sludge cooked in large metal pots along the edges of camp. The children who were strong enough were dispatched to fetch well water in dented cracker tins. It was an ongoing process throughout the day and into the night. In the morning, the dead would be hauled away and disposed of, and the process of trying to survive yet another day would begin anew for the rest.

There was a heartbreaking incident in one of the smaller villages. The village itself seemed fairly prosperous. There was water and some rather robust looking palm trees near the oasis. Some of the villagers had camels and donkeys and seemed, if not well fed, at least showing no physical signs of starvation. Refugee squatters who had come seeking help from anyone who could provide it, lived, and died, in makeshift lean-tos. A few of us reporters moved through the village taking pictures and doing interviews through interpreters. In one dramatic moment, a weeping native woman came to us holding a tiny infant in her arms. She pleaded with us to take her child with us . . . back to wherever we had come from . . . to get it the nourishment and medical assistance the baby needed to survive. It was no more than a few months old. She was willing to give her baby

Somali children with their water tins

away to save it. But it was too late. As was obvious to us, the child was dead. The interpreter told us she had been carrying the baby in her arms seeking help since the previous day, either unaware of or unwilling to accept the fact the baby had died.

We traveled by open truck from village to village or refugee camp to refugee camp. It was always uncomfortably hot and dusty as we bounced through the colorless terrain. Two vivid images remain from these trips.

I had been given a CNN baseball cap by someone on the flight from the states. I was happy to have it in the desert, where intense sunlight posed a threat. It was necessary protection for a balding, middle-aged man. At one point, after we had left one village and the driver had gotten his truck into high gear, my hat flew off, over and out of the truck behind us. Within a second or two it was fifty feet down the road. Then a hundred. I watched the gap widen when I saw a young boy rush to claim the hat in the middle of the road. He clearly knew that it had come from one of the strangers who had just visited the camp and was then somewhere behind the cloud of dust. He scooped up the cap and started running toward us as fast as he could. I waved at him to encourage the effort. But the harder he ran the wider became the distance between him and the truck. After dashing a hundred yards or so, the lad realized the futility of the chase and gave it up. I remarked to one of my colleagues as the boy disappeared in the distance that if the same thing had happened in the States, the kid who found the hat would have been running the other way.

The sights and sounds of Somalia and Kenya were remarkable for a wide variety of reasons, from the colorful and exotic to the tragic and heartbreaking. What may be the most unusual visual memory I have of that visit falls into none of those categories. It bordered on both the comic and absurd. Again, it came from the back of a truck speeding along what passed as a desert road.

From time to time, we passed huts or shacks that nomad families had set up in isolation away from nearby populated villages. Nomads are traditionally an independent lot. These isolated dwellings were undoubtedly home to the most independent of the independent. As wanderers, they tended to collect anything along the way that might be useful to them. Their huts reflected this tendency and were usually comprised bits and pieces of this and that, scraps found along the trail.

On this particular occasion we were traveling in an extremely rural part of the country. It was so far off the beaten track that we had to travel for miles to find a crude Italian airfield of which there otherwise seemed an abundance in this part of the country. We had a rendezvous scheduled with one of the cargo planes. As we approached one of the isolated huts, nothing seemed out of the ordinary. As with all the others, it appeared from a distance to be built of the usual hodgepodge of scraps. It was only when we passed directly in front of the hut that we could see the main component. Remember, we were hundreds of miles from anything that might be called a city, and at least that far from any source of electricity, which was unknown in the Somali hinterlands. Nonetheless, a rather large wooden sign formed most of the front of the otherwise decrepit hut. It read, "VCR's Repaired Here." The point of origin of that sign, and how it got to the Somali desert, remains a mystery to this day.

I have mentioned the gangs of marauding toughs who ranged over much of Somalia. They were called "Technicals." These Technicals comprised a number of irregular armies whose loyalties were to clans, warlords, individual villages, or to no one but themselves. There was little about them that was admirable. They robbed and plundered at will. They hijacked non-governmental organization (NGO) lorries and looted warehouses filled with grain destined for the starving refugees. That which they could not haul away for themselves, they destroyed to keep from their enemies.

Their victims were selected indiscriminately or arbitrarily and included the Red Cross, other non-governmental agencies, and prosperous Somalis. Anyone with anything they considered of value was a potential target. They were heavily armed with weapons of various vintages, with which they were not necessarily proficient. When they weren't stealing outright, they were demanding "tributes" of cash from victims. They had mastered the old-fashioned shakedown. Murder was also in their repertoire. On a return flight from one of our trips to the Somali hinterland I found myself sitting next to a young man I had not seen before. He was clearly in some sort of distress. I tried repeatedly to engage him in conversation but got nothing in return beyond monosyllabic grunts. I soon gave up, believing the fellow was either ill, unsociable, or exhausted. He sat with his eyes fixed on the front of the plane. Frankly, his prolonged silence and refusal to interact during the long flight made me uneasy. I was happy when we landed and he shuffled off with one of the flight crew.

I learned later that day that he was a reporter for an American magazine who had been covering the factional violence in Mogadishu with a photographer. Earlier that day or the day before, as the two of them walked on a street in the capital, one of the thugs who roamed the city calmly walked up to the pair and without warning, shot the photographer in the head. He was dead before he hit the ground. The shooter walked away laughing. There had been no motive for the shooting. There was no indication as to why he had not also shot my traveling companion. It was simply a wanton act of violence. The journalist sitting next to me on the plane was neither ill, unsociable, nor exhausted. He was in a full-blown state of shock over an incident that had occurred only a few hours earlier.

The famine and the lawlessness in Mogadishu ultimately led to the placement of U.S. troops in Somalia as part of an international relief force. Relief efforts had to be protected by a forceful presence. An initial contingent of marines landed at dawn on the beach at Mogadishu within a few weeks of the incident just described. Their arrival was reminiscent of World War II action in the Pacific as they came ashore in camouflage hauling high-caliber weapons. They were not fired upon. Within a year, however, eighteen American troops would be killed by the Somali thugs in desperate combat depicted in the book and film *Black Hawk Down*.

What made these independent militias especially dangerous was not only the fact that they were heavily armed and showed little reluctance to kill to achieve their ends, but also the fact that they were often "high" on the local drug of choice called "khat." Many Somalis and other Africans are addicted to it.

Khat is a plant that is commonly found in East Africa and the Arabian Peninsula. Its leaves produce a narcotic that is a targeted drug for many anti-drug organizations around the world. It's a mild hallucinogenic that can produce a variety of effects including stimulation, euphoria, excitement, emotional instability, tremors, and constipation, none of which is good when the user is already unpredictable and carries a gun.

The African continent is divided by many countries and even more tribes in which there are many inefficiencies that routinely lead to disruptions to commerce and national economies. Nonetheless, the distribution of khat is exported throughout the continent with remarkable efficiency. When the distribution of other commodities is stalled for any reason, khat is not. It is widely used in Somalia, one of the countries where it is grown. Users chew on the leaves of the khat plant.

The Technicals, like many in the Somali population, commonly chewed khat, which may explain some of their more unpredictable behavior. If Technicals could not be avoided, they were to be approached and dealt with extremely cautiously.

During our movement around Somalia we often saw small groups of them moving about in pick-up trucks brandishing a variety of ancient firearms. These were young, local irregulars who were held together by what they could earn "protecting" villages or by low-level looting. They were little more than local hoods, very much unlike their tougher, older, more seasoned and better organized mercenary counterparts who soldiered for clans or political organizations.

The young wannabes in the villages would undoubtedly graduate one day to the next level. On the whole, they seemed a cheerless, sullen bunch whose attempts to look threatening fell just short. They were apparently too timid to consider taking us on whether they were chewing khat or not.

Our single confrontation with the big-boy Technicals came during a visit to the town of Baidoa, an ancient city in south-central Somalia. It was one of the larger cities in that part of Somalia. It was an obvious destination for those streaming in from rural parts of the country seeking food and medicine. It had quickly overflowed with these refugees. Dozens became hundreds, hundreds became thousands. More arrived every day. They squatted on the edges of town in almost indescribable squalor. They built huts if they could find enough scraps of usable material to do so. Even a few twigs were somehow twisted together to give form to tiny structures. Rags, straw, and scraps of clothing, sometimes the clothing of the dead, were stretched across the twigs to give some protection and privacy.

But these were scenes we would only come to see once we entered the city . . . IF we entered the city. It was our intention to report on the United Nations and Red Cross effort in Baidoa. The

The Red Cross in Somalia

number of refugees there was increasing every day and the relief effort to help them had become an international story. No matter how extensive the efforts of relief agencies, they were destined to fall short every day because of the ever-increasing crush of humanity converging there.

In spite of all of the attention, and the scope of efforts to help, access to Baidoa was controlled by Technicals. There was no clear indication as to whom they gave their loyalty. A dozen of them set up a command post at the gated entrance to the town through which our vehicle had to pass. We were in a small pick-up truck. Only a few reporters from our group had decided to travel to Baidoa. The others were being escorted to different locations. As we approached the checkpoint I was wishing very quickly that we had made the same decision.

The men at the gate were distinctly different from the wannabes we had run into in the small villages. These men were older and had better weapons, which they handled so casually and carelessly as to be in itself cause for alarm and potential danger. There was something resembling a command structure or military hierarchy among the men. One of them was clearly in charge. Others repeated his orders, while others followed them. There was no mistaking their intention to stop us. What was unknown was whether they would allow us to continue and if so, at what price?

What was particularly troubling was the fact that these men were high. They were all chewing khat. Their pupils were dilated. They were anything but jovial. Their grins seemed more sinister than sincere. When they spoke they showed teeth that were discolored from the khat leaves.

Once we had arrived at the checkpoint we had, in fact, reached a point of no return. It was now up to this small band of men to determine our immediate future. From my point of view, the options were limited. They could demand of us anything they felt they might get and let us through. They could turn us back or wave us through on a whim. They could do nothing and just keep us there. My biggest fear, and I believed it to be a real one, was that they could become agitated and harm us, even shoot us. I was very frightened. These guys were high, unfriendly, and they had guns. The story of the ruthless and senseless shooting of the photographer in Mogadishu was still fresh in my mind.

Our driver, who was also our interpreter, had told us as we approached the checkpoint to say nothing to these men and to show no sign of impatience. It was strongly suggested that we avoid eye contact so as not to convey any sense of disrespect that might be misunderstood, triggering an unwelcome confrontation. The cameraman was told in no uncertain terms not to take pictures of the Technicals. Some of the Somalis were superstitious about cameras, believing that film could hold their souls captive. We were, of course, using videotape. This, however, was neither the time, the place, nor the people with whom to debate the difference.

The driver, and at one time or another, all of the men outside the truck were soon engaged in an animated conversation. It was an obvious negotiation. There was no way of knowing what was being said or whether anything was being demanded. Our well being seemed very much in the hands of this Somali driver who was also a stranger. I would write later in one of my reports that I learned something about myself in those moments. Instead of giving in to my fear and insisting that we turn back, away from these men and the threat they posed, I did not. I waited it out and was proud of myself for having done so and taken the more challenging course.

All of that was put to the test during the ten minutes or so the negotiation was taking place. Those men not taking part in the discussion were in constant motion around the truck, poking their Kalashnikovs into the bags of grain we had stashed in the bed. They were basically props to reinforce our association with the relief agencies; however, the bags could also be useful in situations such as this one either as a bargaining chip or as a form of currency.

The negotiation finally ended successfully with approval for us to enter Baidoa. It seems the NGOs had some sway over these men, probably by making sure they were well fed. Our driver told us later that the men had demanded the grain we carried. He was proud of having convinced them that some of the people inside needed it more than they did. I winced at that, thanking God he hadn't pissed them off. However, once they were convinced we belonged to their benefactors, we were allowed through without the necessity of any sort of tribute. Had they demanded money, I would have cheerfully turned over the grain and every cent I had in my pockets.

Some time later, when we were back home, I watched television coverage of Audrey Hepburn in Baidoa. She was a special envoy for the United Nations Children's Fund, UNICEF, and active in many humanitarian issues. She, likewise, was there to see how well the relief effort was going. After her visit she wrote:

I walked into a nightmare. I have seen famine in Ethiopia and Bangladesh, but I have seen nothing like this—so much worse than I could possibly have imagined. I wasn't prepared for this. The earth is red—an extraordinary sight—that deep terra cotta red. And you see the villages, displacement camps and compounds, and the earth is all rippled around them like an ocean bed. And those were the graves. There are graves everywhere. Along the road, around the paths that you take, along the riverbeds, near every camp—there are graves everywhere.[24]

Four months later, she was dead. A generation later, many of the problems she, and we, observed, remained.

Our forays into the villages in Somalia reaffirmed something that television news people have to be very careful to remember, and that viewers should understand. What is seen on the screen is not always an accurate depiction of what is actually happening. In no way do I mean to minimize what was happening in Somalia at that time.

Three hundred thousand people starved to death in the early 1990s. Clearly a tragedy by any measure. But I was struck by the fact that the pictures that we had been seeing back home were pictures of the worst of the worst. The dying, fly-besieged men, women, and children were pathetic. What is typically not shown in events of this scale is a somewhat broader view. For every dying Somali whose frightful image filled a television screen, others were nearby who were not starving and likely to survive. Not everyone was starving, yet the news pictures implied everyone was because that is all the viewers saw. That is not to say that others weren't malnourished, or might soon starve, but what the world's audience was seeing was only part of the picture. Perhaps because of that, the world tried to help and might not have if the more fortunate Somalis had been a part of those pictures depicting the horror of the situation. If the lens had zoomed out and that perspective had been broadcast, the response might not have been what it was.

So, what should the journalist do? Give that full perspective or focus only on the worst or most dramatic? A camera's lens can distort. A small group can be made to appear like a mob. A ten-pound fish can be made to look like a monster. Pictures focusing on the devastation left by a tornado or other natural disaster can imply an entire community was erased unless the wider area showing what was spared is also shown. Television audiences should realize that what they see on screen is but a fragment, the Mona Lisa's eyes without the smile, which, of course, makes what we saw in Somalia no less heartbreaking.

Finally, as startling as many aspects of the trip to Somalia were, and as dangerous as some of our situations might have been, one final fright remained before departure. Our hotel on the Indian Ocean coast on the outskirts of Mombasa was by most standards a luxury establishment. It was a typical resort hotel in the sense that a few dozen rooms were located in a single building. Then there were some one- and two-story bungalows scattered among the palms on the extensive grounds of the complex. Winding paths guided guests and staff around the lush park-like setting. A constant ocean breeze could always be counted on and was always welcome there.

Small monkeys populated the trees and were always seen scampering around the lawn and trees much as squirrels do at home. The little creatures were used to the human activity and had no fear of people. In a short period of time, we newcomers became quite used to their coming and going just as they had gotten used to us.

On my final morning as I was shaving before departure, I almost cut my throat in the process when I saw movement behind me in the mirror. Startled, I turned around quickly, taking an unintended swipe at my carotid artery in the process. There on the balcony railing staring at me intently sat one of the little creatures. At first, it scared the hell out of me. He, or maybe she, seemed to show some interest in me in my half-naked state. Perhaps it was intrigued because my face was covered in shaving cream or because I stood immobilized staring back at it. Not yet proficient in protocol when it came to visiting monkeys, I was not quite certain what I should do about this uninvited guest. Quite suddenly, it began to shriek in what I can only believe was a cry of fear, a robust belly laugh, or a call to comrades to "Come have a look at this." I guess I won the staring contest. After a moment or two, it left, scampering up a nearby tree.

A few moments after that, I too was gone. A big C-130 lifted us out over the Indian Ocean, then north to Cairo, London, and, finally, to the United States, a long way from the awful tragedy that was, and remains to this day, Somalia.

USS Missouri

Over the course of a long career in broadcast journalism, there have been many thrills. I have interviewed presidents, show business celebrities, and leaders in the world of science, business, and academia. I have attended historic events that have included Mikhail Gorbachev's visit to the Missouri college where Winston Churchill made his famous "Iron Curtain" speech. I have covered summit conferences, ten national political conventions, and the inaugurations of three presidents. I have had the privilege of meeting a diverse array of people like Andres Segovia and Harry Chapin Carpenter, Martha Graham and Cyd Charisse, Stan Musial and Pete Rose, Nancy Wilson and Leontine Price, Lee Iococca and Michael Millikan, Jerry Lewis and Garrison Keillor.

I don't think any opportunity to rub shoulders with history or those who helped make it is more firmly locked in my memory than the chance to travel to Hawaii aboard the historic battleship the *USS Missouri*. It was her final voyage. The voyage was to be a last hurrah. She was to be a key player in fiftieth anniversary ceremonies commemorating the Japanese attack on Pearl Harbor.

The *USS Missouri* is one of the most famous warships in American history and the last battleship ever built by this country. She spent most of the war years under construction at the Brooklyn Naval Yard but got into the fray in time to participate in the Battles of Iwo Jima and Okinawa where she was struck and shook off a glancing blow by a kamikaze suicide plane. It was on the *Missouri* that Japan formally surrendered in Tokyo Bay in 1945.

The *Missouri* saw action in the Korean War, after which she was decommissioned and put into "mothballs" where she remained for years in ghostly formation with other retired vessels. Life was breathed back into her in 1984 when she was modernized and returned to service. She fired the first shot in the 1991 Gulf War and served with distinction in the Persian Gulf before she was again decommissioned for the last time, having earned eleven battle stars and a rightful place in U.S. Naval history.

USS Missouri berthed at Pearl Harbor at twilight, December 6, 1991

The *Missouri*'s final voyage under her own steam came in December 1991 when she set sail from Long Beach, California, bound for Pearl Harbor and ceremonies commemorating Japan's attack. I was privileged to be aboard. A number of Missouri journalists were invited on the journey to document this historic voyage and honor the vessel named after their state. The Missouri connection went beyond the name of the ship. A number of weapons used in the Gulf War had been built by St. Louis firms. Margaret Truman, daughter of the Missouri-born president who loved the vessel, helped launch the ship almost half a century earlier and later presided over ceremonies when she was re-commissioned after a short retirement. Sterling silver gifts presented to the *USS Missouri* from various nations around the world are housed at the Missouri statehouse. The ties are strong.

There were dozens of print and broadcast journalists from around the country onboard for the journey as well. Former crew members were invited to make the trip, and scores did, including two former crewmembers whose cremated remains were aboard for a burial at sea. As former crewmen, they were entitled to that rite.

A number of other military and civilian dignitaries were aboard, including several naval historians. No one aboard who sailed from Long Beach was unaware of the ship's important history or the nostalgic nature of this final mission.

Scores of sightseers were aboard the vessel when I arrived some two hours before the scheduled departure. They were taking photos on the gleaming teak deck and at the embedded plaque commemorating the Japanese surrender. Several Japanese were among the visitors and stood at the historic spot for souvenir photos just as eagerly as everyone else. There were photos of visitors examining the scar left by that Japanese kamikaze just off the main deck.

We weighed anchor at mid-morning the day after Thanksgiving. Conditions were ideal. Under bright sunshine, blue Long Beach skies, and a snappy, salty breeze, we set sail for the horizon and Hawaii, two thousand miles away. Commander Lee Kaiss, who had been in command throughout the *Missouri*'s Gulf War service, was at the helm. When the Missouri fired the first salvo of that war on January 17, Kaiss' unforgettable words launched the war: "We're going to kick some ass. Everybody stand by."

We left port in perfect sailing weather, but it didn't last long. Within hours, the ship was being battered by fifty-mile-an-hour winds and heavy seas. A general order was quickly issued and was very specific; no one but authorized personnel was allowed on deck. No one had the inclination. The nine-hundred-foot-long vessel creaked and groaned. Huge engines generating 212,000 tons of horsepower pushed 60,000 tons of steel through swells as high as a two-story house. The sea pushed back. Some seasoned sailors onboard said the conditions were the worst they'd ever experienced. The ornamental ship's bell weighing hundreds of pounds was torn from its mount and bounced around the deck tearing big chunks from the thick teak. We could hear it below. It thundered as it roamed the deck like a giant Ahab. Remarkably, it remained onboard.

So-called "small" or auxiliary boats fastened to the side of the mother ship just above the main deck were batted around. Some were partially torn away from their moorings as lines holding them snapped in the storm. They remained partially secured, suspended precariously over the deck below by the few lines that remained intact. The prohibition against going on deck remained in effect all

USS Missouri storm damage

that first day, all that night, and the next day while we rode out the storm. Only those trained to deal with the damage were allowed topside. We waited below until the most dangerous of the damage had been attended to and all was proclaimed secure. By then the *Missouri* was negotiating the tranquil waters of the South Pacific, a welcome change to those of us . . . all of us . . . suffering from cabin fever.

I was not accompanied by any of my colleagues from KTVI. We were allowed only one berth on the *Missouri*. Arrangements had been made for me to share a cameraman accompanying a high-profile anchorman from Los Angeles. The cameraman was a talented photographer and a good guy, but he was not happy about pulling double duty. The arrangement meant he was supposedly at my beck and call as well as that of his partner, whom everyone onboard was soon to call "Hollywood Harold." Harold was a forty-something egocentric creature who pretty much considered himself a big deal. In actuality, he was less talented than he believed, with people skills that hinted he might have been an early charm school dropout. It was obvious from the outset that he was outright hostile to me. He was furious that his bosses had allowed the sharing arrangement.

He made it clear he wanted no part of it and was quite disinclined to honor the deal. This was a problem inasmuch as we were already out to sea and I had no other means of getting the pictures for the reports I was expected to have prepared and ready to broadcast when we reached Hawaii. I was also charged with putting all my material together for a documentary to air some weeks into the new year.

The cameraman and I ultimately worked out a method whereby he would work for me when Harold was otherwise occupied. He promised to overshoot for Harold where he could so there would be video available for me. It proved very awkward. Harold had the photographer for situations in which I also needed him, which meant that Harold controlled what video was shot. I could share it, but Harold had a penchant for putting himself in most scenes. Harold on deck. Harold on the bridge. Harold in the engine room. Harold in the Combat Engagement Center. Harold talking to seamen. Harold in the officer's mess. Harold, Harold, Harold. Different outfits in every scene, perfect hair and teeth. That made much of the video virtually useless to me. Clearly, Harold thought that he, not the *Missouri,* was the story.

Furthermore, as I watched him operate, it was also clear that he had no plan as to what he wanted to do. I can only assume that Harold was more than a little insecure in his role as reporter. Couple that with a colossal ego and each exaggerated the other. He might have been pretty good in the studio, otherwise why would he be making a good living in a major market? That does not necessarily translate into commensurate reportorial skills.

Hollywood Harold was the kind of television person who gives the medium and the people in it a bad name. I once overheard a former colleague giving advice to a young television reporter. This particular reporter had reached a point, as some do, at which he thought he was irreplaceable. He was on television, after all, and people recognized him when he was out in public. The public tends to give people they see on television a higher level of celebrity than those in other high-profile professions or accomplishment. It's one of the reasons people who have just experienced tragedy bother responding to the TV reporter's question of "how does it feel?" That special status can be fairly heady. My colleague tried to get the young reporter back into the real world with these words: "It's not you. It's what you do." She told him that people were reacting only to the fact that he was "on television." It seemed to work with this young man.

Obviously, no one had taken the trouble to pass that lesson along to Hollywood Harold. He was a fixture on West Coast television and undoubtedly made big money. Onboard this ship, however, he was ridiculed for his runaway ego, self-focus, and his continuous attention to personal detail and comfort. The people on the *Missouri* had never seen Harold on television. They could only judge him by how he acted around them. They saw him as a boor and a fop.

The quarters available to us were not plush. We were assigned wooden bunks that were stacked four deep in quarters that were the size of a walk-in closet. There was no room to spare in the bunks. They were hard and narrow, only as wide as the average occupant was wide, and as long as the average occupant was long. It was like sleeping in an open coffin. The digs were not plush enough for Harold, who demanded something more comfortable. Remarkably, he got his wish, if for no other reason than to shut him up.

He spent much of his energy pursuing the only woman onboard. That was Lieutenant Commander Susan Fitzgerald. She was an attractive officer with an impressive résumé. It included a specialty in explosives demolition. She had put it to good use during the Gulf War as a member of the ship's Explosive Ordnance Detachment. While assigned to the *Missouri* during the hostilities, her job was to lead small teams of demolition experts into the Persian Gulf's waters to disarm Saddam Hussein's mines. They had to physically enter the water to do so. Any ship that brushed against the spikes on these bobbing bombs could be seriously damaged or sent to the bottom. Disarming them was both delicate and dangerous.

Harold was a lot less dangerous, and a lot less delicate. He made his predatory intentions clear to any who would listen that he was on an amorous exercise. He predicted success and stated that he would bed her before we arrived at Pearl. Lieutenant Commander Fitzgerald seemed mindful of Hollywood's intentions and managed, with a little help from her friends, to keep him at a somewhat greater distance than she had those floating mines.

While Harold was doing his thing, the rest of us were doing ours. Our days were filled with our own routine. We had our work, and the Navy kept us busy with frequent tours of the ship. Tours were organized from bow to stern, from top to bottom. There was lots to see. We went to the very bottom, twenty-seven feet below the water line where the hull is protected by thirteen inches of armor. Access was through a maze of narrow hatches that impeded progress under ideal conditions. Those who worked "below" were, in fact, submariners. If the ship was struck by a torpedo, a bomb, a mine, or suffered an onboard explosion, their chance of survival was virtually nil.

We visited the turrets from which the guns were loaded. The shells fired from the signature sixteen-inch guns weighed a ton each, about the same as a Volkswagen. They stood chained in rows of cold steel awaiting the call to action. Yet their accuracy was legend. We watched a video showing one of them hit and vaporize a target in the Iraqi desert.

The video was taken from cameras aboard a drone plane. These miniature, unmanned, and unarmed reconnaissance planes were launched from the *Missouri*. Their mission was enemy target acquisition. In-flight video was transmitted to the ship continuously. When targets were acquired, precise location coordinates were also transmitted, allowing gunnery officers to zero in and fire the big guns. Mighty Mo's guns were fired more than eight hundred times during the Gulf War, many times at targets acquired by the drone. Targets miles away never heard the shot and never knew what hit them. The drone found them. *Missouri*'s gunners did the rest.

One of those drone planes was aboard the *Missouri* on our trip. It was flown every day while we were at sea, ostensibly for training purposes, but undoubtedly also to impress the visitors onboard. It was much smaller than a single-engine plane. Its wingspan was no more than twenty feet. It was of such size and configuration that at very low altitude it looked like an actual warplane flying much higher. We were told of an incident during the war in which one of these drones was flying over a small offshore Iraqi island occupied by dozens of Saddam's soldiers.

Those monitoring the video onboard the ship were startled when the pictures showed the soldiers below staring at the drone with their hands in the air. They were surrendering. Helicopters carrying several officers were dispatched from the ship to the island where they landed and processed the surrendering troops. In effect, the Iraqis had surrendered to a miniature, unarmed, unmanned airplane without a shot being fired. Had they not surrendered, and they had no way of knowing it, they might have been visited instead by one of those sixteen-inch shells.

The *Missouri* also carried weapons other than the big guns. Tomahawk and Harpoon missiles were part of the arsenal, along with smaller defensive weapons. They were controlled in what civilians would call a war room, but which was known officially as the CEC, the Combat Engagement Center. The activity and equipment in this room was highly classified. The CEC was located near the bridge. It was a relatively small room and so dark it took several seconds for a visitor's eyes to adjust. Several computer terminals were set up at intervals around the room. Young officers, all of whom seemed to be in their early twenties, sat before them. At first we thought they were playing video games. The graphics on their screens were big, colorful, and animated. One of the officers explained that this was the nerve center for combat operations. Using intricate calculations programmed by this equipment, the officers could target and fire most of the weapons onboard the ship. It was what one of the young men called "gee whiz" stuff that was capable of wreaking enormous destruction very quickly and very accurately.

These young men were the first of the Nintendo generation. They had grown up playing video games and were probably more comfortable using this equipment than their predecessors had been doing it the old-fashioned way. Goodbye Kentucky windage, hello Super Mario Brothers. It answered a question I had had in earlier years about the amount of time my own children had spent playing video games. I thought it was time wasted until I rationalized that there was value in developing hand-eye coordination and value in learning the rules of major sports while playing them on the TV or computer. Little did I know then that the development of hand-eye coordination and skillful use of joy sticks might mean the difference between victory and defeat in the next generation's war.

A ship the size of the *Missouri* is a city. The people who populate it are a community joined in common purpose and in common experience. As we neared Pearl Harbor, it all came into play. It was time to spruce up for the ceremonies ahead. A new life came to the ship. Every member of the crew was put to work giving the vessel a spit-shine inside and out. The teak decks were scrubbed, bulwarks were soaped and hosed, new paint was applied to anything that showed a hint of rust. Sailors were busy everywhere. One of them was a seaman who didn't have to work at all. He had won the lottery not once, but on three different occasions. He was rich, but he loved the Navy.

Sprucing up the ship was a mission within a mission for the crew and a special time in the history of a special vessel. Its final glory was coming. Everything was being done to ensure it would look its best for the final role. By the time it pulled into Pearl Harbor, it was ready for a final close-up.

We were busy too. My Los Angeles colleagues had brought video editing equipment onboard. As part of the arrangement, my photographer would be editing the material I was putting together for satellite transmission to St. Louis upon our arrival. I had written several pieces on the voyage focusing on the ship, the voyage itself, and people from the St. Louis area who were part of the historic event. Of course, Harold had to go first. He took his time, putting me in yet another precarious position. My material was expected in St. Louis as soon as we docked. Arrangements had been made for me to do a series of live reports over the course of the day and evening on the eve of the anniversary of the attack. Fresh material was expected for each one. We managed to get most of the material completed. I took the time to have a look at what Harold had done and was gratified to see that he used a great deal of the material that had been shot expressly for me, including interviews with Commander Kaiss and other officers as well as one or two St. Louis crew members. Of course, there was an abundance of coverage of Harold himself. Not surprising. Also not surprising, was a parting shot from Harold. But ultimately, I had the last laugh.

The arrival at Pearl was unforgettably special in so many ways. Every person on the ship, save those necessary to bring her in, was ordered to the deck as dawn broke. It was a traditional ceremony at Pearl known as "Manning the Rails." It's a tribute to the USS Arizona by ships entering the port. Uniform of the day was dress whites. Everyone who was available ringed the deck and stood at the rails in rigid attention. The sun was coming over Diamond Head as the *Missouri* turned into Pearl Harbor. The golden morning rays lighted the ship as if it had all been staged by a Hollywood director. Battleship gray was transformed into a golden luster. Starched whites turned golden. The sun's reflection played on the gentle waters and painted the Arizona Memorial resting serenely nearby. Yes indeed, the *Missouri* was ready for its close-up. Whistles piped and flags whipped as the ship lumbered toward its berth trailing a golden wake.

Our arrival was during the exact moments of precisely 49 years and 364 days earlier when the Japanese attacked Pearl Harbor. Except for the scene we were a part of, everything must have been very much as it had been that Sunday morning, the tranquility, the lighting, the vulnerability. One could not help but think of that as the *Missouri* docked at a respectful distance from the *Arizona* near the place that years later would become her permanent home.

The silence was broken by the rattle of a heavy chain holding the anchor as it dropped to the bottom. Still to come were the ceremonies in which the president of the United States would preside. The *USS Missouri* was to be the stage. Pearl Harbor and the *Arizona* would be the set for an audience that would watch around the world.

After the unforgettable six-day cruise marked by revelation, frustration, and a little relaxation, it was time to go to work. Arrangements had been made before my departure for a carefully choreographed technical adventure. With the material we had produced on the ship in hand, it was now left to get it home to St. Louis. A technical crew had been hired for transmitting the pieces produced onboard ship by satellite back to St. Louis. I was to introduce those pieces live from alongside the *Missouri* throughout the day during several local St. Louis newscasts.

The site selected at Pearl Harbor offered an impressive view of the docked battleship that had been my home for the past week. The local crew had all the facilities necessary to transmit everything by satellite. And everything went according to plan. Almost.

Part of the arrangement had been that the Los Angeles photographer who had accompanied us on the trip was to actually shoot the live shots. Turned out, he was a no-show. I was to learn later that he was, on Harold's instruction, off shooting something relatively unrelated to anything that involved the *USS Missouri*. This was in direct disregard of the arrangement between his station and mine.

Fortunately, the technicians handling the live transmission to St. Louis had the necessary equipment and expertise to get the job done. So, we were stiffed by the Los Angeles crew (something for which the photographer apologized after I returned to St. Louis) but saved by the technical people in Hawaii. It went without a hitch except for those obstacles concocted by Hollywood Harold. By the way, my documentary on the *Missouri* won a regional Emmy the following spring. In my remarks at the awards ceremony, I did not thank Hollywood Harold. Why he took the approach he did remains one of those mysteries. As I indicated earlier, however, the final laugh was mine.

Following this voyage, the *Missouri* was towed to Bremerton, Washington. She did not steam under her own power ever again. It was less expensive to tow her back. Once at Bremerton she was again decommissioned, and again she took her place among the ghost ships that had served the country so well. Just as in her past sojourn at Bremerton, it was not to be her final resting place. Amid some controversy, she was towed back to Pearl Harbor almost a decade later where she became a floating museum. She now stands as if on sentry duty guarding the *USS Arizona*.

The *Arizona* is a national shrine. It honors those 1,177 souls who went down with her, as well as all who died in the December 7, 1941, Japanese attack.

There's a certain symmetry to these two ladies resting now at that place. The death of the *Arizona* marked the beginning of World War II. As a museum, the *Missouri* is the place where that conflict formally ended. Its role now is as protector of those still entombed below so that they may always rest in peace.

Under Siege

*S*uch are the uncertainties of modern communication technology that one, like myself, is never quite certain of not only how pictures and sound fly through the air, but of who might be listening in. Apparently during my satellite transmissions from Hawaii, someone in Hollywood Harold's town was listening. In this case, it was producer/director Andrew Davis. He was in the later stages of completing a major film, tentatively titled *Dreadnaught*. It was a Steven Seagal adventure film with Tommie Lee Jones and Gary Bussey, among others. I was to become one of the "others" in a very peripheral way. The plot revolved around the terrorist hijacking of a U.S. battleship and the heroic Seagal's successful intervention. It was a film that eventually made more than $100 million and proved successful in theaters, rentals, and VHS and DVD sales. I'm led to understand that at one time it was the number one movie watched in hotels. That may have had something to do with a pretty girl jumping out of a cake wearing nothing but her freckles.

I enjoy telling people that although I did not get the girl, I am still getting royalties fifteen years after the fact. True, they amount to less than ten dollars a year at this stage, but at one time, they added up to a few hundred bucks per annum.

I was preparing to go to the 1992 GOP National Convention in Houston when I received a phone call from someone associated with the *Dreadnaught* production and asked if I might be interested in doing some narration for the film. Of course, I thought it was a joke. The caller persisted while emphasizing that this had to be done quickly. I was finally convinced this was on the level, but I had to explain that I was just about to travel to the convention and would be unavailable for the week. The caller wondered if I could record the lines in Houston if they faxed the script. I thought that was possible and gave her my contact numbers.

There was no contact in Houston. I thought it might have been a prank after all and that my chances for a star on the Hollywood Walk of Fame had sunk to about the same level as having a star on

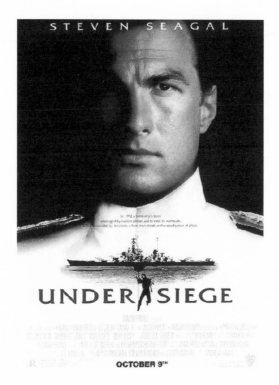

the Walk of Fame in St. Louis. I was only back from Houston for a week or so when I received another call with an apology and an explanation. The script had not been finalized, and producers decided they would prefer to do the recording themselves to ensure the highest possible quality. Would I mind coming out to Hollywood to track the narration? No, I would not mind.

So, within a few days I found myself driving to the airport in the pouring rain for an early morning flight to Los Angeles. Not more than a mile from the airport, traffic came to a halt. There was no obvious reason for the stall. I had left myself plenty of time to get to my gate. I had no luggage for the one-day trip. I didn't begin to worry until the minutes began ticking off and it was getting dangerously close to flight time. It had reached the point where I'd considered abandoning my car on the side of the road, and making for the airport on foot. I gave up on that idea. It was raining too hard and the airport was too far away.

Still no explanation as to the reason for the delay until a radio newscast solved the mystery. President Bush was visiting St. Louis that day. Air Force One had landed at a private section of the airport. All of this was expected and his route into the city had been well publicized the day before so commuters could take potential delays into account. When a president comes to town and is on the move, everything along his route shuts down. Traffic is stopped in its tracks until the chief executive is safely past any given point. The shutdown precedes the president by fifteen minutes or so and continues for several minutes after he's moved on. Then, of course, the backed up traffic has to unsnarl itself before it can get moving again. Presidents probably lose a lot of votes that way when they travel. People may forgive a lousy tax policy. Inconvenience is another matter.

The publicized route for Mr. Bush's travel into downtown St. Louis did not include any of the highways I would be using to get to the airport, so I hadn't worried about any disruption to my trip. The newscaster informed me, however, that on landing Mr. Bush had decided on a side trip into town to take a passerby look at some project in which he was interested. That route did involve my path to the airport, which is why I wound up standing in place when I should have been strapping myself into a TWA jetliner.

My panic level had just reached full gestation and I had pretty much given up on chances of making the flight when traffic began to stir. Slowly, ever so slowly, the automobiles began to move. Ten minutes later, I was running for the gate. I was the last person to board.

A limo was waiting for me at the Los Angeles airport, and I was beginning to feel like a big shot as we whisked off to a studio lot. It is easy to understand how people can get used to this kind of lifestyle. Here I, a nobody, was being as pampered as a Hollywood somebody. I could only imagine what life might be like for a star.

I was taken to the Warner Brothers complex where we stopped among a group of small and identical cottage-like buildings that lined the street on both sides. These were apparently used as the temporary offices for production companies using the Warner Brothers lot and facilities. I was directed to one where I found a few people inside. It was busy with office-like activities involving telephones, computers, and fingernail files. The young lady applying a self-manicure didn't miss a beat as she looked up. I picked up the inquiring eyes but wasn't at all sure that there was an "enquiring mind" that went with them. I gave her my name. She dabbed at the phone buttons, mumbled something, and I waited.

Not long. Andy Davis, the producer/director of *Dreadnaught*, was out of a second room quickly and ushered me in. He was a pleasant but somewhat harried young man who did not fit the stereotype of either producer or director. He was sort of geekish but friendly. We went through the usual pleasantries, then got down to business. He told me the film was in its final stage and that my part was the final element. The film, re-titled *Under Siege*, was to be released in a month.

The script was ready, he said, except for maybe a slight change or two and that if I was ready, we could go over to the studio and get going. The "studio" was more like an airplane hangar, or perhaps even more like a professional hockey rink after the game is over and the fans have gone. Lighting inside was at a minimum. In one corner, about a mile-and-a-half away, I could see some activity and was told that was where the technicians were. I had been expecting a table or podium and a microphone to do the recording. Facilities for voice-overs usually run the size of a small WC. Instead of being taken to a table, I was led to the middle of this huge room where a single microphone hung suspended from a ceiling so high I couldn't even see it.

He gave me the script. It was about three pages long. I figured they'd wind up using a sentence, maybe two, in the film. He told me he was having trouble with one part of the script. The conversation went something like this:

Davis: "Here's the problem. The way it reads now is . . . 'fifty years ago today, the infamous Japanese surprise attack destroyed Pearl Harbor. . . .' What do you think?"
Marsh: "What do you mean?"
Davis: "Well, I'm not sure whether we should say Japanese or Jap."
Marsh: "Japanese is probably more politically correct."
Davis: " I know, but everybody called them Japs."
Marsh: "They did then."
Davis: "Yeah. But this is now. I'm not sure. Jap sounds good . . . but maybe not better. Japanese is okay, but I like the sound of Jap."

He went back and forth on it for another minute or two. Finally, I said, "Why not just say 'fifty years ago today . . . someone invaded Pearl Harbor.'"

I was trying to be funny. He didn't get it and actually looked as if he were considering it. He wasn't. "Let's go with Japanese," he said. "This has to sound like a today newscast."

That was my role. I was to voice-over video of Pearl Harbor anniversary ceremonies showing President Bush aboard the Battleship *Missouri*. I had no idea how it would be employed in the film. I was more certain than ever that only a few of the words before me would make it to the screen. As it turns out, it kind of set the stage for the film very early on. Then, exit Marsh stage right.

The process didn't take very long. Davis thanked me. His last words suggested that I be sure to look for my name in the film credits. That was the last I ever heard from him or his staff. An hour or two later, I was back at LAX awaiting my flight back to St. Louis.

I was eager to see the final product and would be lying if I didn't admit to being a little full of myself for actually being in a Hollywood movie. It was a big deal to me. So, when it finally came out, I, my wife, and two young children were among the first in line. I was thrilled when the film virtually opened up with my narration, and I was surprised that every word I had recorded had been used. It was a pretty entertaining movie too. I was feeling like pretty much the big shot until the end of the movie. My family and I stayed to watch the credits. Everyone wanted to see my name listed among the stars. We were the only people left in the theater when the credits stopped rolling. My name was not among them. Every hair stylist, boom operator, and even the assistant camera operator for the assistant cameraman was listed, but I was not. To quote a song: "Fame if you win it comes and goes in a minute."

Well, I got over it, because a lot of people locally realized I did have a role, however anonymous it turned out to be. From what I've been able to piece together, the narration was an afterthought, a necessary afterthought. For some reason, the original opening, however it was structured, didn't work, and they had to come up with a "device" to get into it. The narration was the device. It had all happened so late in the production schedule, and so shortly before the release date, that all the graphics for the movie had long since been in the can. When Mr. Davis was assuring me of my "credit" in the film, there was no way it could or would be there.

I also learned later that none other than Hollywood Harold, whose material ten months earlier from Hawaii had also been eavesdropped on, was also considered for the narration. However, I apparently had "the sound" they wanted, so I got the gig. To this day, people ask me, "Was that your voice in *Under Siege?*" Eat your heart out Harold.

One final point to my one and only brush with Hollywood glory: Some months later, I noted that *Under Siege* had been nominated for two Academy Awards. Both of them were in "best sound categories." Hey, I thought to myself, I was part of the sound. If *Under Siege* wins an Oscar, it's going on my résumé. I could see it then . . . "Academy Award–winning newsman, etc. . . . ." No such luck. *Lion King* won them both. And you thought Hollywood Harold had an ego!

Humor

*H*umor in most newsrooms and among most journalists I have known would hardly live up to its name in much of polite society. Journalists are generally exposed to so much pain, deprivation, violence, and corruption during their careers that the only way to counter career-long depression is to look at most things through a comic lens. Dead babies and disabilities can get more laughs than a Chevy Chase pratfall. It is a defense mechanism. Learning to laugh at misfortune in any form is the only way many can cope. Journalists are exposed to calamity as part of the daily grind. Even the worst of it is sanitized by copy and video editors before it reaches the breakfast table or the sofa. Journalists see the raw product of news, the worst of the ingredients. If what you see or hear bothers you at the consumer end of the chain, consider what it might do to those on the assembly line. So, dark humor is commonplace.

At least it's humor.

I could recite any number of *bon mots* that would enrage or offend or wear a book editor's red pencil to the nub. However, the best one-liner I may have come across is thirty-five years old, and I still remember it word for word. It is only partially offensive and only slightly crude.

Years ago, a certified weirdo was terrorizing co-eds on college campuses. Was he murdering? No. Was he raping? No. Was he burglarizing their dorm rooms and stealing their jewelry? No. Was he flashing? No. Was he stalking? No. Was he using vile and offensive language? No. What he was doing was breaking into their bedrooms and . . . giving them enemas! That's right. In the dead of night he somehow managed to enter their dorm or apartment bedrooms and give them enemas. No sexual contact. No physical violence. No dialogue.

It is difficult to imagine the kind of mind at work on such a fetish. One might muse over its origin and development, but that brings us back to the dark side again. The villain carried on this activity for a period of several weeks at a number of colleges and universities in Southern Illinois. The number of times he "struck" is not clear, but numerous incidents were reported. It was sufficient to instill a great deal of fear among young women. Little wonder!

The institutions put out numerous warnings and offered advice on means potential victims might use to protect themselves. At one stage, during this reign of terror, one of our news department wags delivered the memorable line. He said that, "This guy should be called public enema number one."

There you have it. Maybe you had to be there. It was a pretty good spontaneous utterance, especially when you consider some potential alternatives. I'll leave them to you. In fact, I'll just leave you . . . but with some final thoughts.

A Reflection

Reviewing the years as I have done is a bittersweet experience. There are literally thousands of Flash Frames in a long career. Some make me smile, some are embarrassing, and of course, there is some sadness for what has become of the business. As I read back over my narrative, I find that I have had a growing tendency to be critical of the profession that has enabled me to pay the mortgage, feed and clothe my family, send the kids to school, and see them on their way to their own series of Flash Frames. Maybe this will help them understand what I have been up to all these years.

It is important to say as I begin this reflection that it has not been my intention to issue a blanket indictment of the industry that I have been a part of for so many years. I must establish that there are some enlightened owners and many very talented and dedicated people in television news. My criticisms and complaints are directed at what I believe is an ever-growing number of people who have put ratings and profits above any sense of responsibility to the communities they serve. Talented and committed journalists are often thwarted in their desire to do good journalism. News programmers, goaded by owners, have in recent years shown an insatiable appetite for irrelevant news that has increasingly tended to focus on random crime, pop culture, and meaningless banter. I see it as a clear effort to pump up ratings and profits rather than to serve the public in a more meaningful way.

My career has taken me from, if not the best of times, then from better times. There was once a much stronger commitment to community and innovation. And a lot of people got into television journalism motivated by a desire to be part of a medium that could use its attributes to the fullest and put a mirror to society to help it better understand itself. This desire began to change in the 1970s and was soon cascading out of control. The line between information and entertainment became increasingly blurred. A new word, "infotainment" was created and insidiously became the bedrock upon which local television news departments built their commitment to the communities they were supposed to be serving.

In the early days of the medium, the job of the journalist was to give people the information they needed to help them make intelligent decisions about their lives and their communities. Now, the mission is to give the audience what it wants. That's because television is a business, and business is designed to make money. If people don't watch, advertisers can't be charged premium rates. Complicating matters is the fact that viewership is eroding and fragmenting as a result of an ever-increasing number of cable television channels, the Internet, and viewer dissatisfaction. The bean counters have determined that audiences want mindless matter, gossip, and pop culture as news. That's why most viewers today know more about Michael Jackson and Anna Nicole Smith than they do about Vladimir Putin or Mahmoud Ahmadinejad. Infotainment has blended news and entertainment so that they are often indistinguishable.

In 1968, a seminal year in American history, the average political sound bite on a newscast ran for forty-eight seconds. They were called "talking heads" and were the words of people interesting enough to be put on television or the radio. The average sound bite in the most recent national election was about six seconds. No one can say very much in six seconds. I can think of a few politicians, however, for whom six seconds is too much time. It is more than adequate for most celebrities.

But content, context, and substance no longer seem the point. The point is to keep the video moving and not slow it down with mere words. In television, it's pictures that count. A quote attributed to comic David Letterman says that "television is not content . . . it's motion." That motion is designed to keep the remote control out of the viewers' hands. Keep them focused. Immobilize them! Given all the technology associated with television these days, the remote control and TiVo may be the most important. The biggest dilemma for programmers is how to keep people from using either to sidestep commercials. Motion that immobilizes is one device.

Emphasis on the aesthetic aspect of presentation has always been important, but it has increased recently. As technology has allowed it, flashing, sliding graphics—the whistles and bells of production—give newscasts the now-you-see-it-now-you-don't look Letterman was talking about. Anchorpersons seem more often selected for their appearance and how well they match the demographics of the audience than for their journalistic credentials or expertise. I knew a line had been crossed several years ago when most of the ten finalists in a Miss America contest said they aspired to be news anchorwomen. I'll wager that every one of them who wanted it realized that ambition. Then, of course, there was the short-lived reality show in which a bikini model was signed on as an anchorwoman for a month on a real newscast at a real station effectively erasing the "info" from infotainment.

Language is also an issue. Writers in an earlier era of broadcasting respected language and knew how to use it, as did the on-air readers of those words. It may have been that they were all educated differently or that they often came from the print media, where words and their meaning mattered. Or it may have been that they were not encouraged, as broadcasters are today, to articulate colloquially. Was it stuffier? Probably. I was once instructed to write "like I was writing for the *New York Daily News* rather than the *New York Times.*" However, what has become less stuffy has become less precise, often misleading, and perhaps even desensitizing.

I often refer to an article by Jim Mitchell I found in the *Arizona Republic* earlier this decade. He refers to television newscasting as a "performance" that "apes its tabloid cousins." I cannot disagree. His words may be a few years old, but they still have relevance. Here are some excerpts from his column:

"We dullard viewers might not know how to react so they tell us. 'A shocking story tonight' they cry. Our shock, if any, has likely worn off since we read the news in the paper or saw it on CNN hours, or even days earlier. Other routine reports are declared 'tragic' or 'heartwarming.'

This overkill ensures its own diminishing impact. If every misfortune must be hyped as 'gruesome' or 'horrifying,' what demeaned adjective is left for airliner crashes and famines and genocide?

Journalist Pete Hamill describes sensationalism as 'expressing horror you don't feel.' Television news writers do it every night, hustling viewers by inflating each story's importance.

This is no mere quibble over style and taste. It raises big ques-

tions. Can broadcasters deceive deliberately at the moment, and report truthfully the next? Can they still claim credibility?"[25]

I will leave the answer to those questions to you.

We often hear a phrase favored by many television producers that, when one thinks about it, seems counterproductive to the overall mission of the newscast. It most often comes when promoting an unusual or offbeat "man-bites-dog" story, usually before the commercial break, or as a lead-in to the story itself. The anchor will say, "You won't believe our next story. . . ." It begs the question . . . if you won't "believe that," why should you believe anything the newscaster says? Does it make sense in an environment in which credibility is the most precious currency to tell an audience that news is being included that is not to be believed? So now, following Jim Thomas's logic, we are not only being told how to react to a story, we are also being told what is not to be believed. Perhaps I'm too picky. Or perhaps it's just another thoughtless use of language.

Fred Allen was right when he said that "television is the sincerest form of imitation." For a medium in which there has been so much creativity since its inception, there has been far too much reliance on copying what succeeds. One need look only at the spate of "reality programs" for confirmation. Risks are less likely to be taken because taking risks that fail has a consequence to the bottom line.

Much of the blame for the quality of programming in general, and news in particular, has been that ownership of broadcast and newspaper properties is now largely in the hands of corporate America whose loyalty first and foremost is to its stockholders. The mission is to keep costs down and profits high. Maintaining effective news departments can be expensive, so they are vulnerable. Many local radio stations don't even have news departments. In the not-too-distant past, television news departments lost money, but they were considered loss leaders. Their mission was to serve the community well in the hope that the audience would be loyal to that station and stick with it through lucrative prime-time programming.

The last television station I worked for in St. Louis disbanded its news department of some forty people in favor of programming syndicated reruns. Buying a year's worth of *Frazier* or *The Millionaire* is a lot less expensive than buying and maintaining expensive equipment and paying salaries to those forty people. Shopworn sitcoms and game shows can generate a lot of revenue. So, on that station today, instead of the six o-clock or ten o-clock news, that's what you get. The company, Sinclair Broadcasting, decided to go out of the news business in St. Louis within days following 9/11 claiming that revenue lost during commercial-free broadcasting in the aftermath of the attack on the World Trade Center was so damaging to the bottom line it had to retool. This, as the nation was about to go to war! Clearly, Sinclair really wanted out of the news business because re-runs were more profitable.

Sinclair, which now owns dozens of television stations all over the country, has also abandoned news in several other markets as well. This, as the nation *IS* at war! What does Sinclair do with the money it makes? It does what other group owners do; it buys more stations and makes more money to buy even more stations.

Sinclair's disingenuous decision to abandon news in St. Louis was contrary to historic precedent in which broadcasters were more inclined, either institutionally or individually, to serve interests other than their own. A generation ago, however, as networks were acquired by Fortune 500 companies and an inflated bottom line became more important, network news operations were the first to suffer. To cut costs, their overseas bureaus were shuttered and correspondents called home to pink slips. Staffs have been further whittled since.

What television does best is cover events as they happen. It discovered itself during the days following the Kennedy assassination. CBS newsman Bob Schieffer says television "came of age" during this period. The country stopped and watched the story unfold on television. Pictures and sensitive commentary, and sometimes even a tasteful lack of commentary, brought the tragedy into living rooms with enormous impact. Millions of Americans watched an *AVERAGE* of eight hours a day during the four days following the assassination when all programming was devoted to the unfolding events. Networks gave up all their commercial time during those four days. They swallowed $40 million in commercial losses. And that's in 1963 dollars! *Are you listening Sinclair?*

Later, the television pictures transmitted into those same living rooms brought an end to a war. They gave the country the information it needed to make an intelligent and informed decision about the direction the country should take. That information did not come easily. You may recall that CBS's Fred Friendly, Edward R. Murrow's producer and colleague, quit the network when it chose to air re-runs of *I Love Lucy* rather than broadcast congressional hearings on the Vietnam War.

Then came the Watergate hearings. Popular afternoon soap operas were pre-empted for hearing coverage. At my station, viewers complained daily about that. On a day in which the afternoon hearing was delayed, even more viewers called to complain about *THAT*.

ABC's *Nightline* was created when Iranian students took Americans hostage in Iran. The program has been on the air ever since, though in form and substance it is less edgy than it once was.

Thanks to ever-improving technology, television was live when the Berlin Wall came down and when we decided to go to war in Iraq in 1991. Throughout, cable television in general and CNN in particular was establishing itself on a more prominent footing throughout the country. Twenty-four-hour news was a convenient plus in times of crisis. The news cycle was 24–7, but when there was no crisis, the cycle still had to be served. That's when it fell into tabloid mode. Pop culture was given a prominent place at the table. So prominent, the audience began to actually believe that celebrity news, crime news, and so called "news you can use" was, in fact, news, even though little of it was really relevant to our lives. Americans found themselves unable to escape every detail, then every detail repeated, of the O.J. Simpson trial, or the minute-by-minute minutia of other trials or the trials and tribulations of people they had never heard of but who would become household words through sheer force of exposure.

On September 11, 2001, the assault on the World Trade Center and Pentagon was the epitome of an event that, like the Kennedy assassination, television was uniquely suited to cover. A return to maturity came when commercial and cable networks quickly and jointly decided it was time to stop repetitive showing of those chilling and disturbing scenes of planes plowing into the buildings and of people jumping to their deaths from the burning towers. That showed remarkable restraint, and although numbed by the tragedy, citizens applauded it. Few wanted to relive the horror again and again. It seemed to me that perhaps we were entering a new, more responsible approach that might even cause local news operations across the country to reconsider their commitment to the mindless, the inane, and the vacuous.

That did not happen. We are living today with the resulting over-coverage of Paris Hilton, Britney Spears, and countless star-junkies and drunken would-be stars when they go in or out of rehab. News of their exploits is conveniently sandwiched between the latest diets, health trivia, and self-promotion that have become a nightly staple. That's where we are today. Attention to and infatuation with the insipid has become our comfort zone. We don't seem inclined to move very far from it.

The Sinclair Broadcasting business model referred to above is not unique. Rather, it typifies something else that is happening in lo-cal television. It's absentee ownership. Ownership of local radio and television stations and newspapers is increasingly in the portfolios of out-of-town corporations who have no loyalty to the communi-ties their properties are supposed to serve. The loyalty is to profit. Network foreign news bureaus and institutional memory have been sacrificed on the altar of the bottom line.

There was a time not too many years ago when local stations were typically owned by civic entrepreneurs and local investors who lived in that community rather than by corporations headquartered on the other side of the country. The local owners and station man-agers likely knew the mayor and other leaders as well as what the community issues were and what made the region tick. Viewers could vent in person when they had a complaint. They had oppor-tunities to confront the owner or the station manager at the barber shop or at the ballgame. They knew they could visit the station and receive a full hearing on what they thought needed fixing. Owners couldn't hide. Now they can, because they are often thousands of miles away unaware of any of the things that are important to the community they are supposedly serving. The inevitable result is less investment and less relevant local programming.

Although today's profits far exceed what might have been imag-ined decades ago, neither the appetite nor the motive changed much. Consider the following excerpted words of the man who set the bar for broadcast journalism, Edward R. Murrow. In October of 1958, he addressed the Radio and Television News Directors Association in Chicago.

Do not be deluded into believing the titular heads of the networks control what appears on their networks. They all have better taste. All are responsible to stockholders, and in my experience are all honorable men. But they must schedule what they can sell in the public market. . . .

We are currently wealthy, fat, comfortable and complacent. We have currently a built-in allergy to unpleasant, disturbing information. Our mass media reflect this. But unless we get up off our fat surpluses and recognize that television in the main is being used to distract, delude, amuse and insulate us, then television and those who finance it, those who look at it, and those who work at it, may see a totally different picture too late . . .

This instrument can teach, it can illuminate, yes and it can even inspire. But it can do so only to the extent that humans are determined to use it to those ends. Otherwise it is merely wires and lights in a box.[26]

There is some potential for change. At the time of this writing, the Federal Communications Commission is weighing a proposal that local stations establish "community advisory boards" to prod local stations into providing more local content. This is the same FCC, after all, that also recently decided that it would be acceptable for newspapers to also own broadcast properties in some markets. This cross ownership, of course, opens the door to having one corporate entity dominate the flow of information in some communities.

The proposed advisory boards would oversee the process and advise ownership on relevant issues. Such programming would be taken into account when stations went back to the FCC at license renewal time. This is a throwback to more than a quarter of a century ago when television stations were required to produce programming that was in the public interest. In those days, public affairs programs dealing with local issues were a weekend staple. That ended when rules were relaxed and broadcasters realized they could sell that time with revenue-generating syndicated or fluffy news programming. While this is an encouraging sign, there is no firm indication at the time of this writing that it will ever happen. In fact, there is considerable resistance to the idea from owners.

I can recall the days when the ABC news program *Nightline* was considered one of the finest, most informative, most important news programs on the air. Yet in St. Louis it had only a tiny fraction of the nightly audience of its on-air rival, *The Love Connection*. And reruns of *TLC* at that. Nonetheless, the entertainment program had about forty times the *Nightline* audience. But that was a choice viewers were making. So, perhaps the blame for the quality of television programming today, news and otherwise, does not rest solely with the programmers or corporate executives who are charged with maximizing profits and do so by minimizing quality and substance. Perhaps, as Murrow put it, the public has been worn down and is ever-more *"distracted, deluded, amused and insulated."* Nonetheless, we audiences have played into their hands by mutely accepting whatever it is *they* decided to feed us.

As Shakespeare (and Edward R. Murrow) put it, *"The fault dear Brutus lies not in the stars, but in ourselves."* Pogo creator Walt Kelly had it right too, when he said, *"We have met the enemy and he is us."*

Yet, recent research published by Columbia University indicates that we want more from the media in the way of substantive information. A quote from the *Project for Excellence in Journalism* at Columbia University indicates that viewers in this country would prefer "issues-based, policy-relevant stories" to the diet of irrelevance we now receive. Yet when a station in Minneapolis tried to deliver something along these lines a few years ago, it proved a brief and unsuccessful experiment.

So, in words that might befit a twenty-first century Pogo or Cassius, one ought to ask . . . if we are not getting what we want, are we getting what we deserve?

Notes

[1] John F. Kennedy *Footnotes*
Berlin, June 26, 1963.

[2] Seymour M. Hersh, *The Dark Side of Camelot* (Boston: Back Bay Books, 1997), p. 395–6.

[3] Sen. Edward Kennedy
St. Patick's Cathedral, New York City
June 8, 1968.

[4] Mikhail Gorbachev
Westminster College, Fulton, Missouri, May 6, 1992.

[5] H. Rap Brown
Cambridge, Maryland, July 24, 1967.

[6] Gov. Spiro Agnew
Cambridge, Maryland, July 25, 1967.

[7] Thanks to the published work of Clayborne Carson of the *Minneapolis Star Tribune* and Cambridge civil rights activist Dwight Cromwell for helping refresh memories of that night in Cambridge.

[8] *Time* magazine, October 1972.

[9] Senator George McGovern,
August 1972.

[10] Bruce Miroff, *The Liberals' Moment: The McGovern Insurgency and the Identity Crisis of the Democratic Party* (Lawrence: University Press of Kansas, 2007), p. 95–6.

[11] *Time* magazine, August 7, 1972.

[12] Thomas F. Eagleton, 1929–2007.

[13] PSI Squad Publication.

[14] NTSB Investigation Synopsis
April 1974.

[15] "Laughter in the Rain,"
by Neil Sedaka and Philip Cody

[16] Sen. Edward Kennedy
New York City, August 12, 1980.

[17] Sen. Edward Kennedy
New York City, August 12, 1980.

[18] Ronald Reagan
Detroit, July 17, 1980.

[19] Wikipedia

[20] Walter Mondale
San Francisco, July 1984.

[21] George H. W. Bush
New Orleans, August 18, 1988.

[22] *Catholic Times,* May 2004.

[23] *Catholic New Times,* 2004.

[24] Audrey Hepburn, September 1992 .

[25] *Arizona Republic,* Jim Mitchell.

[26] Edward R. Murrow
RTNDA Convention, Chicago,
October 15, 1958.

This book is dedicated to my brother, Bill, who launched me on the journey and who helped edit the book. He's also responsible for the Berlin photos. And, to my wife, Julie, who was with me most of the way, and who corrected my tendency to overuse semi-colons. She's still working on my spelling.

Reedy Press, PO Box 5131, St. Louis, MO 63139, USA

No part of this publication may be reproduced or transmitted in any form or by any means, electronic or mechanical, including photocopy, recording, or any information storage and retrieval system, without permission in writing from the publisher.

Permissions may be sought directly from Reedy Press at the above mailing address or via our website at www.reedypress.com.

Library of Congress Control Number: 2008928964

ISBN: 978-1-933370-36-1

For information on all Reedy Press publications visit our website at www.reedypress.com.

Printed in the United States of America
08 09 10 11 12   5 4 3 2 1

To Joan,
I hope you enjoy this.
Nice meeting you.
Don Marsh

Flash Frames

Journey of a
Journeyman Journalist

by Don Marsh

REEDY PRESS
St. Louis, Missouri